Summit
Books

exit wounds

A Story of Love, Loss, and Occasional Wars

PETER GODWIN

SUMMIT BOOKS

NEW YORK   AMSTERDAM/ANTWERP   LONDON
TORONTO   SYDNEY/MELBOURNE   NEW DELHI

Summit
Books

An Imprint of Simon & Schuster, LLC
1230 Avenue of the Americas
New York, NY 10020

First Summit Books hardcover edition April 2025

SUMMIT BOOKS and colophon are trademarks of Simon & Schuster, LLC

Simon & Schuster strongly believes in freedom of expression and stands
against censorship in all its forms. For more information, visit BooksBelong.com.

For information about special discounts for bulk purchases,
please contact Simon & Schuster Special Sales at 1-866-506-1949 or
business@simonandschuster.com.

The Simon & Schuster Speakers Bureau can bring authors to your live event. For more information or to book an event, contact the Simon & Schuster Speakers Bureau at 1-866-248-
3049 or visit our website at www.simonspeakers.com.

Interior design by Lexy East

Manufactured in the United States of America

1   3   5   7   9   10   8   6   4   2

Library of Congress Cataloging-in-Publication Data is available.

ISBN 978-1-6680-7453-4
ISBN 978-1-6680-7455-8 (ebook)

IN MEMORY OF HELEN GODWIN

For my sisters:
Georgina, who lived through so much of this with me.
And Jain, who didn't get to.

"Life is made of ever so many partings welded together."

—Charles Dickens

exit
wounds

Preface

EXIT WOUNDS IS NOT A CONVENTIONAL MEMOIR. ONE OF MY AIMS IN it is to reflect the enduring power of memory. Stylistically, the book tracks the way that memory works, with all its foibles and distortions. It is neither forensic nor objective; it is digressive and partial, rather like viewing life through a fairground mirror. Because of this, and to protect their privacy, I have altered the names and identifying details of many people (other than immediate family) who populate these pages.

Peter Godwin
New York
2024

Happy Tensing

When she turned ninety, my mother sprang a final surprise on us. She started speaking in the voice of a stranger.

Her usual voice is what linguists call RP, Received Pronunciation, the "standard" accent of the British upper middle class, although it's spoken by only around 5 percent of the population, mostly the privately educated. Now, abruptly, she begins to speak in a frightfully mannered, haute Edwardian fashion. Instead of "home," she talks of *he*ome. The "house" is the *hi*se. *Ears* is "yes." *Sex* are "burlap bags" (sacks). A *crèche* is what happens when cars collide or the stock market dives. And rather than being "happy" (something she would never admit to, anyway), she is now *heppy*.

To say *heppy*, your mouth must tense into a horizontal rictus, so linguists describe this posh patois as "happy tensing." It is a memsahib bark that sounds so pretentious that we—my younger sister and I—assume she must be affecting it, as a joke.

"No one really talks like that anymore," I tell my mother. "Even the Queen has brought it down a notch."

We give it a few days, hoping that this antique aristocratic accent will vanish as abruptly as it arrived. But it sticks fast. So we give this new, fancier model of our mother the nickname "Empress Dowager," or "Her Grace" (HG happen to be her initials too—Helen Godwin) for short, while we try to figure out where this alien voice has come from and why it has suddenly shown up.

The most obvious trigger, a mini stroke, is ruled out by her doctor.

Her Grace is not much help in our quest. She denies that her voice has changed at all. "I've always spoken like this," she insists.

Always emerges as *awe*lways.

The Empress Dowager makes two other changes around this time.

The first change is that, for no compelling medical reason, she takes to her bed, as if prematurely lying in state. And she acquires a new bed, one of those hydraulic ones you see in hospitals, adjustable both in angle and in height. Whenever we visit her now, she presses the control panel to elevate the bed, so that she can peer down at us in Solomonic judgment.

The second change is that despite having always been acutely conflict-averse, allergic to embarrassment, oblique in her diplomacy, she now sheds her social filters. Doctors call this "disinhibition syndrome." Like a toddler, Her Grace now blurts out whatever happens to move through her mind, however peevish or splenetic this may be. Indeed, she seems almost to relish causing offense, especially to me, her geographically distant offspring, resident over the ocean in America.

My sister, Georgina, is the proximate one. She does all the dowager heavy lifting. She has carved out a bedroom for our mother, who cannot manage stairs, by erecting an office partition across the sitting room of her Canfield Gardens duplex in North London; a partition that brutally bisects the beautiful bay window, destroying the aesthetics of symmetry and reducing the remnant sitting room to little more than a corridor, the sole furnishing in which is a Zanzibari daybed, whose crimson cushions Bella, her hyperactive English springer spaniel, has ripped to shreds in lieu of flushing and retrieving the pheasants she was bred to hunt. Georgina and her teenaged daughter, Xanthe, congregate instead in the small, dark, subterranean kitchen, like Victorian belowstairs domestics.

To assuage my guilt at being the absent son, I frequently fly over from New York. And, as I always do, I overcompensate, sitting beside my mother's bed for hours at a time, chatting brightly and reading aloud to her, in the belief that this will help her stave off dementia. But mostly I am trying to convince myself that I am a good son.

There is a sad symmetry to our relationship. I spent the first decade of my life trying to summon my mother's attention, and she has spent the last decade of hers trying to summon mine.

At ninety, my mother measures her longevity against two pacers. Her Majesty the Queen, who is eight months her junior and whom she considers a colleague—they both served in the WRENS (the Women's Royal Naval Service) during the Second World War. And her nemesis, Robert Mugabe, who misruled Zimbabwe for the last thirty years my mother lived there. He is one year her senior, and she is determined to outlive him.

Today I am reading to her from the *Times*, a news story about her erstwhile president.

My mother is always on the lookout for signs of a decline in Mugabe's health. Having ruined Zimbabwe's healthcare system, once Africa's finest, in which my mother served for fifty years as a doctor, Mugabe regularly jets (privately, of course) to Singapore, secretly to be infused there with fresh blood. Vampiric analogies maraud my mother's mind.

In recent TV coverage of him, seated at a table, Her Grace has spotted the president's swollen ankles peeping from under his trouser legs. She diagnoses right-side heart failure. Doctors never really retire.

Neither do African presidents, it seems. Africa has the world's youngest population but its oldest leaders.

"Mugabe's losing it," she says cheerfully. "Have you noticed how his kaftans have pictures of his own face all over them?"

"They're not kaftans, they're dashikis."

With age I'm inheriting my late father's proclivity for pedantry.

"Well, whatever they're called, I think he wears pictures of himself to remind him who he is. He's getting dementia, I tell you."

I worry that my mother is merely mirroring her own fear of succumbing to dementia before Mugabe does.

From the news report I am reading to her, she harvests more evidence for her diagnosis. During a ceremonial tree planting, Mugabe cannot figure out where to deposit his small silver spade of soil.

"In the hole, at the base of the sapling, Your Excellency," his aides urge.

I am still in mid-flow of the *Times* article when my mother holds up her hand, imperiously palming me into silence. She regards me sternly over the rims of her bifocals.

"I can't help noticing you *speak* rather *oddly*," she says.

I refrain from pointing out that this seems rather rich coming from the late-onset Empress Dowager.

"What accent is that?" she inquires.

"Well, I suppose it's a sort of Zimbabwean one," I say.

The white Zimbabwean accent, a tiny subset of Anglo African accents, is fast becoming an archaic artifact of linguistic curiosity as whites continue to leave—some call it, "bred and fled"—dwindling to fewer than twenty thousand now.

But small though it is, Zimbabwean English ranges all the way from the Afrikaans-inflected, where "affluent" sounds like "effluent," to over-elocuted, faux RP English. My own Zimbabwean accent amplifies according to several catalysts: how recently I was in Zimbabwe, how tired I am, and how much I've had to drink. After any of these I start pronouncing the "ish" sound as *ush*, "fish" evolving into *fush*, and "ill" as *ull*, "mill" becoming *mull*.

Today, it's jetlag that fushes my fishes and ulls my ills.

"I *speak* like this," I remind her, "because I was born in Zimbabwe—where *you* decided to give birth to me. And raise me."

"Ah," she says, noncommittal, as if taking it under advisement, that this may—or may not—be true. "Livestock is raised," she points out. "Children are brought up. You've been in America too long."

She cracks that central *r* like a bullwhip. Or, as I would call it, a "sjambok."

Georgina speaks much posher than I do. She had elocution lessons from Mrs. Venning at school in Zimbabwe. At seventeen, Georgina had arrived at Mountview drama school in London, dressed in bright, vegetable-dyed cotton—fine for the Zimbabwean sunshine, but not great for the English damp. In an era when vintage was not yet cool, her only climate-appropriate articles of attire were Dad's old trilby and Mum's old tweed coat, scratchy and heavy.

At Mountview, Georgina had briefly embraced Mockney—the fake mash-up of Cockney that the progeny of the upper middle classes used in a vain effort to gain street cred—before settling on the Queen's English. Georgina speaks proper now, she e*nunc*iates.

Finding that two pages of the newspaper are stuck together, I lick my thumb and forefinger to separate them.

"*Really*, Peter," says Her Grace, dripping disdain. "How *awfully* vulgarian."

In her new voice my name has become Pee-*tar*.

Peter is already a problematic name in America, where the *t* morphs into a *d* to become *Pee-der*. When I announce myself to doormen and receptionists using the Anglo version, with its tent pole *t*, they frown in puzzlement.

I ignore her, continuing to read from the newspaper, until I notice she is examining my profile, her eyes rheumy with inquisition.

"How would you describe your forehead?" she wonders aloud.

My brow *is* rather prominent, a dashboard abutting a windscreen, so, in jest, I reply, "Neanderthal?"

"Yes," she promptly agrees. "That's the word I was looking for."

"Good grief, Mum, that's enough now!"

She looks astonished.

"I don't mean that in a *bad* way."

"What other way is there?"

She shrugs.

"Anyway," I say, stung into defending my Neanderthal brow-bros, "new DNA research shows that *sapiens* didn't follow Neanderthals on the evolutionary curve; they overlapped and interbred with them. Apparently present-day Caucasians have up to three percent Neanderthal genes. Mine must have lodged in my forehead."

Her sardonic mien tells me she has been highly selective in what she's deigned to hear, harvesting only the bit where I cop to being neo-Neanderthal.

"Furthermore"—I am warming to my theme—"it turns out that Neanderthals have had a bum rap. They weren't the violent, knuckle-dragging analog to our genteel, intelligent *sapiens*. Quite the opposite. Neanderthals were the more artistic, the gentler, and we *sapiens* were the violent, homicidal ones." I pause. "Nature's thugs won out, and we are their heirs. As usual, history is curated by the victors."

Her Grace is clearly dubious of this update from the annals of anthropological antiquity.

"You *lect*ure at university, don't you?" she accuses.

"No, yes, well, sort of," I admit. "But not on palaeoanthropology, and I'm only part-time, an adjunct professor."

"I *knew* it," she says.

• • •

Seeking to deflect from my defects—my accent, my looks, my déclassé habits—I examine the pastel seascape above her bed, a painting she has hung there in various landlocked Zimbabwean homesteads, from the Eastern Highlands on the border with Mozambique, to the lip of the Zambezi Escarpment, to the capital, Harare. It tries to capture the way the waves obstinately hurl themselves against the rocks. "[A] sea, swelling, chafing, raging, without bound, without hope, without beacon, or anchor. Torn from the hold of his affections and fixed purposes, he floats a mighty wreck in the wide world of sorrows," as William Hazlitt described King Lear. And I can't help thinking there is an element of Lear in this recently arrived Empress Dowager.

"Why do you always have that painting above your bed?" I ask.

She cranes up at it, appraising. "It reminds me of the systole and diastole of a heartbeat, clenching and unclenching," she says. "But mostly, I just like colors."

"It's not exactly high art," I murmur. I feel instantly ashamed, but my mother is unperturbed.

"Ah, art," she sighs, "ruined since the time of Eden by self-appointed critics, inserting the worm of doubt into the joy of creation."

And she begins to recite the bard of high Victoriana, Rudyard Kipling, her *s*'s assuming a hissing sibilance:

> And the first rude sketch that the world has seen was joy to
>   his mighty heart,
> Till the Devil whispered behind the leaves; "It's pretty, but
>   is it Art?"

I accept my rebuke silently.

To tune me out, Her Grace turns on the television. Her favorite show, *Life on Earth*, is playing. She finds natural history comforting. David Attenborough is intoning earnestly about lemurs. He explains that the lemur gently bites the giant millipede, triggering it to secrete defensive fluid that the lemur ingests "for narcotic effect."

"Wow, lemurs get stoned by sucking shongololos—who knew?" I say, trying to row back from my earlier art attack.

"There's a lot you don't know," my mother says, as though she has always known of this lemur drug-huffing habit.

Shongololo is what we call the millipede in our part of Africa. It comes from the Nguni word "ukusonga," *to roll up*, which is what it does whenever it senses danger. The roll-up defense is one of the oldest in animal evolution, going all the way back to 500-million-year-old tri-lobites. Pangolins and hedgehogs still do it.

I wonder if my mother is doing it too, by taking to her bed, re-treating from a disorienting, dangerous world. When we try to entice her out of the house now, she declines.

"I'm latibulating," she says.

Apparently, it means to hide in a safe corner until conditions im-prove.

She pulls her purple peony-print duvet up to her chin, like a tor-toise retracting into its shell, a defense copied by Roman soldiers in their testudo formation, joining their shields overhead to create a shel-tering roof against the incoming shoals of enemy arrows.

• • •

The arrows unleashed at my mother during her half-century in South-ern Africa have been many and sharp. She was overtaken by Zimba-bwe's civil war, in which her only son and her husband fought, and which claimed the life of her elder daughter, my sister Jain, at the age of twenty-seven, and Jain's fiancé, when they drove into a Rhodesian army ambush three weeks before their wedding. My mother served as a doctor in Zimbabwe's biggest hospital while HIV ravaged the population, before there was any effective treatment.

She saw a lifetime's savings, pensions, and careful investments zeroed out by the worst hyperinflation the world has ever seen (the Zimbabwe dollar halved in value every day), reducing her to humiliating penury in old age. For a pittance, she continued to work well into retirement as a doctor, ministering to the medical staff she couldn't bear to abandon in a hospital that was starved of resources and collapsing around her.

The final arrow, the one that pierced my mother to the quick, was the death of my father in 2004. In his last year, his feet were ravaged by gangrene from diabetes. He would sit on his bed while my mother knelt on the floor to unwrap the sodden bandages from his rotting feet while I tried not to vomit at the smell. Yet he refused to countenance amputation.

My father's final wish was to be cremated. But the only crematorium, Warren Hills, where we had buried my sister, no longer worked. So, I begged permission from the local Hindu pandit to burn my father at their open-air site, and then had to help build the pyre and wait through the night while he burned, to collect his remains. It turns out that flames are no match for the femur. Loading one's father's bones into a bucket, I can report, graphically reinforces one's own sense of mortality.

After that, my mother came to England for a hip replacement and spent six weeks recuperating with Georgina. But when it came time to fly home to Zimbabwe, she just couldn't bear to return to the shell of her former life, overwhelmed at the idea of coping in a failed state without her husband. So, she never did.

She was cheated out of her house, her sole remaining asset. Now she finds herself in England with no income of her own besides a miniature pension from her Second World War naval service a lifetime ago.

A doctor accustomed to being the one who cares for others, she hates the idea of being a burden. But now she must rely on her children for her own survival.

And though we're happy to provide, and we tell her that often, she insists on contributing, spending her days applying for little parcels of charitable money from professional and religious organizations, money that is constantly audited and which she must repeatedly reapply for, even as she grows befuddled by the burden of the bureaucracy.

Her Grace, who grew up in England, now finds it confusing and depressing, a place she no longer recognizes, whose culture and values now seem foreign. For her, the past is another country.

She still misses her husband desperately.

"Do you know," she tells me wistfully, "your father drew me a special map of how to drive to the hospital from home without ever having to turn across the traffic, because he knew how I hated that. And a separate map for the return journey."

Now she must navigate her life without his specially drawn maps.

One of the very few visitors my mother will let into her latibulation is Alison, a music teacher in her sixties, who went to high school in Zimbabwe with my elder sister. Alison helps fill the Jain-shaped hole in Mum's life. And Mum is around the age Alison's mother would be. Each serves as a substitute for the missing. Their psychological puzzle pieces press perfectly into place.

• • •

There's an old Jewish proverb that only those who have been forgotten are truly dead, but I have trouble remembering my older sister now. She was an elementary school teacher, and I keep her photograph and her craft work on my wall—batiks and collages, mostly. Like a little shrine, I suppose. They are so faded now, and tattered, it's hard to make them out. One is a grove of trees, constructed of string glued to canvas. Sometimes, when I pass by, I trace my fingers over it. Touching something once touched by her.

Whenever I do, I try to manifest her. Seven years older than me and sixteen years older than Georgina, Jain was more maternal to us than our mother. I can picture the upward curl of Jain's smile, her lighthearted exasperation with the slowness of others, hear the peal of her laughter. But not the whole. She's been dead now longer than she was alive. And when she was killed, I lived on a different continent, saw her irregularly, so her death didn't present itself to me daily. Rather, it crept up on me, and still does, in accumulating waves, breaking over me, drowning me in her absence.

I can still remember the moment I heard the news. Cambridge in spring, April 22, dawn. I am lying in bed, half-awake; the alarm has already gone off and there is half an hour before my eight-man crew will take to the tranquil River Cam to row.

There was something about rowing that helped calm me after military service; this was my therapy, exercise until exhausted, five or six times a week. The consoling dip and splash of the blades, the nudge of speed as the lacquered shell leapt at the catch of each stroke, and the flick of the synchronized finish as eight blades cleared the water and feathered together. Interdependent oarsmen in a galley, the atavistic thrill of teamwork.

The black-suited porter bangs on the door to say there's a long-distance call for me. I pull on sweats and follow him downstairs through a quad billowing white with cherry blossom. He slides open the glass partition to the porter's lodge and hands me a black Bakelite receiver, shiny with wear. My father's voice is flat and tight as he tells me, without preamble, "I have terrible news, Pete. Jain has been killed." Then his voice trails off, and all I can hear is a bass groan, agonizingly heavy, ponderous and final. I am a dead weight, falling and falling and falling, into this nihilistic sound.

Years later I heard a recording of a black hole, a star imploding in on itself. And I recognized it, that same dystopian symphony, those massive, terminal groans as the whole universe turns in on itself and is swallowed by nothingness.

Only afterwards did I realize that I was the one they had expected to die. This is my survivor's guilt. If any of us had to be ritually sacrificed to the gods to keep the rest of the family safe, it was supposed to be me. I was the one who went to war at eighteen, straight from high school. Drafted in due to a sudden law change (by a Rhodesian government short of white conscripts) that ended military service deferments for students studying abroad, just before I could make my escape.

I wrote about my war in *Mukiwa*, my coming-of-age memoir, and I find it hard to go back into it all. Suffice it to say, what I saw sucked the youth clear out of me and set me on a new trajectory. And when I eventually made it to England, I was different. I was altered in ways I still don't fully understand, as I don't know what kind of man I would have become had I not gone to war. But somewhere I grieve for him too, that man I might have been. I was so young, understood so little of life. I was reading a Leslie Thomas novel at the time, *The Virgin Soldiers*. And I remember thinking, Lord, please don't let me die before I have known love. Before I have loved and been loved.

"Do you remember how *you* heard?" I ask Georgina.

Of course she does, each moment is chiseled into the marble of her memory.

She was eleven, just out of hospital for tonsil removal, when Mum woke her to tell her Jain was dead. You're pulling my leg, said Georgina. She had just read that phrase and was using it for the first time. No, said Mum. It's real. They bundled her into the car and drove straight to the death site, near Shamva.

Georgina finds one of Jain's shoes inside the crushed car and the other one in the bush nearby. They are flatform flip-flops with rainbow soles and white straps, and though bloodstained and too big, Georgina slips them on. She wears them continuously until they fall apart. She wears them to an Eisteddfod music festival, though the dress code calls for black gowns and bare feet. The shoes are ugly and distracting, the judge scolds. Georgina bursts into tears. But her duet with her best friend Ellah still wins first prize.

Among Jain's clothes she also finds a jokey T-shirt that has the slogan *Handle with Care* printed across the chest. Georgina has yet to develop breasts, and the T-shirt is much too big for her. When she wears it, the words are over her stomach.

"What should we handle with care?" someone teases her.

"Me," she says. "You should handle *me* with care."

Growing up in "colonial" Africa, we were taught that sentimentality was to be despised, that we had to be tough, to bear our mantle of responsibility. To whom much is given, much is expected, my mother used to say. Noblesse oblige. My father was more succinct. Belt up, he said whenever we showed signs of weakness or emotion, which were the same things to him. "Get a grip."

We Godwins are paragons of stoicism. Pain is something we pretend happens to other people. Our threshold is so high that catastrophe barely registers on the Richter scale of our forbearance. We continue to feel privileged, fortunate, even as adversity sideswipes us.

It reminds me now of the notices posted on Japanese roller coasters when they banned screaming because it spread Covid. The notices ask riders instead to "Please scream inside your heart." And that's what we did as a family after Jain was killed. In our separate ways, we screamed inside our hearts. Never out loud, and never together. We suffered in silence, alone. The light behind my parents' eyes went out, and it never really burned again. They switched from robust middle age to being abruptly old.

———

My father is dead more recently than Jain, sixteen years now, but already I can no longer conjure him. Until recently I could do so effortlessly. The Gold Leaf cigarette smell of him, his eccentric uniform—safari suit and desert boots, his walrus mustache—the timbre of his over-precise English, learned as a foreign language. The way he chewed his tongue in the side of his mouth when concentrating, as I'm told I do. His engineering exactitude, despising sloppiness in all things. His allergy to sloth.

But slowly the corporeal essence of him is slipping away. I am losing him for a second time as he leaves for that limbo occupied by the memory of Jain. Both are becoming spectral. Vague, mythical. I now miss the *idea* of them, as much as the physical persons.

Jain's death, though more distant, leaves perhaps the deeper wound. Maybe because it is a preview of my own death. A curtain-raiser to my own mortality. A sibling's death does that even more than a parent's. When a parent dies, especially of the same gender, it places you next on the disassembly line. When a sibling dies, then death is right at your elbow, jostling you directly, without a generational buffer.

But the loss of Jain is something deeper too. It's a premonition of cosmic loneliness. The soul-sucking sadness of solitude. A glimmer of the worst the world has to offer. Not that it harbors any particular hostility towards you, but worse, far worse, that it is supremely *indifferent* to your fate.

Thunder Is Not Yet Rain

FOR THE FIRST FEW YEARS BACK IN ENGLAND, MY MOTHER MADE herself useful by taking care of Xanthe, doing as a grandmother what she had never managed to do as a mother—parenting. But then one day she fell, and her confidence fell with her. And as Mum grew frailer, less mobile, Georgina spent more and more time looking after her.

"I promised her I'd never dump her in a residential home," she explained to me at the time. "But it was like having an extra child, one who would not grow up, an unwell person who would never get better. I resented her. I found myself wishing she would die."

Finally, doctors agreed that she qualified for home care, and one day Gina appeared. To Georgina, she was "like an angel," a godsend. To Her Grace, not so much. Gina is not her real name, but that's what she asked us to call her. Georgina says that, just as Gina is composed of part of her name, so Gina took over a part of her life. She comes from Latvia, one of those Russian settlers marooned in the Baltics after the Soviet Union collapsed. Tall, big boned, with ash-blond braids and hands the size of saucepans, she has pale blue eyes and a melancholy manner.

My mother complains about her constantly.

Today she claims, quite seriously, that Gina has been stealing her socks and shoes—my mother's orthopedic compression socks and her bespoke shoes; the right one has a built-up sole after her hip replacement shortened that leg.

"Why on earth would Gina want your old footwear?" I ask. "They have no resale value, and they're not even her size."

As well as level legs, Gina has much larger feet than my mother.

"What could her motivation possibly be?"

"To create *mayhem*," says my mother dramatically.

I try to point out how irrational this is, but my mother's narrative, like a photographic film, has become quite fixed in the darkroom of her mind, and no other impression can affect it now.

This morning she beckons me to her bedside and addresses me in a stage whisper.

"Now Gina has stolen my engagement ring."

She says this with complete conviction, eyeing me minutely for inklings of incredulity. I feel myself pulled into the palace of paranoia where my mother increasingly dwells.

"How do you know?" I ask. "Did you see her steal it?"

"I know. I just *do*."

The engagement ring is made of white gold, as my mother still calls platinum, with a one-carat diamond clutched in a little claw. As well as being of sentimental value, it's the most expensive thing my mother owns; it's the *only* expensive thing my mother owns. It was smuggled out of Poland after the war by a father-in-law she never met.

"You've probably mislaid it," I sigh.

She lifts the thin gold chain from her neck, unharnessing it slowly like a bridle over a horse's head, and hands it to me. At the end of it is a small silver key.

"Unlock the filing cabinet," she commands. "Top drawer, at the very back."

I slide open the drawer. Behind rows of bottles of Eucerin moisturizer, "for extremely dry, compromised skin," and various prescription drugs she's been hoarding, she has secreted a matte-black mini safe. I unlock it. Inside is a small jewelry box.

"Bring."

I deliver it to her, and she snaps it open. The scarlet satin furrow within is empty. No ring.

"You *see?*" she says triumphantly.

"That just proves it's missing."

"Gina's the only one who could have taken it," she insists. "The only one who would know where the key is, who would have the opportunity, while I was sleeping, to get it."

"You've probably put it somewhere for safekeeping and forgotten where. Happens to me all the time."

"Nah-uh."

For the next week, I rummage through her room, searching for the damned ring. It is nowhere to be found.

"What do you want me to do?" I ask.

She just shrugs.

"If I accuse Gina, she'll be furious. She'll probably storm off. And rightly so."

"I don't like her anyway," my mother mutters.

I approach Gina when she is alone in the kitchen microwaving a meals-on-wheels for my mother, a plastic tray of shepherd's pie.

"Oh, Gina," I begin, trying to sound all nonchalant, "you haven't by any chance seen my mother's engagement ring, have you? She seems to have mislaid it. You know how forgetful she can be."

"No," she says quickly. She knows I'm accusing her of stealing the ring and she cocks her head to one side, appraising me with her unnervingly blue eyes. Eyes that give nothing away.

I leave it a day. Then I tell Gina I will have to register the ring's loss with the police to make an insurance claim.

"It's only a formality," I explain. "But it's possible they *may* need to interview the people who live and work here. So, I wanted to give you a heads-up. It's nothing to worry about, just British bureaucracy."

I give a brittle little laugh that she declines to join.

"How did it go with Gina?" asks my mother when Gina has left for the day.

"How do you know I spoke to her?"

"I'm old," she says. "Not stupid."

The next day, when Gina's shift is over, I take my mother an afternoon cup of coffee. In a cappuccino world, she still prefers instant. I dock the *World's Best Grandma* mug, a birthday present from my sons, into her clutch. Her hands have become translucent. They are an anatomy lesson. Vein and bone, metacarpal and sinew, muscle and cartilage, all plainly visible. As she grasps the mug, her hands begin to tremble, but she persists, rushing to park it on the ledge of her substantial embonpoint, upon which she has spread a fuchsia floral face cloth to receive the rim of the mug's hot base.

Once she is situated, she nods me to her bedside table. The cabinet key nestles there in its coil of gold chain.

"Well, go on," she says.

I unlock the filing cabinet again, navigate through the thicket of lotions and pill bottles, pull out the matte mini safe, unfasten it, retrieve the velvet jewelry box, and click it open. Just as she foretold, slotted snug in its satin slit sits her engagement ring once more, the winking diamond securely clenched in the embrace of its white-gold claw.

I turn to my mother. She has one eyebrow cocked. It is sufficient. Gina never returns.

• • •

On her last day, when she thinks the pincers of the law are closing in on her ring heist, Gina double-doses my mother with Warfarin, the blood thinner—mistakenly, or deliberately, we don't know. What we *do* know is that when Her Grace scratches herself, she bleeds like a Romanov.

The Warfarin overdose also causes diarrhea. That night she has trouble getting back into bed after using the chair commode. She topples over but declines to press the alarm button that hangs around her neck for just this eventuality. She doesn't want to wake the household, doesn't want to "be a nuisance," she explains later. Instead, she sits shivering on the floor all night. Come morning, Georgina finds her there, freezing and bleeding, and heaves her back up onto her bed.

When I visit her later that morning, I find my mother sitting in bed, crooning softly to herself, hugging her knees to her chest, rocking. Her eyes are open, hooded and birdlike, darting—but blank and un-focused. Her mind has snapped shut; her circuits cut off.

I greet her and she looks up, sees me.

"What time is it?" she asks, though the giant numerals of a digital clock glow red from her bedside table.

"Ten o'clock," I tell her.

"In the morning, or the evening?" she asks. The curtains are open and sunlight streams in golden from the garden. She has lost all sense of time, lost her circadian rhythm.

I sit with her through the day. She seems in shock and says little.

Georgina walks into our silence with builder's tea. She places it on Mum's bedside table.

"Everything all right?" she asks cheerily.

Her Grace nods and Georgina withdraws. Her Grace sips her tea thoughtfully, then looks down at me.

"I know who you are," she says, "but who was that who just came in?"

"Mum! That's Georgina, your daughter. You live here with her!"

"Oh, yes," she says, with an embarrassed laugh.

A beat, then she speaks again.

"And who is the *father*?"

That evening, as a treat, we order in from Nando's, peri-peri chicken like we used to eat on the coast of Mozambique, washed down by raffia-netted bottles of Mateus Rosé. Mum attacks a chicken leg, ripping it with her incisors, cracking the cartilage with her molars. She eats fast, with a feral ferocity, as though someone might try to snatch the food away. I half expect her to growl protectively when I approach.

When I put her to bed, she asks me to check for tokoloshes. Despite being an Anglican-educated chaplain's daughter, she has absorbed elements of rural Zimbabwean superstition, now resurfacing in her trauma.

I tell her—seriously—because it's clear this is a sincere belief, that tokoloshes don't like newspapers, and I wave a copy of the *Guardian* at the end of the room. She accepts this; her only quibble is that the *Telegraph*, with its wider-page format, might be a more effective deterrent. I reassure her that the bed legs are mounted on bricks—they are not—and so she is safe from tokoloshes. It is a well-known piece of tokoloshe lore that these little goblins cannot scamper up bricks. They are hydrophobic too, so to make a bed completely tokoloshe-proof you must place its legs in tins of water.

I sit with Her Grace until her breathing becomes regular and she sleeps. Then I get ready to leave for the Airbnb apartment I've now rented, having delayed my return to New York to help deal with my mother's mental malaise.

"Do you occasionally feel when Mum is looking at you that she wishes you were Jain?" I ask Georgina as I leave.

"No. Why, do you?"

"I find her looking at me with a certain wistful expression, and I feel like she's still thinking that the wrong child was killed," I admit.

It is the first time I've said it out loud.

At Finchley Road Underground Station I stand alone on the platform, waiting for the southbound train. An announcement crackles over the loudspeaker system. The accent is instantly recognizable as Zimbabwean.

It sounds like home.

"Kwasarwa ani?" *Who is left?*

That's how Zimbabweans often greet each other when they meet in the diaspora. So many are now working abroad to feed their families back home.

• • •

My small Airbnb has that musty bouquet typical of British basement flats, just above rising damp, just below outright mold. Everything about it trumpets transience. Generic heritage England photos on the wall: St. Paul's Cathedral, Tower Bridge, Windsor Castle. Random mantel tchotchkes: a snow globe of Big Ben, a plaster bust of Shakespeare, a ceramic British bulldog, a smiling porcelain pig. Union Jack tea towels in the narrow galley kitchenette. Faded red paper roses in the vase on the small blond Ikea dining table.

The dribbling shower confirms American prejudice against English plumbing, barely rinsing the shampoo from my hair. The steam sets the smoke alarm whooping.

The gap-toothed bookshelf is populated by a smattering of paperbacks. They lean upon each other for support, airport thrillers—Dan Browns, Tom Clancys, Lee Childs—discarded by other birds of passage.

I climb into bed and sleep soon submerges me.

Then, suddenly, I am awake. A dazzle of light and screaming, shrieking. Clearly a child is being murdered nearby. Where am I? What country? Confused, I leap out of bed, instinctively crawl across the floor to take cover under the window. Now I remember, I'm in a North London basement.

I draw the net curtain to see that feral foxes are fucking in the backyard and have triggered the motion-activated security light. In the time I've been away, garbage-rich London has been invaded by these once shy, rural animals. So much so that they have developed into a vulpine subspecies. The dumpster-diving urban fox has a shorter, stouter muzzle, the better to rummage through the plastic packaging of discarded fast food.

I force open the sash window and berate them. They break off their amorous activities to appraise me with insolent eyes of briefcase brown, then they saunter away. Urban foxes have smaller brains too, as inert trash is a less challenging quarry than rabbits and other wily rustic rodents.

No sooner have the foxes left the yard than full-throated birdsong breaks out, plangent and plaintive, resonating through the cool night air across the sleeping suburbs. The clock says midnight, dawn yet a distant prospect. Apparently, it is not only my mother who has a misplaced circadian rhythm. This robin has too—confused by light pollution. That, and possibly the traffic roar that has made it difficult for London's diurnal songbirds to hear each other during the day. Now the males have taken to trilling their calls at dead of night when their song is more likely to be heard by potential mates.

I lie in bed unable to sleep, taking stock of my restless, unsettled existence. It seems to me that leaving is what's most wrenching in life. I wonder if that's what has happened to me, that my life has too many discontinuities, too many fractures and faded friendships. That too many farewells may have broken me, so that I no longer have a coherent character.

I remember the "hostile environments" refresher course the BBC ordered all war-bound correspondents to attend years ago. Having been in the military, I was already familiar with most of it, though it is an entirely different skill set surviving when you are not armed, no longer part of a trained military team. So, I found myself in the English West Country with a squad of ex–special forces soldiers instructing us in the fine art of staying alive in conflict zones.

There was Major Jolly, a combat surgeon with twenty-five years' experience in the Royal Marines, the only soldier to be decorated by *both* sides in the Falklands War. When he had performed surgery on wounded Argentine soldiers, they were astonished to be operated upon. They had expected to be tortured.

For us, he spooled through his "gallery of nasties"—gory close-ups of corpses and their various wounds—and showed us the many ways we might be killed. From Northern Ireland, there was a man shot in the head, and an accused collaborator tarred and feathered.

Feathers usually come from duvets these days, he explained. Though so many are now filled with man-made fibers, which don't have quite the same aesthetic.

Jolly was well named.

Never stand near a blasted building, he warned. Someone opens the window, the glass pane crashes down and decapitates you.

One of the most insidious injuries, he said, is blast lung. It can take hours to develop. You think you're fine, but suddenly you're drowning in your own blood.

On and on he went, cataloging the many ways of dying in war, and how we might try to avoid them. Of course, the best way to really avoid them is not to go to wars in the first place.

Jolly was at pains to puncture the portrayal, in thousands of TV shows, that a car door supplies an effective shield against gunfire.

On the shooting range, we took turns firing rifles at said car door. From a thousand to 750 yards, there's some protection. But closer than that, unless it's up-armored, you're getting the double whammy of the metal shrapnel the bullet picks up as it passes through the door.

This is how a bullet normally kills you, he explained: it enters your body like a ship, setting up a bow wave in front of it, flinging away tissue and creating a vacuum behind it that sucks skin and clothes into your wound cavity.

Jolly showed a slide of a man shot in the abdomen. The entry wound was small and pursed. It looked survivable.

But the entry wound isn't usually your problem, explained Jolly. Once the bullet hits you, it starts tumbling . . . He clicked his remote, the carousel rotated to the next slide, a rear view of the same man. The bullet had punched a huge hole out of his back.

It's this exit wound that'll get you, Jolly said. It's the exit wound that kills you.

• • •

At Georgina's Canfield Gardens apartment, I redouble my reading duties, conducting what becomes a bedside poem-a-thon. I am a reverse Scheherazade; if I keep reciting poetry to my mother, she will live on, she will remain lucid. Mostly I take my cues from her. I am her personal poetry Shazam, ready to hunt down a poem from the slightest literary clue.

My mother has benefited from a classical English education. She spouts shards of Keats, Byron, Pope, Shelley, Tennyson, Coleridge, Wordsworth, Southey, Blake, Yeats, Milton, Stevenson, Browning, Dryden.

She makes me realize the privilege the educated have in old age, chancellors of a cultural exchequer to plunder at will. So long as they can access it. She is having persistent problems pinning down the provenance of poems. We agree, Georgina and I, that Her Grace's mind is dimming, not because of dementia as such, but because she just hasn't been exercising it enough. Thunder is not yet rain, as the Kenyan proverb puts it.

I assume the role of drill sergeant in a mental boot camp to clear her synapses, a cerebral chimney sweep, a neural Roto-Rooter. As she recovers, you can almost hear her dusty synapses crackling back into use. Her emotional repertoire expands too. She becomes by turns funny, wry, indignant, critical, wheedling, mordant, mischievous.

Once I start reading, her pump is primed and she will often recite along with me from memory. She squinches her eyes, reaches back into her youth, and somehow retrieves word-perfect gobbets.

The poem-a-thon becomes a poetry survey course for me too, a serendipitous retrieval of my own cultural canon, a core curriculum of prewar poetry. Georgina jokes that we should compile the poems into a compendium and call it *Poems to Die By.*

Her Grace, whom we think to be asleep, overhears. "*Poems by Which to Die,*" she corrects, without bothering to open her eyes.

Anything can cue my mother's poetry by association. Looking at an early Christmas card adorned with cherubs and angels, she declaims, "Not Angles but angels," but knows not from whence it comes. Soon we are neck-deep in the works of the Venerable Bede, a Benedictine monk from Northumbria.

Her Grace reminds me that in his book *A History of the English*

Church and People, published in 731, Bede became the first historian to articulate the idea of Englishness, treating all the inhabitants of lowland Britain—Saxons, Jutes, and Angles—as one "English" nation.

"The origins of perfidious Albion," I joke.

"What?" She turns on faux deafness when it suits her.

"Perfidious—"

"Yes, yes. I heard you the first time. Albion, white, from the chalk cliffs of Dover."

"And perfidious because the English betrayed the French Revolution," I suggest.

"Pah, that's just Gallic propaganda," she says. "They've never forgiven us for setting fire to Joan of Arc, who, by the way, was an epileptic. She saw God during her seizures."

Her Grace, the former physician, has a keen eye for diagnosing the medical ailments suffered by historical figures; ailments, she avers, that explain their behavior. Michelangelo, she believes, was autistic. Samuel Johnson had Tourette's. It's obvious from his face, she says, that Abraham Lincoln had Marfan syndrome. Churchill was bipolar. Newton, psychotic. Tolstoy was a manic depressive. I'm not sure how she knows all this, but she's quite adamant.

•   •   •

Once, my mother had been a *great* narrative diagnostician. It's an art increasingly lost by modern, tech-dependent doctors. As a boy I used to watch her work. She was a GMO—government medical officer— and the only doctor for thousands of square miles along Zimbabwe's eastern border with Mozambique. In her rural clinics she didn't have access to blood tests and scans, so she had to elicit the malady from the person in front of her. I saw the way she would put patients at ease by creating a sympathetic space, slowly coaxing embarrassing details from them, examining them meticulously. And how she made no distinction for status, paying the same attention to all, trying to figure out what ailed them, even as the queue coiled around her rondavel clinic.

She had supervised a tuberculosis sanitarium, and a leper colony at Biriwiri, which I visited regularly as a child. The lepers used to let me play tsoro with them. It's an African strategy-based game, over a thousand years old. You move pebbles between rows of holes in a piece of wood or in the ground, move them very fast. Many of the lepers were terribly disfigured, their features eroded, their fingertips or whole digits missing, but that didn't slow them down.

When I had children of my own, I found myself questioning the wisdom of my mother letting me hang out with lepers as a kid.

"Didn't you worry that I'd get infected?" I asked my mother.

"They were dry lepers, not wet ones; they weren't infectious," she said. And then, because she couldn't resist it, she added the grinning caveat, "by and large."

The Biriwiri lepers had a big radiogram perched on fluted wooden legs. They turned it up loud and danced, almost ecstatically, to up-tempo simanje-manje music. And they smoked sweet-smelling cigarettes which they rolled themselves from pages of the *Umtali Post*. It took a few more years for me to recognize the sweet smell as mbanje—weed—and to realize they were all high.

When Georgina asked Mum how she never recoiled from the terrible afflictions—putrid open wounds, pus-filled cysts, goiters, rotting gangrene, rabies—with which she was routinely confronted, we were both surprised by her answer, given that she was not overtly religious, seldom went to church.

"I saw Jesus in every patient," she said. "I imagined each one might be Our Lord."

Those long lines of patients, the tuberculosis sanitarium, and the leper colony meant my mother was always late to collect me from school.

I would wait alone on the red cement veranda, doing my homework at the stone balustrade, long after all the other day students had gone home. Eventually the night watchman would arrive to hoist the hissing Tilley lamps onto the lantern hooks. And still I waited for the welcome crunch of tires on gravel that would announce the arrival of Dr. Godwin, still in her white coat, smelling of disinfectant, with a stethoscope stuffed in one pocket. Dr. Godwin, aka my mother.

One day she knelt in front of me, her eyes level with mine, and she told me that what she *really* needed was for me to be a "big boy," to be independent and "grown-up." And so I was. Because I wanted to please her, to earn her love. But of course, her goal was to no longer have to pay attention to me, to no longer need to worry about me, so that she could do her real job, her vocation. I was proud of her, and I understood that she had more important things to do than to take care of me. I was a loyal child.

Then the war came to Chimanimani, heralded by the death of our next-door neighbor, ambushed up near Skyline Junction by a guerrilla group called the Crocodile Gang. My parents sought special permission from the Ministry of Education for me to board at school. I was six, two years younger than any other boarder, and small for my age. Bullied and homesick, I cried myself to sleep each night and began wetting my bed. I drew a prison-style calendar and taped it to the inside of my metal locker door, crossing the days off until the first permitted parental visit—an exeat—six weeks later.

When my parents arrived—late—in their dusty ivory Austin Westminster, I was ready, my black tin trunk with GODWIN stenciled on it in white capitals, all packed. I ran to the car, dragging the trunk behind me, wrenched open the car door, leapt in, and burst into tears, begging to go home.

It never occurred to me that once they saw how unhappy I was, my parents might make me stay. But they did. The war made it too dangerous to do otherwise, they tried to explain over tea and rusks in the Chimanimani Hotel lounge.

I can remember every detail of their departure later that day. The cawing of the crows in the cypress trees, the evening breeze picking up off Green Mount, the precise way the taillights of the Austin glowed briefly red as my father braked and then accelerated away past the banks of morning glories and into the gloaming. In that moment, I understood that I was really on my own.

From then on, I was raised in uniform, in boys-only institutions, boarding schools further and further away from home (followed by the army, and even a males-only Cambridge college). At school I became almost feral, going for months without a one-on-one conversation with an adult.

And I never really trusted my parents again.

• • •

This morning, Her Grace is in the mood for some Thomas Babington.

"Thomas Babington?"

"Aka Lord Macaulay," she says in her superior way. "'Horatius at the Bridge'?"

At seventy stanzas, "Horatius at the Bridge" is a marathon recital. Several dozen verses in, as the battle flows interminably back and forth around the contested Pons Sublicius, I am ready to concede defeat myself. It is a bridge too far.

"Jesus, this is taking longer to read than it would to fight the battle itself!"

At this she takes hold of her monkey bar, pulls herself upright, and begins to declaim in a surprisingly vigorous voice:

And how can man die better
Than facing fearful odds,

For the ashes of his fathers,
And the temples of his Gods

Exhausted by the effort, she falls back upon her paisley pillows and closes her eyes.

Nema, the new carer sent by the agency to replace Gina, pads into the room in felt slippers. She is Sudanese, in her thirties, an observant Muslim who wears a black hijab snug to her skull. Before reheating my mother's ready meals, Nema scrutinizes the ingredients list. If they contain pork products, she refuses to open them.

Back home in Khartoum, Nema was a high school teacher, but her qualifications aren't recognized here in England. So now she visits my mother twice a day instead, bathes and feeds her, tidies her room, and empties her commode. She is supposed to do all this for ten pounds an hour—after the agency has taken its cut—but we top it up, because we want her to be nice to Her Grace.

My mother warms to her at once, and soon they are chatting away like close comrades. She tells me that Nema came to London a few months ago as part of an arranged marriage. But she doesn't like her husband and is secretly taking contraception.

When I leave for New York, I try to press a roll of notes, a £250 tip, into Nema's palm. I have a little thank-you speech prepared. But Nema looks down at the money, aghast, and tells me that she can't possibly accept it.

"I really *like* your mother," she says. "She is my only real friend here."

My mother, hale now, her brio replenished, clasps my hands in hers and asks, as she always does, with big eyes and a manipulative tremor in her voice, "When will you return?"

"Kure ndokuna amai, kune mukadzi unofa wasvika," I reply in jest. I have been collecting Shona aphorisms my whole life.

"What does that mean?"

What it means is: "Far is where the mother is, where the wife is, you risk death to reach." What I tell her it means is: "The way you calculate the difficulty of any journey depends on your desire to take it."

She casts me a look of mock horror that morphs into a lopsided grin.

"Good boy," she says, even though my hair is now garnished with gray. When I reach to hug her, she stiffens with discomfort and pats my back awkwardly, as though trying to burp a baby.

Tribes Without Flags

NO ONE IS MORE SURPRISED THAN I AM TO FIND MYSELF IN AMER-
ica. I never aspired to it, yet here I am, living on my third continent.
America was Joanna's dream. She'd wanted to get here ever since she
read American studies at the University of East Anglia, ever since
she directed *Saturday Night Fever* at the drama club there. And when
the *Guardian* offered her the New York bureau, she jumped at it. I'd
just left the BBC, was working on my third book, could live anywhere, so a two- or three-year posting in New York seemed an interesting intermission. I had not expected to be here twenty years later.

Joanna and I met at the late Café de Paris, in Piccadilly, introduced by
Jane, a mutual friend who had described her to me as "the rudest woman
in London." Jane meant it as a compliment, and I took it as such. Indeed, Joanna *was* bracingly candid, unplagued by that crippling British
trait, fear-of-embarrassment. *Private Eye*, the satirical magazine, would
soon confer upon her the definite article, in French no less: La Coles.

Back then, we still greeted one another with mutual cries of "Ahoy!" like shipmates. ("Ahoy" had been the way Alexander Graham Bell suggested phones be answered, but Thomas Edison's "Hello" won the day.)

Back then she still had wild Titian tresses that were a suspiciously similar shade to my mother's—paging Herr Doktor Freud.

Back then she still had a little gap between her front teeth, about which she was sweetly self-conscious. Whenever she smiled too broadly, she would quickly remember and retract it. I found the net effect terribly attractive, a smile that played fleetingly across her face. Tentative, some might say, dentative. It was a smile you had to earn.

I would gently tease her about Chaucer's gap-toothed Wife of Bath, a woman of insatiable lust. And reassure her that ever since the European Middle Ages, a gap between front teeth—diastema—has been regarded as a thing of beauty in a woman. In many parts of Africa, it still is, as well as a sign of fertility. So much so that some women get gaps between their front teeth cosmetically carved.

Once in America, Joanna quickly had her teeth recapped and whitened, giving her a wide, white, gapless reef, a TV anchor smile, fleeting no more, bold as high-beam headlights. And as dazzlingly deployed.

Her hair changed color too, from red to platinum blond. I can always spot her in a crowd. Among the browns and blacks and dirty blondes, a lone shimmering dandelion. And she had it chopped into a bob, a bright white helmet that became part of her new image. Because it naturally curls, she summoned groomers to the apartment weekly to tug and stretch it into compliance, often with the aid of hot Japanese tongs.

Watching the hairdresser and the makeup artist work around her, snipping and spritzing, brushing and blowing, painting and powdering, reminds me of a Formula One race car pulling into the pits, where a crew changes its tires against the clock.

She is like an actor prepping for a role, strapping on a prosthetic mask, and she sees the irony of it. We exchange surreptitious eye rolls; this creation is "work Joanna," the one she needs to be out in the corporate world. The prodigious networker, the whale swimming through the social sea, trapping bold-faced krill in the bristles of her baleen. This is Brand Joanna, not *real* Joanna.

Armed with a clothing allowance, her wardrobe has experienced an extreme makeover too, filling up with designer clothes: her favored outerwear, a Sgt. Pepper brocade coat. I joke with her that while the Devil might now wear Prada, the Devil's husband still wears Gap.

America changed her in other ways too. It was a just-add-water fillip. It boosted her drive, made her ultra-decisive. Her approach to the world was so binary, quick draw, that it released a bounty of mental energy, the energy that I wasted balancing options, playing out scenarios, and trying to hold mutually contradictory views in my head at the same time.

The States billowed the sails of her ambition. It freed her from the doldrums of English faux self-deprecation, of the humblebrag that often goes awry when Brits try it in America. She agreed with Chekhov that an essential quality of civilized people is that they do not disparage themselves to rouse compassion.

The States helped her fizz like human Alka-Seltzer, snare-drum like an Energizer Bunny. British newspapers weren't big enough to contain her, and she jumped ship to join *New York* magazine as a features editor, and then to the poop deck of editors-in-chief, dominated by other Brits—Anna Wintour, Tina Brown, Glenda Bailey—at the helms of US *Vogue*, *Vanity Fair*, and *Harper's Bazaar*. Joanna edited *Marie Claire*, then *Cosmopolitan*, and soon she became editorial director of all Hearst's magazines. As she shinned the corporate mast and increased her earnings, I took over more of our domestic life, including our two American-born boys.

I sold my Notting Hill flat, and with the proceeds we bought a ruinous prewar apartment with high ceilings and good bones on Manhattan's Upper West Side.

Even then I didn't think we were really *settling* here—it just didn't make financial sense to rent once Joanna stopped being a foreign correspondent with an accommodation allowance.

Because we weren't married yet, for the first five years of Joanna's posting to New York I was a temporary sojourner, living here on a tourist visa, making sure that I exited every few months so as not to violate my status. Then I began the protracted process of applying for a green card as an "alien of exceptional ability."

"A bit of a reach," my father had teased at the time.

But in due course I got it. Then, 9/11. And as soon as city hall reopened, Joanna and I married during her lunch break. She was eight months pregnant with Hugo, our second son. We joked that for our wedding vows I pledged to give her access to my US citizenship, and in return she pledged to give me access to her corporate health insurance. Afterwards we strolled over to Bubby's in Tribeca, ordered a half bottle of Veuve Clicquot and a couple of salads, and then both went back to work.

• • •

The Beaux Arts apartment buildings along Riverside Drive, where we bought our dilapidated ground-floor apartment, were built at the turn of the nineteenth century by wealthy Jews excluded from the grand co-ops that line Park and Fifth Avenues. The pro forma constitutions there, in these Upper East Side vespiaries, stipulated: no Blacks, no Jews, no entertainers (Sammy Davis Jr. would have been a triple threat). Our own apartment served as the end of an underground railroad for refugees—a landing pad for newly arrived Soviet Jews.

The apartment looks out over Joan of Arc Island, a small tussock off Riverside Park, presided over by a twice life-sized statue of Jeanne d'Arc herself, the medieval virgin warrior and patron saint of France, inventor of Joanna's signature bob hairstyle, burned at the stake by the English and, according to Her Grace, an undiagnosed epileptic. From her rearing steed with its flared nostrils, she brandishes her broadsword at the New Jersey Palisades, a mile away across the Hudson River. In 1915 she became the city's first monument to a historical woman, sculpted by a woman too, Anna Vaughn Hyatt Huntington.

It is early September, and I am jogging along the riverbank, as I try to most days, hoping that exercise will quiet the demons in my head. Our dog, Phoebe, runs at my side—she's a beagle-cross, a refugee from a kill-pound in Georgia, Confederate not Caucasus. Dungaree-clad animal activists swooped in to save her just before she was scheduled to be gassed. They drove her north in their bus with dozens of other rescued puppies. Phoebe still radiates the infectious energy of a dog who knows she's lucky to be alive. But she's an erratic running partner, apt to dart across me to pursue squirrels.

On the Hudson, the last of the summer sailboats bob at anchor, their stays clinking against their masts like ice cubes in sundowners.

Upriver, the colossal cables of the George Washington Bridge, supposedly still the busiest river-crossing in the world, look as fine as filigree lace. The steel struts of its turrets are entirely exposed, without the planned limestone and granite cladding, because it was still being built in 1929 when the Great Depression struck.

The Hudson was once so toxic that brigs sailed up it to burn the barnacles off their hulls. But slowly it has been getting cleaner, and the giant Atlantic carp, so-called Albany chicken that grow to fifteen feet long, once again swim here.

The indigenous Mohican called this river "the water which flows both ways," as it is tidal as far as Poughkeepsie, seventy-five miles up-stream. The driftwood logs, floating south from as far as Canada, move north again as the tide turns.

And at a certain point each day, the Hudson's seaward flow is met by the incoming Atlantic tide and the river achieves perfect stasis, hanging in exquisite suspension for a short, magical moment. And when this stasis happens at sunset, as it does today, the light plays upon the surface of the water, beveling it into coppered facets, like a hand-beaten cauldron. And then the moment passes, and the river takes up its restless journey once more.

Ahead, a crowd of people block our path. They appear to be throwing things over the railing into the river and blowing something that sounds to me like a vuvuzela. Forced to a halt, I see that it is a curled ram's horn, a shofar.

"What's going on?" I ask one of the obstructors, a bearded, middle-aged man, dressed all in black.

"It's Tashlich," he explains, "the first day of the Jewish High Holidays. To atone, we write down our sins of the year on a piece of paper and then cast it into flowing water, preferably with fish in it. Fish have no eyelids, you see, so their eyes never close; they see all things, just like our Creator."

He tears a page from his notebook and offers it. "Would you like to atone?" he asks.

I realize I haven't been to Catholic confessional in, what, more than a decade? "Phew, I may need more than one page!" I say.

He laughs, tearing off a second one. "You don't have to *actually* write your sins down," he says. "It's symbolic."

I take the paper, scrunch it up as instructed, and throw it into the water. But it just sits there.

"The Hudson isn't flowing at the moment," I point out. "Maybe this won't work."

He surveys the stationary river.

"Don't worry," he says. "The tide will turn."

• • •

On Friday afternoon, as we do most Fridays now, we head north from New York City, up the Henry Hudson Parkway, past the Manhattan Mini-Storage billboard that warns, "If you leave New York City you'll have to live in America," and onto the narrow, winding Taconic State Parkway, statistically New York State's most dangerous road. I feel free, steering our leased Volvo XC90 through a series of switchbacks we call the luge. White lines on the road ahead rush towards us, opening it like the teeth of a giant zipper. I am effectively on my own. Joanna pecks at her phone next to me and, in the back, our two sons, Thomas and Hugo, are subsumed in their own screens. We are alone together.

Behind the wheel I find the agency that now seems lacking in the rest of my life. I drive fast but accurately, accelerating into the bends to take advantage of centrifugal force, as I was trained to do in the police driving course decades ago in Zimbabwe. I am one with the machine, exhibiting, I would claim, excellent SA—pilot-speak for "situational awareness."

"It would be a shame to break Volvo's unblemished run," Joanna says without looking up.

I have boasted to her that no one has ever been killed in this model Volvo—it has a fatality-free record. Ergo, we are immortal while ensconced within its steel-ribbed sarcophagus.

Joanna calls me an aggressive driver. It's not my driving itself she objects to, but what she regards as my episodes of road rage. I maintain that I'm simply an adherent of the George Carlin school of speed: "anyone driving slower than me is an idiot and anyone driving faster than me is a maniac." I never actually *do* anything aggressive. I merely mutter harmlessly hostile harangues. I'm a paper tiger. My roar is muted, neutered. My French cousins have a phrase for the kind of person I have become—"un mouton enragé"—a furious sheep, a normally calm person who sometimes, suddenly, completely loses his shit.

"Fat Cat will vomit if you go on driving like this," Joanna warns, without losing eye-screen contact.

Annoyingly, Fat Cat emits a protest yowl on cue.

Fat Cat couldn't be further from his rapacious capitalist archetype. He's a shelter cat, a gelded marmalade mongrel with lazy, cinnamon eyes. The boys named him Ginger as a kitten, but it never took. His Fat Cat moniker is now well deserved; he's so fat, the protruding pouch of his belly drags along the floor gathering dust, fallen paper clips, stray Post-it Notes, desiccated spider carcasses, and other random debris. He's a feline Swiffer.

We are heading for Indian Orchard, set on a steep slope of Bird Peak, one of the highest peaks in northwestern Connecticut, where we now have a modest weekend cottage.

At the bottom of the hill, we stop to release Phoebe. She bolts from the opening car door like a greyhound from a rising race gate, her pumping palomino haunches quickly disappearing around the bend as she romps for home. When we pull into the drive, she meets us, breathless, beaming at having chased resident chipmunks down holes and squirrels up trees.

· · ·

I have come to rely on Indian Orchard as a rural refuge, a shelter. Up here, like my mother does in Canfield Gardens, I am latibulating from the pain of my last book, *The Fear*.

For that book I traveled back to Zimbabwe, which is not easy for me to do. Back in 1984 I had to flee arrest in Zimbabwe and was declared an enemy of the state for reporting on the Matabeleland massacres, when Mugabe unleashed his North Korean–trained Fifth Brigade soldiers on the Ndebele people in the south of the country, who had supported a rival political party. He called it Operation Gukurahundi, the "spring rains that flush away the debris." More than twenty thousand civilians were killed, maybe many more—we still don't know because there has never been an accounting.

Twenty-five years later I went back in to document the pro-democracy activists, many of them friends, seeking to unseat Robert Mugabe's repressive kleptocracy through elections. The notebooks I brought back from this long, under-the-radar reporting trip brimmed with details of Mugabe's industrial-scale campaign of torture. Zimbabweans called this time "Chidudu"—*The Fear.*

It was important, I thought, to record the bravery of those opposing the dictatorship. But the northern world was watching football and soccer and scrolling through social media. They were playing video games and going to Marvel movies, golfing and working out at the gym. They were doing all the things you do when you have freedom. And peace. And money. All the normal, happy, pointless things. And few cared about a small Southern African country. Why would they? So, the promises I proffered to the people I'd interviewed, that I could help draw attention to their situation, proved to be inflated.

When I was a boy, just post-toddler, my father-the-engineer decided that the best use of one of our rare moments alone together was to teach me the arcane science of metal fatigue; part of his occasional efforts to convert me into the STEM son he'd always wanted.

This was the man who gifted me the detailed manual to a Suzuki 125cc motorbike for my sixteenth birthday. And then opened the garage door to the bike's parts that he had disassembled and laid out across the floor. I put them together in such a rush that there were several components left over, so I had to start again. But after that, I knew the bike inside out, which, of course, had been his intention.

Looking back now, I think he took solace in the solidity of science, the immutability of its rules in an otherwise capricious and unreliable world.

For the metal fatigue lesson, he sat me down at his workbench and handed me a piece of broad-gauge wire, instructing me to bend it back and forth. After a considerable time—to me, at least—nothing had happened, and I asked to stop. He ordered me to continue. The wire slowly heated up, and then, quite suddenly, it snapped.

Metal fatigue, he explained, is caused by "repeated variations of stress." Once a "fatigue crack" opens, it grows with each loading cycle until it reaches critical size, when the "stress intensity factor" exceeds the "fracture toughness." That is when the material breaks.

Mental fatigue, it seems to me, works in much the same way. I sometimes wonder if I am approaching that breaking point. As a journalist covering conflicts, you are conditioned, like emergency medics and ER doctors and cops, to compartmentalize, protect your core from the horrors you witness, so you can continue to do your job efficiently. You cultivate a carapace, a kind of controlled schizophrenia to shield yourself from the repeated variations of stress. You must, otherwise you will snap.

I found myself sitting up here in the sanctuary of Indian Orchard, a place of palpable peace, writing about appalling violence. The disconnect was extreme, producing in me a malaise, a kind of cognitive dissonance. I tried to joke with Joanna (editing *Marie Claire* at the time and fresh from the Paris fashion collections) that she was now an expert on *cout-ure*, while I was an expert on *tort-ure*. But mostly I was unable to talk about it. It was just too dark. I didn't want to rain on our family parade.

For though I hadn't admitted it to myself yet, living through and writing *The Fear* had left me shaken and depleted. I still feel self-conscious to mention its effect on me. My psychological wounds are *so* much less than the *actual* wounds of the astonishingly brave people I was describing.

Zimbabwe is not just another story for me. It pierces the protective husk of the foreign correspondent because, to me, it is not foreign. It is personal. As I marshalled the material and relived the experience, I seemed to succumb to some kind of empathy-overload. The weight of others' suffering stopped me from inhabiting my own life, from having *fun*. Whenever I tried, a veil of guilt descended—more than a veil, a portcullis, hurtling down to cut me off from contentment, consigning me to a state of mind I now know is called anhedonia. My own preoccupations were utterly inconsequential compared to the people I was writing about.

And I felt a rift opening. Back in America, Zimbabwe seemed so obscure, so far. It seemed a world away.

I felt closer than ever to my sons. They were my escape. Parenthood, I realized, had made me more sensitive and emotional, tender even. I was less worried that the pram in the hallway—as Cyril Connolly put it—was the enemy of promise, than I was of the promise of enemies. I lost my appetite for all that, lost my tolerance for danger, for risk.

When my son Thomas was born, I had looked at him and thought of Yeats:

> *Come away, O human child!*
> *To the waters and the wild*
> *With a faery, hand in hand,*
> *For the world's more full of weeping than you can under-*
> *stand.*

Some say that you become the parent you needed as a child. A sort of retroactive wish fulfillment. Selfish as it sounds, I sensed that being a hands-on father might help me heal too. That through the balm of the boys, I could somehow be made whole again. They were my life preservers, cork rings floating on a sea in which I was floundering.

• • •

The sanctuary on Indian Orchard was a terrible purchase. Built in the early 1960s, it's a squat, ugly, dun-roofed, berm bungalow, burrowed into the hillside, hobbit habitat. Joanna had fallen in love with it while I was away in the Kalahari on assignment for *National Geographic* among the San people, and I was persuaded to do a remote sign-off based only on photos, a description, and her giddy enthusiasm.

The day after we closed, the American property market tanked. By the time we moved in, the house had already shed a third of its value. That was without factoring in the right-of-way I discovered deep in the deeds. It went across our lawn to a neighboring, undeveloped plot, a lien that would perpetually plague our property value.

Things started to go wrong at once. The house needed a new roof, new windows, and outside doors; the chimney stack was structurally cracked; the mudroom turned into a small river every rainstorm and snowmelt; the fireplaces smoked if not handled with excruciating care; and there was radon resident in the schist beneath. And, initially, no internet—it was too far from the last phone-line booster.

And when I ventured into the attic, I discovered, in addition to insulation installed the wrong way round, an old ophidian map showing that this *precise* location was a protected breeding ground for timber rattlesnakes, which turn out to be one of America's most venomous reptiles. I would wake up at night convinced I could hear the sinister susurrations of their malign maracas as they fucked in the attic.

Rattlesnakes aren't the only local wildlife. The edge of our yard is the boundary of New York's Taconic State Park, which runs sixteen miles along the Taconic Mountains and merges in the north with Bash Bish Falls State Park in Massachusetts. There's no fence of any sort— you just walk across unhindered—and these reserves burst with bears, bobcats, beavers, coyotes, foxes, deer, otters, skunks, hares, and wild turkeys. When the animals gravitate south, the first human habitation they encounter is this little cottage dug into the hillside.

Up here it feels like we live in their world, not they in ours.

As soon as you enter Indian Orchard, the view surges in to meet you. It's visceral, physical. You instantly forget what a terrible investment this house is, its structural defects and its leaks and its awful exterior aesthetic.

In the foreground, a lush sward slopes steeply down to a split cedar rail fence, which tees up a rustic panorama: first the prow of Indian Mountain and then the rest of the Taconic ranges, folded tight, one behind another, in a spectrum of fading blues. They are punctuated by patchwork paddocks carved from the New England forest. This is the kind of landscape that inspired the early transcendentalists—Henry David Thoreau, Ralph Waldo Emerson, and Margaret Fuller—in their belief that nature radiates the divine.

And when the sun slants from the west to silhouette the distant crenellations of the Catskills, it reminds me of the luminous Chimanimani Mountains on the Mozambique border of Zimbabwe, mica-sparkling sentinels of my childhood, my Ithaca, the place that will always be home in my head, even as it grows more distant in time.

Joanna arrives in the bedroom to interrupt my reverie. She's mounted on red-soled Louboutins with heels like oil derricks.

"In the future," I wonder aloud, "will we look back at high heels, circumcision, and religion as foot-binding, genital mutilation, and witchcraft?"

She ignores me, her face basking in the blue light of her cell screen. "Can you change the music?" she says. "This stuff is so . . . maudlin." She picks up my phone and scrolls through my playlist. "Why do you only listen to people with no nations?"

She has a point. There are a lot of tribes without flags on my playlist. As the Irish say, the victors write the history, the vanquished write the songs. Many of the artists here are from remnant peoples, marginal, unrequited nations. The history-diced, the dominated, the divided. Scatterlings of Roma, Berbers, Kurds, and Tuaregs. Mandinka, Wolof, Fulani, Ndebele, Herero, and Igbo. Ashkenazim from the Eastern European diaspora playing Yiddish klezmer music on clarinets and cimbaloms. Sahelian griots plucking their koras, Jeli striking their balafons, Manyika malleting mahogany marimbas, Ndau thumbing the metal tines of their mbira, San trance-chanting incantations from a time before language. Troubled troubadours, their voices tight with yearning, accompanied by weeping guitars and the haunting cadences of talking drums that echo the prosody of the human voice.

Maybe I'm drawn to their elegiac tones, laments infused with the loss and sadness of exile, of being without one's own home, of the unfinished business of belonging.

Joanna kicks off her Louboutins, slides into Gucci shearling mules, and skitters downstairs. She appears to be walking on squashed squirrels.

I turn my music back up. Playing now is "True Sorry," by Ibrahim Maalouf, a refugee from the Lebanese civil war who can coax from his trumpet the minutely calibrated quarter-tones necessary for Arab maqams. He seems to blow the trumpet as softly as one would a flute.

• • •

I go back to researching my latest project, a biography of the enigmatic nineteenth-century figure Emin Pasha. I became intrigued when I saw a photograph of him in a book on Henry Morton Stanley. With his small oval glasses and his claret fez, complete with black silk tassel, Emin Pasha looked like a sepia Shriner. Why hadn't I heard of him before? I'd been raised on tales of the English-speaking "explorers," John Hanning Speke, David Livingstone, Mungo Park, and Richard Burton. But never Emin Pasha.

I became determined to unpack him because he reminded me of my father, a cultural shape-shifter, moving between religions, languages, nationalities. Looking back now, I think that I imagined writing about Emin Pasha might help me understand my father.

Like a Matryoshka doll, Emin takes some unpacking. Born

Eduard Carl Oscar Theodor Schnitzer, a German Jew, he trained as a physician, converted first to Lutheranism, then Islam when he worked for the Ottoman administration in its dog days. He became a naturalist, anthropologist, linguist, abolitionist, found his way to Egypt, where he took the name Emin Pasha, a Muslim honorific. The British general, Robert Gordon, who ruled over Sudan, sent him to govern Equatoria, its vast, southern province that included what is today South Sudan and northern Uganda.

Emin was an unlikely governor, diminutive, intellectual, a skilled player of chess and, on the piano, of Chopin and Mendelssohn. Yet he managed to command a detachment of sullen Egyptian officers for whom service in the wilds of Equatoria was a punishment posting, an alternative to a prison sentence. Equatoria was beyond the reach of the navigable Nile, blocked by the Sudd, a shallow swamp choked with papyrus and water hyacinth, infested with crocodiles and hippos.

A few years into Emin's posting, a Sudanese carpenter, Mohammed Ahmed, declared himself Mahdi, the Last Prophet, and led an uprising of so-called whirling dervishes against the British, slaying General Gordon at the Battle of Khartoum in 1885, declaring a caliphate, and sweeping all vestiges of British rule from Sudan.

Or so the Western world assumed. But three years later a letter that Emin Pasha smuggled out of Equatoria arrived in London. Cut off from the outside world, 1,200 miles from the coast, Emin and his ragtag garrison continued at their post. Emin had "gone native," like Captain Kurtz at the head of the Conradian river. The world was agog. Newspapers in Europe and the US awaited Emin's sporadic updates like missives from the moon.

Joanna finds my choice of subject odd. She thinks I'm deliberately courting obscurity with this Quixotic endeavor.

"No one has the slightest idea who Emin Pasha is," she complains.

"Emin's obscurity is the whole *point*," I say.

Joanna is not to be deflected. "If you must still focus on Africa, what about writing something on George Clooney and Darfur?" she suggests.

"Hmm." I affect to take this seriously. "But which period? There are four distinct periods of colonial Sudanese history."

"Huh?" She reemerges from her cell phone, a rabbit startled out of a lettuce patch.

"Pre-Clooneyal, Clooneyal, Post-Clooneyal, Neo-Clooneyal."

She rolls her eyes. "I'm only trying to save you from your own irrelevance, you know. Oh, and, by the way, Clooney has used most of the millions he earned for his Nespresso ads to pay for satellite surveillance time over Darfur, which has been highly effective in cutting down the atrocities there. You, of all people, should be aware of that."

"I know, I know. You're right." I feel bad for singling out Clooney. "But why do we always need celebrities to get attention for Africa? It's as though we need brand ambassadors, celebrity sponsors for each humanitarian crisis. George has Darfur, brought to you by Nespresso; Ben Affleck has eastern Congo; Angelina's all over Ethiopia and now, Namibia—she even gave birth there, on the Skeleton Coast. Oprah's into South African education; Denzel's supporting African kids with HIV; Charlize helps rape victims in South Africa . . ."

Though appearing to listen, Joanna is tapping on her rose-gold iPhone, shellac clacking on glass, overlaid by the retro typing audio she's now enabled. She's nostalgic for the antediluvian, analog days when we began as reporters, when you still hit keys that flicked levers, that pushed raised letters onto inked ribbon, that indented paper with text. Wherever she goes, you can find her by following the faux mechanical clatter of an old Olivetti.

My train of thought is derailed by a howl of pain from the lawn below. I run down to find that Phoebe is trying to kill a chipmunk, her muzzle moist with its blood. The chipmunk has nipped her on the nose and now the dog has backed off. I hold Phoebe's collar while the chipmunk limps away into its nearby hole, to die down there in the dark, beneath the ground. I pull the dog indoors, turn off the lights, and climb the stairs to bed.

Joanna is already asleep. I slide in beside her, careful not to wake her. But there is really no need for caution, she's snuffling gently in her earplugs and eye mask. The place could burn down and she wouldn't wake.

• • •

Somewhere deep in that Taconic night I am awoken by the hooting of an owl. Once awake, I lie there, worrying. The Swedes have a word for this dead-of-night angst. Vargtimmen. Wolftime. I conduct a quick circuit of the stations of the cross, mentally genuflecting at each of my various anxieties.

I think about how different my life might have been had I stayed in Southern Africa, or if I'd remained in England where I lived for more than fifteen years, all told. How different our children would be had they grown up in the damp, etiolating English climate, speaking in quaint Anglo accents, affecting to be allergic to enthusiasm. My sons are away at boarding school now. American ones. Having attended Dickensian boarding schools in Zimbabwe, it troubled me that they'd both chosen that path, and I'd done my best to dissuade them. Until a friend of mine, a pediatric shrink, tiring of my lament, reminded me of the golden rule of child-rearing. Parent the child you've got, he warned. Not the child you were.

I backed off after that.

Now, shockingly, our younger boy, Hugo, is nearly fifteen. He seems to be growing an inch a week, like a backyard weed. Already he's north of six feet. His complexion is swollen with testosterone, stippled with a light crop of acne despite his diligent scrubbing, or perhaps because of it, his face an aggrieved red from his daily ministrations. He lollops along, distracted by devices, leaving a plume of forgotten items behind him: keys, wallets, ID fobs, books, chargers, clothes, and basketball boots as big as boats.

His energy levels oscillate wildly. One minute he is impulsive, compulsive, frenetic. The next he speaks as though drugged, which in a sense he is, by his own hormones. Hair sprouts from the various junctions of his body. His legs gangle like a colt's, not yet grown into themselves. His features are changing their proportions, altering his appearance each time I see him. He is a chrysalis, about to burst into a different cycle of life, a pupa wriggling to discard its childish husk to emerge pinkly massive and adult.

Yet just as we think he is really maturing, he'll regress. When we'd taken him out from school for Sunday lunch, he interrupted Joanna in full flow to inquire whether we knew that, during the Middle Ages, people thought if you trapped your farts in a jar and then inhaled them, it would cure you of bubonic plague.

"Jesus, is that what we get for paying to have you privately educated?" asked Joanna.

"No, I read it on the web," Hugo replied mildly, ignoring her ire.

He treats us like old, inherited furniture now, benign if vaguely embarrassing. Unless we get in his way, then he erupts as though he has stubbed his toe on us. We are fading already to the edge of his cosmos, suns he once orbited, reduced now to mere moons. All we can hope to do is to modulate his emotional tides.

This is the all-important final act of parenthood, and it's the hardest one. This is the act where you let go, you walk away and allow your children to ripen into their own people. Accept that they are the vines to our trellises, let them grow up and over us, obscuring us with their own fertile luxuriance. Like the espalier fixed to the stucco wall of the house here, woven with pear tree branches that, come summer's end, become so laden with fruit they wrench the espalier from the stucco.

It seems only last week that we were watching Hugo the toddler in the school's annual nativity play, cast as a diminutive shepherd in taupe hessian robe, a checkered keffiyeh corded to his head, gasping at the star-of-wonder, star-of-night, star-with-royal-beauty-bright, while his older brother, Thomas, played Balthazar, one of the Three Kings, with powdered gray hair and fake sideburns, presenting Joseph with the gift of myrrh.

As we'd sat like Brobdingnagians on Lilliputian school chairs among lines of cooing parents watching the nativity tale, I found myself wondering what happened to myrrh, blood of the wounded tree, holy oil, balm of Gilead, balsam of Mecca, sweet cicely. It has been reduced to an ingredient in mouthwash. No longer fit for Jesus's baby shower, just a morning gargle.

The soft oblivion of sleep, that merciful release from consciousness, still eludes me.

I think of the horror movie script I am writing on spec. The one set in the luxury African safari lodge. How shall I pitch it? An African *Deliverance*? *The Shining* in the savannah? *Don't Look Now* on safari? *Rosemary's Baby* in the bush?

Many rural Africans still believe in witches and wizards, in apparitions and spirit-possession. But the challenge is to make a Western, urban audience buy into these apparitions too, or at least suspend their disbelief of them. In most narratives it's usually only in a malarial fugue or some other Conradian fever dream that northerners in Africa succumb to local belief in the supernatural. To make this script work I need a skeptical northern protagonist to be utterly convinced—taking the audience with him—that he's witnessed one of these African golems.

The more I consider possible plot lines, the more I realize that the scariest thing of all is not that you have *seen* the monster, but to suspect that you *are* the monster. That the madness is inside you, the monster within.

Outside, the coyotes begin to howl from the forest above the cottage. Call and refrain. One, and then an answering howl, and then a chorus of them. I feel the hairs on my arms hackling, a primordial horripilation in reaction to the baying of predators beyond the circle of firelight, beyond the pale. Fat Cat appears outside at the windowsill, bug eyed, stiff tailed, scratching frantically at the screen. For all his feline bravado at being able to survive out there in the wild, he's just a kibble-fed kitty at heart, a beta *Felis catus* cowering in the cave of his *sapien* sponsors.

I pad over to the window to let him in.

• • •

In the leavening light of morning, I Skype London to wish Georgina a happy birthday. It's hard to know when to call, as her job requires strange hours.

She's had an interesting career: to qualify for the actors' union Equity after drama school, she spent a year as a children's entertainer, Georgie Porgie, dressed as a clown in an outsized yellow onesie with big, multicolored polka dots (sewn for her by Mum). She soon dropped the clown makeup. Peak Georgie Porgie made the children cry, and passengers on the Tube shrank from her.

Eventually Georgie Porgie broke into the lucrative Japanese birthday party circuit, entertaining the kids of bankers recently arrived from Tokyo, where there is no culture of musical statues and it was seen as an appealingly exotic, English folk ritual, like Morris dancing.

There followed a stint in local theater, touring provincial seaside towns with a saucy production of *The Tart and the Vicar's Wife*—Georgina was the tart—and then she went home to launch a career in radio. After also falling foul of the Zimbabwe regime, for helping to start an independent radio station in a country where all broadcast outlets were state controlled, she bounced back to Blighty to work for Radio Africa, which transmitted into Zimbabwe remotely. She has been a radio presenter ever since.

For the last few years, she has worked for Monocle Radio, and she naps at odd hours to make up for her 4:45 a.m. alarm call, to get to the studio, often in the dark, having already digested the morning's papers and written the intros and questions for her current affairs show, *The Globalist*. And she talks to authors weekly for her other two shows, *Meet the Writers* and *Monocle Reads*. Writers love her because she rigorously reads their books. She also moderates at book festivals and judges literary awards and so, on average, she consumes four books a week, sometimes on audiobook, speeded up while she yomps Bella across Hampstead Heath.

Now Georgina gives me a visual tour of her recent redecoration of the Canfield Gardens apartment, taking in Xanthe's purple-walled bedroom, the shy piebald cat in the doorway, the plastic tube of LED lights snaking down the stairwell banister and, finally, to our mother lying high up in her bed as if upon a Victorian litter.

"It's Peter," Georgina tells her. "He's calling to wish me happy birthday."

Our mother squints suspiciously at my image on the phone to verify my identity. Once satisfied, she launches into the circumstances of Georgina's birth—an unexpected one for a forty-three-year-old rural doctor who thought her breeding years were well behind her. Then she segues to mine.

"You're very lucky to be alive at all," she reminds me and goes on to recite my origin story, something she does from time to time. In this origin story she tells of how her first obstetrician urged her to abort me and have a hysterectomy because an earlier surgery to scrape the embryo of my stillborn older brother from the lining of her womb had left it lethally weakened. Another pregnancy was likely to tear the womb open, with hemorrhage and death for both mother and baby.

She tells of how another doctor (hat-tip to the good Dr. Sachs) decided she could risk it. Of how I was allowed to grow under his careful watch and then whipped out by cesarean section the minute I was viable, a pale borlotti bean with a thick fuzz of dark hair. How I was placed in a Plexiglass box for the next three months, where I contracted a violent case of whooping cough that nearly killed me.

So far, I'm familiar with this origin story. But then, in another outbreak of her late-onset candor, my mother adds a new chapter, one I haven't heard before. Initially, she says, the nurses presented her with a robust baby boy. They laid this bonny, red-haired cherub upon her breast to bond. At the time she had long, Titian-red hair. The nurses cooed at the match. After a while, she can't remember how long now, the nurses rushed back in and detached the bonny, red-haired cherub and substituted it with a jaundiced, dark-haired runt.

"What was your reaction when they handed you the real me?" I ask.

"Disappointment," she says without demur.

When You See Me, Weep

I FIND THE UPPER WEST SIDE A STRANGE PLACE TO HAVE WASHED UP. Anchored in the north by Columbia University (where I am teaching) and in the south by the Lincoln Center for the Performing Arts, most of its two western avenues—Riverside Drive and West End Avenue (and the fifty cross streets between them)—was declared an "historic district" in the 1980s, which means nothing old can be torn down and nothing new can be put up. Dominated by prewar apartment blocks, it is frozen in time.

As well as hosting one of New York's biggest Jewish communities (by repute, intellectual and creative Jews live here, and Wall Street Jews live on the Upper East Side), the Upper West Side is home to the most eclectic assortment of public memorials I have ever seen, a theme park of statuary thrown up in the space of a few years, mostly in the early 1900s, part of New York's bid to rival the grand old cities of Europe.

The monuments flow by as I run north. At 79th, flanked by Hotchkiss Cannons, stands the Soldiers' and Sailors' Monument, a vast classical cupola erected to honor the Union soldiers of the Civil War. Now barricaded because its crumbling edifice is leaking.

Inside Riverside Park at 84th is the site of a memorial that never was. The American Memorial to Six Million Jews of Europe was approved by the city in 1952, but the funding was never raised. In the city with the world's largest Jewish population, that's all that's here, seventy-five years later. Surrounded by rhododendrons and a low iron fence, a granite plaque in the boulevard, declaring this is where the memorial *would* have been . . .

At 100th Street stands a large bronze frieze set in limestone, commemorating the New York City Fire Department, including its fire horses. After 9/11, in which 343 firefighters died, it became a vigil site. I took two-and-a-half-year-old Thomas there, hoisted him on my shoulders to see all the cards and candles laid out on the plaza. He associated them with birthday parties and began to sing "Happy Birthday" in his innocent, piping voice and was astonished when it made the people around him weep.

A fifteen-foot-high, medieval Japanese figure in a huge bowl-shaped takuhatsugasa hat and missionary robes, clutching a staff, stands under the portico of the nearby Buddhist temple at 105th Street. In the basement dojo here, the boys learned karate, Thomas peaking at brown belt, Hugo perfecting a blood-curdling yodel and bailing after purple. The figure is Shinran Shonin, founder of the Jodo Shinshu sect. His bronze statue somehow survived the Hiroshima atom bomb, unscathed, and was shipped to America in 1955 to promote world peace. There had been a brief scare that he might still be radioactive, but he was Geiger counted and deemed safe.

I notice, as I run, the thin length of fishing line strung taut, twenty feet high, between utility poles, refracting the sunlight into a rainbow spectrum. It stretches almost invisibly from pole to pole, without a break, mile after mile. It is an eruv—short for eruv hazerot: mixing of domains—which allows Orthodox Jews to undertake domestic tasks (carrying prayer books, reading glasses, and keys, using wheelchairs or strollers) that would otherwise be prohibited in public on the Sabbath.

I turn for home, my T-shirt sticking wetly to my back now and my calves aching, and pause at the small carved urn inside a modest enclosure on the edge of Riverside Park, at 122nd Street. It is easily overlooked, but since my children's births it has always stopped me short. This is the Amiable Child Monument, placed here by the grieving father of a five-year-old boy who fell to his death from these cliffs more than two hundred years ago—before Frederick Law Olmsted smoothed them out into a sylvan esplanade with the railroad buried beneath it.

On the urn's pedestal, its chiseled letters rusty red now with lichen, is a reminder from Job 14:1–2, of how fleeting is our time here: "Man that is born of woman is of few days and full of trouble. He cometh like a flower and is cut down; he fleeth also as a shadow and continueth not."

Back at my desk, freshly showered, I am absently looking out of the window when into view meanders a line of preschoolers. There are five preschools in the surrounding blocks. These toddlers wear fluorescent-orange safety vests with reflective silver stripes, their hands tethered to toggles from a central rope, tottering up Riverside Drive. Their minders lead them in a medley of nursery rhymes. Above the song rises the wailing of several kids, inconsolable as they drear along the sidewalk, a manacled millipede of tiny humans, a New York shongololo.

The toddler file draws even with an elderly man who has paused on the sidewalk. He is very pale and gulps for air. He is having a heart attack. The children regard him with interest, even the wailers distracted into silence. The man sways on his feet and then keels over onto the sidewalk, his head striking the curb with a crunch, audible even to me, his eyeglasses skittering into the road, where they are at once crushed by a passing car. He lies on the sidewalk, blood haloing his head and reddening his pleated cream guayabera.

Two of the teachers kneel to help him. Another reaches for her phone as she tries to move their tethered millipede away from the bleeding body, but the kids hang back, craning at the prostrate figure.

I start to dial 911 too, but an ambulance is already whooping up. The medics leap out and work on the old man for a couple of minutes, but it is clearly too late. They pull a space blanket over his head and load him onto a gurney and up into their rig. A teacher picks up the squashed eyeglass frames from the road and hands them to a medic. He bags them, hops back aboard, and the ambulance draws away.

A co-op handyman, who has been watering the shrubs nearby, quickly hoses the blood from the sidewalk. An hour later, when I take the dog out, there is nothing to tell of the recent event, nothing but the glinting slivers of the dead man's eyeglasses on the road.

"He cometh like a flower and is cut down; he fleeth also as a shadow and continueth not."

I pick up my phone and call my mother.

• • •

Her Grace answers in her memsahib bark.

"This *is* a surprise," she says. "Is everything all right? I wasn't expecting to hear from you today."

Her new accent is even more marked on the phone. "Hear" is *hee-ar*. I've noticed that her new voice has made her act posher too.

Saul Bellow said, "Tell me where you come from and I will tell you what you are." But in Britain you don't even need to say where you come from to reveal your place in the world. As soon as you open your mouth, it becomes clear. The cruel cryptology of class kicks in. The Sorting Hat of hierarchy. In Britain, accent still reveals antecedents and education, and it goes a long way in determining your life's trajectory.

My mother's place, by this calculus, even though she has spent the last fifty years in Africa, would be in the first estate of 1930s England. Part of an upper middle class who were privately educated but unmaterialistic and venerated public service.

They were heirs to one of the most extensive empires the world had ever seen, made possible by history's largest navy, a navy that was instrumental in projecting Rule Britannia, allowing Britain to construct her global empire. An astonishing feat for a small, soggy island nation.

A list of countries that bellicose Britain has invaded is quicker to draw up in the negative. Over the years, she has warred with all but 22 of the world's 193 countries. Genghis Khan once complained that conquering was easy, it was getting down off your horse that was the hard part. Yet the British dismounted and stayed on in many of the countries they conquered. Their empire, Kipling's "dominion over palm and pine," lasted more than four hundred years.

My maternal grandfather, Christopher Godwin Rose (after whom I was given a middle name, and, ultimately, my surname), played a small part in this floating behemoth. He joined the Senior Service in 1913 and served aboard HMS *Colossus* in the First World War, when it was hit several times in the Battle of Jutland, the largest naval engagement in history, and the one that turned the tide of the war, thereafter cooping up the German navy in its home ports.

My grandfather died twenty years before I was born. And though my mother was only eleven years old at the time, he seems to have played an outsized role in her life. When I was growing up in Zimbabwe, she would drop odd snippets about him, how he had named the rooms of their Kentish vicarage after the ships on which he'd served. He'd placed their signs above the doors, insisting those rooms be referred to as Royal Arthur, Ramillies, Pembroke and Vernon, Columbine, Colossus, Courageous, Warspite, Victory, Revenge.

For a country so excruciatingly class conscious, the role of accent as a prime signifier and social shibboleth is oddly recent. It was only with the advent of mass media in the 1920s that socially stratified accents really became countrywide. And the RP of BBC English was not an entirely organic development, it was shaped by an Advisory Committee on Spoken English set up by the BBC's first head, Sir John Reith.

We challenge Her Grace, to see if she could qualify as a 1920s BBC newsreader. At that time, candidates had to audition by reading the following passage, unprepared:

> *Penelope Cholmondely raised her azure eyes from the crabbed scenario. She meandered among the congeries of her memoirs. There was the Kinetic Algernon, a choleric artificer of icons and triptychs, who wanted to write a trilogy. For years she had stifled her risibilities with dour moods. His asthma caused him to sough like the zephyrs among the tamarack.*

Of course, she nimbly clears all jumps, including the early triple, Cholmondely, which, naturally, is pronounced *Chumley*.

English is full of such land mines, we realize anew in trying to help Nema learn it. All these silent letters in this bastard language, the DNA of loan words from the tongues of dozens of other peoples. Residual genetic material from Greek and Latin, Norse and Jute, German and French, sitting there silently now, to sabotage strangers. Trying to explain them to Nema makes me acutely aware of these hidden barriers to entry, these shibboleths to separate ingroups from outgroups, velvet ropes erected to keep her out.

———

Today Nema is describing where she lives in Khartoum, and the bridge that spans the Nile there: "the silver, old, big bridge."

"It's the big, old, silver bridge," I correct, as she has asked us to do.

"That is what I said."

"Yes, but not in that order."

"Why does the order matter?" she asks, exasperated.

"It shouldn't, but it just does," I say.

Later when I've looked it up, I tell her that adjectives must be in this order: opinion, size, age, shape, color, origin, material, purpose.

"How do you remember all that?" she says.

"Well, native English speakers know it without learning it; they grow up with it."

"I will never learn this accursed language," she wails. "It is full with traps to catch foreigners, to stop us from being ever accepted."

The ancient provenance of shibboleths and their global span show just how tribal humans have always been. I remember learning about them at Jesuit high school, that in Hebrew the word "shibboleth" means *an ear of corn*, and it was deployed as a password by the Gileadite sentries to expose their Ephraimite foes, as recounted in Judges 12:5–6: "Then said they unto him, Say now Shibboleth: and he said Sibboleth: for he could not frame to pronounce it right. Then they took him, and slew him at the passages of Jordan . . ."

South African xenophobes do the same to suspected Zimbabweans and other Black Africans who have migrated there. They make them count in Afrikaans and burn them alive if they cannot. In the Dominican Republic, the Spanish word for parlsey—"perejil"—was deployed to reveal Creole-speaking Haitians, thousands of whom were then killed in the Parsley Massacre of 1937. And in the Second World War, American night sentries in the Pacific used "lollapalooza" as a password because Japanese soldiers struggled to pronounce the letter *l*, rendering it as an *r*.

• • •

With Indian Orchard we inherited the services of an itinerant gardener called Murphy. She became my temperate safari guide. The guru of the garden, an expert botanist who could teach me about North American flora, so that it might become as second nature to me as the African bush, so that I might feel like I could belong here, just as she did—secure and comfortable because it was her home.

Murphy appears to live in her mud-streaked, hearse-like station wagon, a forty-year-old Volvo 200 Series—the longest car they ever built—which she shares with two large black dogs and several black garbage bags of blue jeans, plaid flannel shirts, and earth-toned cargo pants.

She is of indeterminate age, with a weather-beaten face, and moves slowly and deliberately, her gait like that of a chameleon, carefully scoping out each footfall before committing to it.

Communicating with Murphy is a challenge. As well as cycling through phones, she eschews email. And she usually works on our property during the week when we're seldom there. On the occasions I do manage to intercept her in person, she appears startled by the sound of a human voice. I realize she must go for days and days up here without talking to anyone. Yet, ask her about the natural world and she transforms, becomes animated and authoritative, her conversational cadence kicking up several gears.

My parents were avid gardeners, convening each day after work to walk their acre of land with their dalmatians, though their flora was tropical: aloes, euphorbia, msasa and avocado, canna and flame lily—the national flower. Frangipani was my father's favorite; native to Southeast Asia, it is considered a symbol of immortality because it can still flower even if uprooted. And they would always end their tour by sitting together on a little wooden bench they had placed next to a soft pink kapok bush that they'd transplanted from Jain's garden after she was killed. This was their botanical balm, all protected by a big bower of bougainvillea, interspersed with sharply serrated sisal, until it burned down one night, exposing them to the busy main road.

I think I may be trying to channel that botanical balm, as it is something that calms Joanna too. Like birdwatching, gardening is something that sneaks up on you with age. We find ourselves doing our own garden walk-throughs, sometimes with Murphy as our pastoral guide. The more I know about what I am seeing, the more connected to this land I hope to feel.

Murphy's first assignment at Indian Orchard was to help fend off the one blight to its pristine panorama. The neighbor to the east, an architect, had erected a startling, eye-achingly white, postmodern, topography-taunting ziggurat of a house. It is as priapic as ours is reticent, a giant middle finger to the natural order. We call it Terminal Four.

Murphy suggested we move the half dozen rhododendron trees already growing on our property to screen it out.

I quickly agreed.

Once she had moved them, Murphy doused the shrubs with deer repellant and, come November, wrapped them tenderly in burlap bandages like wounded soldiers, to shield them from the frost-flecked winds sweeping down off the mountain.

Murphy's rhododendron transplant took, and the shrubs survived in their new home. I took solace from that. Maybe I too would be able to sink roots into this northern earth in which I found myself transplanted, and with the right amount of water, fertilizer, and winter burlap bandages, I too might survive, settle, prosper even.

But once in their new home, the rhododendrons proved laughably diminutive, an attenuated avenue of dwarf trees that is no match for the ziggurat.

I wrote to Georgina about our epic rhododendron fail.

"You can't say rhododendron," she reminded me.

We have this running gag dating back to Zimbabwe's independence in 1980 when Robert Mugabe set about removing all references to Rhodesia, the offensive ancien régime named after Cecil John Rhodes—the only colonizer I know of to name a nation after himself. The rules of our semantic Rhodes Must Fall dictate that all words that begin with "rho" must, according to Mugabe's mandate, be replaced with "zim." All Rhodes lead to Zim.

Hence zimdodendrons.

Any "ro" (without the *h*) is fair game for zimification too: robots (which is what Southern Africans call traffic lights) to zimbots, but only if consonants conjoin or syllables elide.

Words starting with "ro" that are already derogatory, like rodent and robber, roué and rotten, acquire an *h* to become rhodent and rhobber, rhoué and rhotten.

Sometimes an *r* followed by a vowel other than an *o* can be included in this rhogues' gallery. Rhats, for instance. And rhubbish.

Those "ro" words that reek of white elitism survive, but only with an added *h*, to point up their privileged provenance. Hence, Rholls-Rhoyce, rhoyal, Rhomanovs (the white Rhussian dynasty), and Rhomans (imperialists themselves).

• • •

Joanna also tasked Murphy with planting daffodil bulbs. She wanted to echo the Yorkshire Dales of her youth where jocund banks of daffodils trumpeted each spring.

"How many?" asked Murphy when Joanna explained the effect she was after.

"A hundred?"

"That won't fill up that area," Murphy pointed out. "More like a thousand."

I could only roll my eyes at how long this operation would take.

Yet when they burst from the hillside on the first warm day in April, it all seemed worth it. Even the boys were impressed when I walked them through the dancing ranks of yellow. We lay down among the flowers, and Hugo examined a flower head, peering at the small inner golden crown surrounded by six paler tepals.

"Daffodils belong to the Narcissus genus," I told him. "Did you learn about the ancient Greek myth of Narcissus at school?"

He shook his head.

"He was that vain dude," ventured Thomas. "Who looked in the mirror and fell in love with himself?"

At Hugo's request, our bedtime story that night was my version of the myth of Narcissus. Only now do I recall that it's from Ovid's *Metamorphoses*, so a Roman invention, though set in ancient Greece.

"There once was a beautiful wood nymph, Echo, who lived in the mountains," I improvised. "She angered the gods by talking too much, so they punished her by taking away her voice, allowing her only to repeat the last words of other people.

"At the foot of the mountains lived Narcissus, a handsome, haughty hunter. People were always falling in love with him, but he never loved them back. He didn't believe in love. This angered Eros, the god of love.

"One day Narcissus was hunting up in the mountains when the wood nymph, Echo, saw him. Eros notched a love-arrow into his bowstring and shot her, so she too fell in love with Narcissus. He was singing and talking to himself, and Echo repeated the last few words of each sentence, in his own voice.

"'What a magnificent voice,' Narcissus thought."

"Didn't he recognize his own voice?" asked Hugo.

"Or realize it was repeating the same words as he'd just said?" added Thomas.

Tough crowd.

"Apparently not," I said. "Your own voice sounds different to you because you hear it internally, through the bone of your skull, and not through your ears like you hear other voices.

"Anyway, Narcissus looked for the source of this magnificent voice, until he came to a pool. When he looked down at the water, he saw a handsome young man and fell in love with him."

"He didn't realize it was just a reflection?" said Thomas.

"How did he think he was breathing under the water?" said Hugo.

I had not expected that the myth of Narcissus was to be this rigorously fact-checked.

"It's a myth, Tom," I said, frustrated. "It has gods and nymphs and stuff. It's like a fairy tale or a fantasy movie. When you watch *Harry Potter* or *The Hobbit*, you don't actually believe them, but you still enjoy the story. It's called 'suspension of disbelief.' That's what you need for myths too. Don't take them literally."

Thomas looked unconvinced, but I plunged on.

"Narcissus pined by the pool for his fickle new love, and the forlorn Echo watched him from the nearby forest.

"Eventually, the townspeople sent a rescue party up into the mountains to look for Narcissus. But all that remained of him by then was a flower, which they named Narcissus, in his memory. Echo too had wasted away. The only thing left of *her* was her voice, which you can still hear to this very day if you go into the mountains and call out."

"Wait a minute," Hugo said, finally making the connection. "An echo is called after a Greek wood nymph!"

I switched off their lights and said goodnight, but as I left, Thomas tossed a final query after me: "Dad, if the facts of the story aren't true, shouldn't it at least have a moral? Otherwise, what's the point?"

"Well," I said, returning to their moon-drenched room, "you already figured it out. You shouldn't admire yourself too much. If you fall in love with yourself, there's no room to love anyone else."

"Or for anyone else to love you," added Hugo.

"True. And as well as giving his name to the flower, Narcissus also gave his name to the word 'narcissist,' which is someone who thinks the entire world revolves around themself. Narcissists are so self-absorbed they can't even imagine what it's *like* to be anyone else."

"What if you don't even really like *yourself*?" asked Hugo. "What's the Greek myth for that?"

Later he found an online listicle entitled "The 13 Biggest Assholes in Greek Mythology." To his disappointment, Narcissus didn't make the cut.

• • •

"What books did your parents used to read to you?" Hugo had asked at the time. And to my shame, I couldn't bring one to mind. So I'd called my mother, and the only book she could remember reading me was a droll Victorian volume called *Ruthless Rhymes for Heartless Homes*, by Colonel D. Streamer.

"I was trying to toughen you up," she jokes. "Scare the sentimentality out of you."

"That seems somewhat sinister," I say.

"You alliterate rather a lot, don't you?" she replies.

"Well, yes, I suppose I do; I like the prosody of it."

"You know what they call alliteration?" She answers her own question before I can draw breath. "Poor people's poetry."

"A phrase which is *itself* alliterative," I can't help pointing out. "And who are these *they*?"

But she has already ended the call.

• • •

It took a full year for the artful intricacy of the garden at Indian Orchard to reveal itself. An orchestra of flowers, striking up from different sections in a subtly color-coordinated symphony. The whites of snowdrops and crocuses, clethra and lily of the valley, hawthorn and pear blossom. The yellows of the daffodils, forsythia, leucanthemum, scabiosa daisies, and holly potentilla shrubs. The purples and mauves of hyacinths, bearded iris, veronica speedwell, heliotrope, and wisteria. The pinks of tree peonies, of lilacs and liatris, echinacea, tamarisk, and rhododendron. The full-throated reds of oriental poppies, flowering quince, and climbing roses. And finally, the cortege of black tulips.

In that year, more of Murphy's equipment accumulated around the edges of the garden. A rusty red wheelbarrow with a flat tire, a battered yellow mower "awaiting parts," and a diminutive John Deere garden tractor in a fading shade of jade, oozing oil. Though she earnestly resolved to remove these each time we chatted, fingers of foliage slowly spread over them, until they disappeared like relics of a lost civilization, to be discovered by post-Armageddon archaeologists who will puzzle over the strange agricultural tribe that once worked these Taconic hills.

Murphy's abandoned implements did eventually serve a useful purpose.

One day, as I knew it would, a large sign appeared at the end of our drive announcing the neighboring property as for sale. Zoned for a four-bedroom house, its new owners would have to drive through our yard to reach it. I watched in horror as a real estate agent paraded a posse of potential purchasers across our lawn to reconnoiter the adjacent land. And an evil thought took possession of me.

I called the boys to explain what I had in mind.

We called it Operation Appalachia.

Together we drew up ambitious battle plans for a range war in defense of Indian Orchard by transforming it into a hillbilly reliquary. Suspending Murphy's grass mowing until further notice. Dragging out the contents of the garage—logs and planks, drums, car parts, paint tins, and old batteries—and scattering them around the lawn where prospective buyers would walk. Parking our old, olive Jeep in the driveway, with the universal distress call of a raised hood. Emptying the garden shed of broken fence poles, bales of wire, bags of fertilizer, old window frames, tiles, shingles—and strategically placing these around the lawn, together with random garbage, surreptitiously weighed down with rocks and other windproof detritus. Positioning two speakers, face-out, at the windows and instructing the boys that, whenever they saw visitors, to open the sashes and play, at full volume, their usually verboten, oath-sprinkled rap playlist. Erecting a store-bought "Beware: Dangerous Dog" sign.

Because I'd made a bet with the boys not to cut my hair until I'd finished my current book, I already looked the part of a muttering mountain-man, shaggy salt-and-pepper locks down to my shoulders, and beard unkempt. At the time of the bet, I'd anticipated book completion was a mere month or two away, but it proved to be more than a year distant.

Joanna declined to take part in Operation Appalachia, not out of moral scruples, but because she found it impossible to scuttle her sartorial standards, even for a redneck ruse.

Operation Appalachia, I realized, was a classic example of Batesian mimicry, common in the natural world. I explained to the boys that we were faking an aposematic signal, making ourselves look like people you might be afraid to live next to. We were pretending to be a more "dangerous" kind of species than we really were. Like the defenseless African grasshopper that mimics the stinging ant to discourage predators.

Unsurprisingly Hugo was a little confused. I told him about a study that researchers were doing on cattle in Botswana. (I had taken the boys to Southern Africa—Botswana, Mozambique, and Zambia—as part of a feature piece about kids on safari. Hugo spent much of the time with his nose in *Scatalogue*, a wildlife turd recognition book—a "poodunnit," he called it.) These free-range cows were being attacked by lions.

So, the researchers painted big pairs of eyes on the buttocks of some of the cattle. They found that these ass-eyed cows were attacked far less often than the others. Because lions are ambush predators, they rely on the element of surprise to sneak up behind their prey. If the lions think that the cows have spotted them, they usually break off their attack.

The boys were used to this by now. Used to me scouring natural history for analogs to explain human behavior. I didn't realize I did this until I had children. I think it's the long legacy of growing up in rural Zimbabwe. Curiosity about my surroundings as a salve for solitude, just as exercise helps lift depression.

Now that I had completed my "teachable moment," Hugo, who had patiently listened to the disquisition, had two pressing points. That's a long way to say "bluffing," was the first. The second was to suggest we paint eyes on our own bums. He ran off chortling.

Months passed and the neighboring plot stood stubbornly unsold. The real estate agent, an ex-Marine, called a truce, suggesting a summit at the Irving Farm coffee shop in Millerton to discuss terms. He cut the asking price to one we could almost afford, and we took out a second mortgage to buy a property we did not want, to defend the one we already had.

Once we had closed on the new domain, I tried to walk our acquisition, two acres of uncleared Taconic hillside, but I was unable to make much headway, so densely thicketed was it. I decided to just leave it be, to serve as an impenetrable barrier—our own little Darién Gap, an arboreal moat defending Fortress Indian Orchard.

. . .

From London, Georgina sends me a photo, captioned *Canine geriatric care.* It is of her dog, Bella, lying on Her Grace's bed, guarding her. Her Grace wears an expression of benign surprise. Surprise at the fact that, at ninety years old, she finds herself alive still, when most of her cohort, including her husband, are not. On this she's in accord with Trotsky, that old age is the most unexpected of all things that can happen to a person.

I call her to check in. She nudges her glasses down the bridge of her nose to take a better look at me on the screen.

"You look like Struwwelpeter," she harrumphs.

Struwwel—shockheaded—Peter features a boy with wild, bushy hair and dirty, uncut fingernails. It's the lead story in an 1845 compendium by the German psychiatrist Heinrich Hoffman, with tales built like the ones in *Ruthless Rhymes for Heartless Homes*, where kids behave badly and reap disastrous consequences.

I make a vain attempt to pat my hair down and distract my mother by asking how she's feeling, knowing this will unplug a torrent of medical details. I've tried to cap her recitation of symptoms, for she can kvetch with the best of them, owing to her medical expertise. She reads her symptoms much as a gnarled farmer would read clues to the weather, picking her way expertly through an almanac of ailments.

It reminds me of veterans swapping war stories. For aging is the final battle in a war we all lose. Bette Davis was right, old age is no place for sissies. And there is something chilling about these elderly emissaries from our future, ancestral auguries that this decrepitude will soon descend upon us too—unless we are lucky enough to die young.

When autumn arrives at Indian Orchard, we marshal the boys alongside the new plot for our fall ritual, the recitation of "Beech Leaves," by James Reeves. Our family tradition demands they pull on their boots and stomp through the crispy leaves to the thumping rhythm of the lines:

I am a giant, and my steps
Echo and thunder to the sky.
How the small creatures of the woods
Must quake and cower as I pass by!

The last couplet they declaim at the shout, trying to strike fear into the hearts of any adjacent rodents. It is late afternoon, and through the deciduous forest of elm and pine and oak, bare now of their leaves, I catch a brief, tantalizing glimpse of the sun sliding behind the bald, brooding brow of Winchell Mountain. It is like one of those vast Thomas Cole oil paintings of the Hudson River School, a russet range with ramparts celestially backlit. There are stunning sight lines here to the west and I am seized by the notion that, with a bit of judicious paring, we just might be able to liberate our sunset.

I summon our local arborist, the aptronymic Mike Root.

The dense foliage, he explains when we walk the new plot, is unnatural, man-inflicted, the result of farming or building disturbing the earth and unleashing a chaotic, anarchic ingrowth. Parasitic bittersweet vines (*Celastrus orbiculatus*) have metastasized here, coiling round the mature trees. Native to Asia, bittersweet extends fifteen feet a year, becoming as broad as a builder's bicep, and eventually throttling its host.

We hack our way through the head-high, thorn-guarded multiflora rose, not a rose as such at all (by any other name, nor smells as sweet), but an invasive, scrambling shrub (also an immigrant from Asia) that chokes all competition. And the mesh of honeysuckle that has grown between the throng of saplings. Root ties neon-yellow tape around the tree trunks—mostly first-growth ones—which he deigns to pardon. He condemns the rest because they are too crowded or diseased. They must be killed, he insists, to breathe new life into this old copse.

Root's crew get to work on the forest, festooned now with what looks like police scene-of-crime tape. They shoot their slingshot over the fork of each condemned tree and pull the pilot line over to rope it to a winch. With a chainsaw they amputate the trunk. The swirling yellow-ringed interior is shockingly exposed, sap bleeding down its severed neck into the dark Taconic earth. They feed the growling woodchipper with branches. It strains to digest each new helping. A Bobcat mini-dozer guns back and forth, tugging at the tangle of foliage with its iron claws. Cracks and pops ring out across the hillside in fusillades like an infantry skirmish.

As the wrenching deforestation continues, my misgivings grow. After all, I am the architect of this destruction.

And then, for the first time in decades, sunlight breaks through the thinning overgrowth to dapple the forest floor. And I no longer feel guilty. We are liberating the forest within. As the men cut and pull and hack and dig, I begin to feel lighter. Crimson cardinals swoop down on the bounty of worms presented by the newly peeled earth. Squirrels and chipmunks scamper up trees and under granite ledges, rattlesnakes slither away from the din.

How the small creatures of the woods must quake and cower as I pass by.

Freed of vines, older trees appear to reclaim their domains. At the crest of the hill, an oak tree emerges into sight, seventy feet tall, queen of all she surveys. Mike Root estimates she's a hundred years old. As the land opens around her, she seems to exhale. Her sun-seeking boughs reach high, like the arms of a revivalist preacher. I rub my palms over her gnarled bole. Up near her crown she bears a jagged lightning scar, an old war wound. It has healed now, with new bark folding over to create swollen keloid labia, crimped at the edges like a singed empanada.

• • •

Once the foresters have gone, I notice remnants of old wire all over the new plot, looped around trees, embedded in their bark, and buried in the ground. I pull up yards and yards of it from the loamy earth and roll it into rusty bales, like the poachers' snares we used to collect in Gonarezhou game reserve in southeastern Zimbabwe.

The next weekend, as I drive up Indian Orchard hill, I see Murphy waving from inside the tennis court next door at Terminal Four. Reticent to the point of reclusive, this is oddly gregarious for Murphy. I lower the window and wave cheerily back as I roll by. Instead of being assuaged, Murphy waves more urgently. Strange, from someone who so prizes economy of motion. Then I see the cause of her uncharacteristic energy. A black bear is standing on its rear legs, front paws on the chain-link fence of the tennis court, trapping her inside. I drive slowly over, honking and flashing my lights, and the bear lopes off up the hill.

Murphy opens the gate sheepishly.

"Whoa, that's a big fella," I commiserate. "Hope he didn't have you trapped for too long?"

"A few hours. He's only a teenager," she says, apologizing on behalf of the bear. "I think he just wanted to play. But I decided it was safer to shelter inside the court."

As I walk her back to her car, I ask about the wire I'm finding in our newly cleared plot.

"It's from the roosting pens," she says. "There was a big turkey farm here once."

I find this ridiculous. Indian Orchard is so self-evidently bucolic, we can't possibly be living on the site of some industrial fowl battery; Murphy must be confused.

But sure enough, when I go to the Salisbury Historical Society, I find an old black-and-white photograph of the Shagroy Turkey Farm. And I'm astonished to see the Indian Orchard hillside intensively latticed with roosting cages, and even, down the hill, a multistory tenement building for migrant workers who killed and cut and canned the turkeys. What had happened to it all? I wonder.

It turns out that one morning in the early 1960s while the fowl were outside in the farmyard, a small plane buzzed low over them. They panicked at the sudden, skyborne sound and rushed headlong into the base of a granite cliff. Most were killed outright. (At full tilt, a turkey can scamper at over twenty-five miles an hour.) The rest were maimed and had to be destroyed. Eight thousand turkeys died in the stampede that morning, causing the farmer to run into a financial cliff of his own. He later tried, and failed, to commit suicide in his car by carbon monoxide poisoning.

I pull on my workman's gloves to pluck the last strands of rusty roost wire from the earth, and I worry that the great turkey self-slaughter and the suicidal farmer karma might still somehow blight this land.

• • •

In a call to Her Grace, I mention my surprise that we are living on top of an old industrial turkey plant at Indian Orchard. And how is it that you can live somewhere and not really know who the previous occupants were? That you are just the latest tenants?

"Ah, palimpsests," she says. "Mother Earth has many secrets, if you only know where to look."

She dials so rapidly between wisdom and waffle these days that I can't quite recognize which mode she's in.

"We are seeing many of them here in Europe with the big drought. The hunger stones have spoken," she says grandiloquently, as though assuming the role of augury herself.

I have been reading in the papers that Europe is suffering a devastating drought, with rivers dropping to record lows, but I hadn't heard of these previously submerged "hunger stones" being exposed. Her Grace explains that they had been placed there some four hundred years ago as an early-warning system, to alert us that famine would soon follow their appearance. Apparently the oldest one is a boulder deep within the River Elbe. On it, a message is chiseled in German: "Wenn du mich siehst, weine." *When you see me, weep.*

In the usually rain-doused isle of Britain, she says, drought has left the land so parched that from the air could be seen, for the first time, distinct traces of ancient land usage, invisible at ground level. The ghostly outlines of old roads, walls, and ditches, gardens and paddocks, houses and barns, all began to appear. They had always been there, hiding beneath the earth's pelt, a ghostly pentimento. Even after all these years, they still informed the landscape, becoming visible only in desiccated extremis. The memory of landscape is long. The ax forgets but not the tree . . .

Our shock at being presented with the long-forgotten usages of a shared place is like sitting in a time machine that remains stationary but travels backwards into history. We are confronted with our reverse chronology, like the strata of an archaeological dig. The earth reminding us that we are nothing but an ancient accretion, piled one atop another, jostling each other out of the way, supplanting ourselves over and over. A Dagwood of humanity, each ingredient spread onto the crust of its predecessors. In our case, the roosting cages of the forgotten Shagroy Turkey Farm.

· · ·

In late summer, a new inhabitant appears on the grass turnaround midway up Indian Orchard Road. Dressed in a florid floral aloha shirt, khaki cargo shorts, a natty cream Panama, and aviator shades, he lounges in a camp chair, complete with a cupholder bearing some sort of green-garnished cocktail. Behind him, parked in the meadow, stands a spinnaker-blue Ford Taurus with Sunshine State plates featuring a blushing pair of oranges.

I don't pay him much attention on my first couple of passes, returning his vague waves reflexively. But when he's still there after three days, I become curious about this blithe interloper.

"Who's the dude camping out on the turning circle?" I ask Murphy, my voice flecked with suspicion.

"Oh, that's my father," she says apologetically. "He used to own the top farm on Indian Orchard; it's where I was raised. He sold it and moved down to Florida, years ago."

"Oh . . . How nice he drove all this way up to visit you," I say, abashed.

"He's got stage-four cancer; he's come home to die." Her voice is neutral. It registers no sadness or regret. It is simply the natural order of things, like a salmon returning to the head of its native river.

A few days later the Sunshine State Taurus is gone, and with it, the camp chair and its aloha occupant and his terminal cocktail. Murphy looks up from her bulb-planting to confirm that her father has duly died. She had delivered him to Sharon Hospital in her protracted Volvo.

Tell It to the Bees

"NEMA IS PLANNING TO RUN AWAY FROM HER HUSBAND," MY MOTHER announces.

I am sitting by her bed, back in Georgina's house in London to visit her, and to conduct more Emin Pasha research at the British Library.

"The problem is that her husband's family will pursue her, such would be their humiliation. And she would be cast out by her own family too, for the dishonor she would have heaped upon them."

"Good Lord, how can we help?"

"She's sworn me to secrecy," says Her Grace. "She's thinking of changing her name and moving out of London. Perhaps to Europe. But she's worried that she can't speak any European languages."

"Maybe Ireland?"

Our conversation stops abruptly when Nema taps on the door with tea.

I begin peeling a banana for Mum's afternoon snack. I can soon tell from the purse of her lips that she finds something about my actions irksome.

"You're doing that all wrong," she sighs finally.

I bite my lip.

"The proper way to peel a banana is not from the stem, but from the opposite end."

"That's about as petty as the war of the eggs in *Gulliver's Travels*," I say.

"Which war was this?" asks Nema.

"It's a novel by Jonathan Swift about a fictional war among tiny people—six inches tall—called Lilliputians, and the Blefuscudians," I say. "They went to battle over which end you should crack open a boiled egg—the big end or the little end."

Nema tinkles with laughter.

"Jonathan Swift meant his egg war as an allegory for the religious quarrels between Catholics and Protestants," I say.

Nema reaches into her improbably fluorescent-pink Hello Kitty backpack for her spiral notebook. "An al-*egg*-ory?" Her pen pauses its fluid movement across the page from right to left in Arabic script.

"It's not another egg word, that one," I say. "It only has one *g*: a-l-l-e-g-o-r-y. It's a story with a hidden meaning, a sort of metaphor."

"And what is this thing, a metaphor?"

"The observation of affinities in objects where no brotherhood exists to passive minds," Her Grace says grandly. "That's how the poet Wordsworth unimprovably put it."

"Wordsworth is a good name for a poet," Nema concedes, but she remains understandably puzzled.

"A metaphor is when you describe something as something else that somehow reminds you of it," I try.

"Can you give me an example?"

"The Lord is my Shepherd," says Her Grace from on high. "Psalm 23."

As Nema is Muslim, I try to think of a more appropriate metaphor. "Wine-dark sea. It's from the ancient Greek book the *Odyssey*, by Homer."

"I don't drink alcohol; it is haram, forbidden," says Nema. "But still, I know that wine comes in three colors: white, red, and rose. Which one did he mean?"

"It's not rose," I correct gently, "it's rosé. The *e* has an acute accent. It's French for pink."

Nema jots in her book. "I thought 'acute' was an angle," she sighs.

"That's *exactly* right," I say. "And the accent over the *e* is a little line, set at an acute angle."

"Yes, it is opposite of oblique, that angle," says Nema, encouraged now. Only she pronounces it *obli-cue*.

I withhold my counsel; this must already be infernally confusing.

Her Grace has no such compunction. "It's pronounced ob*leek*," she says.

• • •

Her Grace has been rummaging around her family papers and wishes to show me what she has found. Though she doesn't speak much about her family, her father obviously had a huge influence on her. At home in Zimbabwe, she kept a thicket of his high school athletic trophies on a silver tray in the dining room. I used to examine them as a boy, one of the few material manifestations of my own antecedents. His boyhood achievements were so much greater than mine. Christopher Godwin Rose could run a mile in four minutes and forty-six seconds. He had been head boy at Weymouth College and then gone to Cambridge on a math scholarship.

His family had been wealthy Wiltshire landowners, and then suddenly they weren't, so he'd done what recently impoverished upperclass young men did back then, joined the clergy or the military—in his case, both.

I already knew that the Reverend Godwin Rose became a radically progressive prelate. He was an active member of the Churchmen's Union, which was to Anglicanism almost what liberation theology was to Catholicism. And in 1924 he had authored a pamphlet for the Marie Stopes Foundation, entitled *The Christian Case for Birth Control*, in which he condemned the Anglican bishops' recent ruling that contraception was against the teaching of the Bible and morally harmful because it interfered with the will of God. To this, my grandfather drew a mocking comparison:

> *When lightning conductors were first introduced, they were regarded as impiously interfering with the will of the Deity, who, if he wished to strike a building with his fire, should be allowed to do so. If a man who thought this had put a lightning conductor over his house, he would have been committing an act which was morally harmful to himself.*

Now Her Grace hands me a copy of the book her father had written, *Antecedents of Christianity*, published almost a hundred years ago. I had paged through this disintegrating hardback as a boy. And sometimes when I'd lost faith in my own muse, I'd found solace in his writerly DNA. But only now do I read it all the way through.

It is an extraordinary document for a clergyman to have written back in 1925. For it does a daring dance, *just* this side of heresy. Essentially, he looks at the development of Christian ideology through the lens of Darwin, applying the tools of social anthropology before it had been recognized as an academic discipline.

He peels Christian belief back to the studs to find its theological ancestry, demystifying it. He traces how the Church had borrowed, plagiarized some might say, many of its best tunes from prior productions; that much of Christianity is simply a reprise, a portmanteau of pagan beliefs, and of Judaism, Hinduism, Confucianism, Buddhism,

Taoism, Shintoism. And in that way, religion too is an accretion, with Christianity a cultural sapling grafted onto a trunk of preexisting beliefs.

My grandfather courts danger constantly in the book. Take the subject of human sacrifice and religious cannibalism: he draws a straight line from the human sacrifices of Aztecs through to the "body and blood of Christ" in Communion wafers and wine—eating your God.

• • •

I am spending several hours a day in the British Library reading room, trawling through Emin Pasha's journals. He is stranded in Sudan, trying to learn a new language and customs, much as Nema is trying to do in England.

Back in Britain, an expedition was organized to "rescue" Emin, even though he was reluctant to be rescued. Chosen as its head, book contract in hand, was Henry Morton Stanley, who'd been sent by the *New York Herald* to "find" David Livingstone back in 1871.

I'm fascinated by the contrasts between the two: Stanley, the bombastic, self-glorifying nemesis of the thoughtful, cultured Emin Pasha. They personify opposite sides of the Western "explorer."

Like my parents, Emin Pasha seemed motivated by some idea of public service. But having plowed through his diaries, I have found almost nothing (in common with most Victorian journals) about how he *feels*. Like my father, he seems to be surrounded by an emotional force field. The one thing he *does* get excited about (as my father did too) is botany. Emin cataloged many of East Africa's flora, helping to create a Western scientific taxonomy, and sending samples to museums in Germany.

Stanley did indeed rescue Emin, who left Equatoria reluctantly, loath to abandon his men, not just his Egyptian officers, but the so-called One Elevens, Nubians who were Muslim converts with three vertical tribal scars etched into each cheek, 111, hence their name. His garrison was a substantial town, ten thousand strong, plus their wives and children.

Stanley put Emin and his daughter (from his now deceased Ethiopian wife) on donkeys and trotted them south to Bagamoyo, on the coast of German East Africa (what is today Tanzania). There they were feted at the three-story coral commissary, serenaded with a tuba band and a twenty-one-gun salute from a German cruiser anchored in the bay. Unused to any structure of more than one story and rendered woozy by several flutes of Krug and schnapps chasers, Emin wandered onto the roof terrace for some fresh air. There he lost his footing and, as Evelyn Waugh later described it, took "a header off the balcony," breaking his skull on the flagstones below.

Emin fell into a coma and Stanley, irritated that he couldn't return in triumph with his human trophy, sailed back to Europe empty-handed to embark on a lecture tour recounting how he had heroically "saved" Emin Pasha!

Much to his doctor's surprise, Emin slowly recovered and, although nearly blind, insisted on setting off back into the interior to fetch his men. En route he was waylaid by Arab slave traders, who beheaded him.

Today Emin languishes as a faint footnote to Stanley's solipsistic account of his own rescue expedition, a hatchet job in which Emin is painted as an incompetent ingrate, the ultimate passing Jew, a shape-shifting man of no nation, no fixed religion, who dials rapidly through competing identities—Christian, Muslim, German, Ottoman, Briton—belonging to none.

My intent is to mount a second rescue mission, this time saving Emin from the mists of undeserved obscurity and righting an historical slight.

•　•　•

On my return from the British Library, Her Grace announces that she would like to visit the bees. The apiary, a pine box with framed screens slotted within, is in Canfield's common garden, a mere hundred paces from her bed. Over the years, at her request, I have often walked, then wheeled her to visit them. She is consoled by the bees' intense focus and the urgency of their mission—I think it reminds her of her own professional life, and the sense of purpose she misses.

"If bees disappear, there will be an apocalypse in four years," she says. "It was Einstein's greatest fear."

The resident beekeeper tends the hives in a beige cotton bee suit with hood and veil. When he arrives in the garden square, the kids follow him like the Pied Piper, chanting "Bee-man! Bee-man!" And they watch as he swaps out screens full of honey for new ones laced with a syrup made of rainwater and sugar.

According to the apiarist, the bees face many threats. Parasitic mites, for one. And American foulbrood, an aggressive bacterial infection. Then there are Asian murder hornets, which came ashore in the South of France a decade ago stowed away inside terra-cotta vases from China. With bright orange faces like samurai masks, they are bigger, more aggressive, and more venomous than Euro hornets; their sting can penetrate a bee suit and kill a human. They eat bees, snatching them in flight like raptors attack smaller birds.

And there is a new kind of pesticide (neonicotinoids), which is genetically implanted in crops and ingested by bees when they pollinate blossoms. It seems to interfere with their navigation system, disorienting them so they get lost and die outside when night falls, as they cannot fly in the dark. Banned by the EU, the bee-man fears that post-Brexit UK will start using it again, and the bees won't be able to find their way back home.

· · ·

I go to say goodbye to my mother before leaving again for New York. She is sitting upright in bed watching the news. She watches a Taiwanese plane clip a bridge and plunge into a river. She watches ISIS jihadis parade a Jordanian air force pilot they have shot down. They have dressed him in an orange, Guantanamo-style jumpsuit and locked him in a cage, and now they are about to set him on fire. And as she watches all this, she slowly plucks plump green seedless South African grapes off a bunch at her bedside and pops them into her mouth, one by one.

"Promise me, Peter," she says, "that you won't go back to the Middle East."

What she is requesting is that I no longer cover conflicts. I nod vaguely.

But my mother has nothing to worry about. The truth is, I have lost my capacity for conflict. I have withdrawn from the fray. Latibulated from life. Retreated. Retired hurt. And Indian Orchard is more than ever my refuge.

• • •

I am not the first to use this Lakeville eyrie as a sanctuary. Artie Shaw, the clarinetist and swing band leader, fled here more than forty years ago, escaping a triple threat: showbiz burnout, the House Un-American Activities Committee, and the IRS. Shaw added the downstairs studio with its adze-scored barn beams and glass doors that slide open onto a flagstone terrace and a pergola poised upon diminutive Doric columns. And wreathed them with wisteria.

My playlist of troubled troubadours doesn't feature any of Shaw's music, so I set about rectifying this. It turns out he deserves to be on it—in his signature tune, the eerie "Nightmare," he coaxes a sound from the clarinet that hails straight from the Jewish Pale, a haunting, Hassid sound, melancholic and unsettling.

I've always associated this kind of clarinet with Jewish klezmer. Which is no coincidence. Artie Shaw was born Avraham Arshawsky to Jews who fled the East European pogroms for the Lower East Side of Manhattan, where they worked as jobbing tailors.

Shaw was born with an astonishing talent. More than perfect pitch, he could distinguish between quarter and even eighth tones. After leaving school at fifteen to turn pro, he surfed the crest of the swing band era, rivaling Benny Goodman, crisscrossing the country, packing huge venues. He was the first bandleader to hire a front singer of color, Billie Holiday, and with her toured the segregated Jim Crow South in 1938.

There must be something in the well water up here on Indian Orchard, for Shaw wrote an autobiography, *The Trouble with Cinderella: An Outline of Identity*, here. And his eighth wife, Evelyn Keyes, wrote her own memoir here. I largely wrote two books here too, *When a Crocodile Eats the Sun* and *The Fear*, as well as a lengthy introduction to a rereleased edition of Dambudzo Marechera's *The House of Hunger*.

And Joanna edited scripts here for *The Bold Type*, a TV drama that ran for five series and which she executive produced. The show follows the staff of *Scarlet*, a women's magazine based on *Cosmo*. (They had wanted to call the magazine *Steinem*, but Gloria threatened to sue.) *Scarlet*'s editor in chief, Jacqueline Carlyle (played by Melora Hardin, star of *The Office* and *Transparent*), is Joanna's alter ego—kindly but authoritative, generous and wise, a mentor to die for. JC is not so much *The Devil Wears Prada* as *The Angel Wears Gucci*. Jacqueline's husband is a British war photographer, a small part, and they have two young sons.

And now Joanna is writing a kind of self-help book here, called *Love Rules*. She describes it as a diet book for relationships, a compendium of "love hacks." The book is subtitled *How to Find a Real Relationship in a Digital World* . . .

• • •

There is one moment from the extraordinary arc of Artie Shaw's life that I cannot shake. An indelible image that comes back to me whenever, like tonight, I lie in this Indian Orchard bedroom, sleepless, the same bedroom Shaw lay in. It arrived via a journalist friend, David Kamp, who interviewed Shaw in Ventura County, California, shortly before he died alone at the age of ninety-four, having long since succumbed to his inner curmudgeon.

Fifty years earlier, at the age of forty-four, Shaw had concluded that his clarinet playing had peaked, that his fingers weren't quite as felicitously fast as they'd been the day before. Wanting to set aside the instrument before his virtuosity waned, he stopped cold turkey. Publicly, he said he'd taken the instrument as far as he could. Perfectionists, he lamented, finish last.

Kamp asked if he missed the clarinet.

Not at all, Shaw said quickly. Too quickly.

There was a long pause. Then Shaw continued. Sometimes, he admitted, in the dead of night he would wake to realize from the positioning of his fingers that he'd been playing an imaginary clarinet in his sleep, pressing the phantom keys of an instrument he had made his own, only to abandon it at his apogee.

There's an African footnote to Artie Shaw's famous clarinet, the one that he continued to play up here solely in spectral form. The wood from which it was fashioned is called African blackwood, one of the densest woods in the world. It comes from the grenadilla (*Dalbergia melanoxylon*), a small, gnarly, purplish tree (part of the rosewood genus, not to be confused with ebony, to which it is superior) that takes up to a century to mature. Now endangered, it's indigenous to the part of Zimbabwe I am from and is likely where Artie's clarinet barrel originated.

I love the looping ellipsis of this, the way that, in the end, we are all raveled, resonating to subtle, secret notes. If we only know what to listen for, we can still hear them above the clanging of false gongs.

Twenty-five years after I came to America, I still seize upon the African blackwood in Artie Shaw's clarinet as a win for the home team. Even as I have been drawn to the magnetic north, I still use Africa as my true south. I continue to distinguish east from west by visualizing which sides Mozambique and Angola would be on as I look north from wherever I am. I know this is absurd. And, especially in America, it exposes me to the incoming fire of large-caliber cultural criticism.

I am white. Worse than that, I'm an oxymoronic, African white, marooned by colonial history—native, but not Indigenous. Neither am I poor. I have no hillbilly elegy to deliver. I am patently privileged (Indian Orchard is our weekend house, after all). I am a laggard in the grievance stakes. There is only the "inherited trauma" of my father's family being gassed by Nazis in the Holocaust, revealed by my father at his own deathbed "confession" of his hitherto hidden Jewishness. That, and my experience as a teenaged combatant drafted into the Rhodesian civil war, the one in which Jain was killed.

My ancestors did not come from Africa to America against their will; they were not shackled in the fetid holds of slave ships, pursued across the ocean by shivers of esurient sharks. My parents were not smuggled out in a leaky, listing boat on the South China seas. I sailed here from England aboard the *QE2* (on a media freebie). And I have no language issues—I arrived preloaded with English software.

So, I am not a refugee. But nor am I an immigrant. True immigrants energetically reboot and re-root, propelled by poverty, driven by necessity, motivated by opportunity.

I am not an expatriate either, dropping in for a Yankee drive-by, like many pukka Brits who never relinquish their real residency, popping back to the Home Counties for Christmas, sending their kids to

British boarding schools to imprint Anglo accents and preserve their prepositions before days of the week.

What I am is an émigré, I suppose, an exile. And we exiles tend to remain deracinated, to drag with us an ineffable sense of loss, exuding an aura of melancholy, a sickness of the spirit—unmoored from our new surrounds. It is harder for us to "move on." We're still tethered to our history, even as it grows ever more tenuous.

• • •

Virginia Woolf understood the vice of the past, how it can burn more brightly than the present. "The past is beautiful," she wrote, "because one never realizes an emotion at the time. It only expands later, and thus we don't have complete emotions about the present, only about the past."

Louise Glück goes even further in her poem "Nostos": "We look at the world once, in childhood," she says. "The rest is memory."

I fear that I may be stuck in just such a loop, still unwrapping antique emotional packages, presents from my past.

But for a few sartorial foibles (a lingering weakness for veldskoens—Boer bush boots; kikoyis—bright cotton wraps from the Swahili coast; and a trio of brass bangles I still wear because the Kalahari Khoisan shaman who slipped them over my wrist during a trance dance predicted personal mayhem if I were ever to remove them—and, like my mother's residual belief in tokoloshes, I'm *just* superstitious enough to be scared credulous), it's probably my accent, my mash-up Anglo-Zimbabwean accent, which remains my chief external identifier. By the time I came to the US, I was in my late thirties, and accents, linguists tell us, are fully imprinted by about thirteen.

The moment I open my mouth, I betray my alien provenance, my exotic terroir. Almost anywhere in the world, people ask me, where are you from? By which, of course, they also mean, you are not from here. You are from somewhere else.

"A man who changes his country is like a dog who changes his bark . . . not to be trusted," James Michener wrote in *The Drifters*. In which case, my family is so untrustworthy as to have changed breed entirely, from bark to howl. In two generations we have spanned five countries on three continents. But maybe, at some level, my fidelity to my old Zimbabwean accent (itself bastardized), and my inability to code-shift, reveal an unwillingness to betray my old bark.

• • •

Another flying visit to London, a stopover from a magazine assignment in South Africa.

My mother unrolls a two-foot-square parchment and smooths it out over her counterpane. On it, in hand-scrawled, tiny, spidery ink, is one branch of her family tree—the Sidneys. It's almost illegible in parts, so I read it to her. At the top is William, Duke of Normandy, aka William the Bastard, aka William the Conqueror, the first king of England, after beating Harold Godwinson (Duke of Wessex) at the Battle of Hastings in 1066.

A Sidney started Sidney Sussex College, Cambridge; a Sydney was the governor of Australia. But my mother's favorite Sidney, the one she wishes to discuss today, is Algernon, the political philosopher who championed civic rights against arbitrary power, for which he was convicted of treason in 1683 and executed by King Charles II.

There was only one witness against him at his trial, she says, and as at least two were required for a capital offense, the prosecution used his unpublished manuscript, *Discourses Concerning Government*, as its second "witness," the judge ruling, "scribere est agere," *to write is to act*—a motto, we agree, that I should be proud to inherit.

Before his death, Algernon said, "The King can make a snuffbox from my arse." And from the scaffold he declared, "We live in an age that makes truth pass for treason." In a sense he wrought his revenge postmortem on the British monarchy, as his works went on to inspire the American revolutionaries Thomas Jefferson and John Adams.

My mother reminds me how she'd insisted on taking me and Georgina to the Tower of London years ago, to march us through Traitors' Gate, where Algernon was conveyed to his death. By then its direct entry from the Thames—to bring condemned prisoners in by barge—had been bricked over. But we followed Algernon's footsteps from the bottom of St. Thomas's Tower, past the oak-latticed Traitors' Gate itself, to his place of execution.

"Traitors' Gate is in our blood," she had insisted then. "It's our family tradition. We're proud to be nonconformists."

Her Grace reminds me she is also descended from Harold Godwinson, so we have a genetic stake in both sides of the Battle of Hastings. Despite our name, which comes from her side of the family, I'm not sure this is true. After all, the Sidney family tree we have been looking at starts with William of Normandy (responsible for the death of Harold).

Tiring of the Sidneys before they make it to the eighteenth century, she asks instead to see photos of her grandchildren, her genetic future, in whom she generally shows no great interest.

I'm scrolling through my laptop when suddenly up pops a wide shot of my father's funeral pyre. I accidentally zoom into it. A tower of flames is swirling around my father's sheet-shrouded body and, before I can minimize it, I can't help noticing that the fire has already eaten away the end of the shroud. The soles of my father's feet are burnt black.

I think I've managed to click away from the close-up image before my mother sees it, but I can't be sure, so I try to distract her by joshing. "You know, according to the ancient Hindu tradition of suttee, you—as his widow—should have been burned on the pyre as well."

"I wish you *had* burned me with him," she says vehemently.

And I realize that she is being quite serious.

Familiar Finches

On the plane back to New York I fall into one of those disassociated, high-altitude funks. The image of my father's scorched black feet and my mother's angry death wish have tapped the well of sadness and loss in which my family resides yet refuses to acknowledge. Mostly I concede that our shield of stoicism is necessary for us to survive what Wordsworth called "Thoughts that do often lie too deep for tears."

Sometimes, though, like now, I feel I'm choking on it all, that I need an emotional Heimlich maneuver to eject the gristle of grief from my airway, to let me breathe again. I'm tired of wearing an invisible lei of loss around my neck like some secret garland, some slow-acting noose.

In *Mourning and Melancholia*, Freud warns of the danger of not bestowing grief the respect it's owed. Grief is greedy. It demands to be fed fulsome obsequies before it will loosen its grip on your throat. That's why all cultures insist on funeral rites. Without proper grieving, you can get stuck in the limbo of a love lost.

In the army we had to practice carrying the inert bodies of fellow soldiers over an obstacle course. It was intended to train us to carry our dead and wounded from the battlefield. No man left behind. I sometimes think we carry our dead with us for the rest of our lives, hauling them in our heads, if not on our backs. If we fail to grieve them adequately, they become ghosts that accompany us.

Maybe it is too late now for me to grieve what, and who, is gone. Maybe there is no way back. The bridges to the past burn behind you as you cross them. Maybe my Sisyphean task is the perpetually unfinished business of belonging. Or maybe I have already been struck down by what Chaucer, in *The Parson's Tale*, describes as "acedia," a listlessness, a despondency, a mortal mental lassitude, a terminal torpor.

Acedia is sometimes called "departing monk syndrome." When a monk left (not even the order, but just for another monastery, merely an inter-office transfer), the remaining monks would often plunge into a prolonged melancholy.

And yes, I know this analogy shouldn't apply to me as it is I who have left for other monasteries. So why do I miss my prior cloisters so much?

It may be akin to the malaise that afflicted some of the local bearers hired by early white Victorian explorers of Africa. Once these porters reached the horizon, they cast their cargo down upon the ground and refused to go further. They had to wait, they said, for their souls to catch up with them. Only later, much later, did scientists speculate that this self-imposed range restriction flowed from the logic of localized genetic malaria resistance (a phenomenon only recently recognized by northerners). If the local porters ventured beyond their own terroir, they were more likely to be felled by fever.

In my case, such sickness is a spiritual one, it simmers just beneath the ground. Like an emotional aquifer, it can spring to the surface at the slightest signal. A snatch of song. A sough of breeze. The murmur of a mourning dove. The drumming of rain on the window, a sound I associate with the loneliness of stormy boarding school nights, a sound that reminds me of that bittersweet line in Faulkner's *As I Lay Dying*: "How often have I lain beneath rain on a strange roof, thinking of home."

At evensong, which back then we still called vespers, we filed into chapel to sing Latin canticles when the day's heart still beat, to find, at our exeunt, that the day had died, and darkness had descended.

Any of these can nudge me into a reverie, abruptly disassociated from the here and now; transported back to the there and then.

Most often such sadness seems to surge at sundown. The stretching of the shadows, the languishing light, the hills captured within their own silhouettes. And then, above, the pulsing glow of the galaxy, its remote vastness reducing us to cosmic irrelevance.

This dusk-triggered dolor has a name: Hesperian melancholy, a heartache that usually eases when night arrives, only to return at the next setting of the sun.

You'd think Manhattan, sundered from circadian cycles by sun-blocking high-rises and nightlong streetlights, would be immune to the curse of Hesperes, but no. "[A]s only New Yorkers know," Dorothy Parker wrote, "if you can get through the twilight, you'll live through the night."

Though diagnosed as Hesperian *depression*, I prefer to backpedal it to a melancholy—a low-cal, drive-by, short-term depression, a tristesse amuse-bouche without the carbs of a "real" depression entrée.

I think Emily Dickinson must have suffered from Hesperian depression. Without calling it such, she describes it perfectly.

> *There's a certain Slant of light,*
> *Winter Afternoons—*
> *That oppresses, like the Heft*
> *Of Cathedral Tunes*

Dickinson didn't name it because no one had, back in the late nineteenth century. It was only labeled later by Eugène Marais, an extraordinary Afrikaans ethologist before ethology—the study of animal behavior—even existed as a discipline.

He called it Hesperian after the Greek for the land of the west, where the mythical Hesperides, a squad of sunset nymphs (Echo's soul sisters) were stationed, on the far side of the Atlas Mountains, the western edge of the known world. Beyond which, they believed, the sun was doused each night in the Atlantic Ocean. There, with the help of a hundred-headed dragon, the Hesperides guarded the tree of immortality—bestowing golden apples belonging to cow-eyed, alabaster-armed Hera, Queen of Olympus, a woman so vain that when Antigone claimed to be as comely, Hera turned her into a stork.

• • •

I first chanced upon Marais when I was based in South Africa, reporting on the last years of apartheid in the late 1980s.

Night after night, we correspondents worked the Black "dormitory" townships where armed police confronted activists trying to organize a labor boycott. We had to get inside these segregated cities each day before the battle lines were drawn. Once in, we often waited hours for conflict to coalesce. I would sit in our dusty gray Passat inherited from my predecessor, recalled to London because he was asthmatic, allergic to tear gas, a staple of our diet by then.

The Passat became a mobile library, littered with secondhand books I would dole out to resident kids. Huge, gantry-mounted arc lights loomed over the townships like prison towers. They blazed all night so that darkness never fully fell upon the jostling rows of identical matchbox houses, disrupting the circadian rhythm of their residents. The lights were bright enough to read by, even in the dead of night.

From the passenger footwell one Soweto winter evening, murky and coal-smokey, I retrieved a battered paperback by Eugène Marais. He stared intensely from the back cover, side-lit, with shaven head, widow's peak, bell-brow, gaunt cheeks. His club collar starched white. His bow tie, tuxedo, and eyes implacably black.

Marais, I learned from Robert Ardrey's lionizing introduction, was a journalist who became a barrister, then a psychologist, specializing in hypnotism (he could pull off that rarest of achievements, hypnotizing unwilling subjects). And then a drug addict—treating his own neuralgia with opium, and graduating to morphine.

The book I held, his unfinished masterpiece, *The Soul of the Ape*, is based on the three years (from around 1903) he lived with a troop of chacma baboons in the Waterberg mountains, north of Pretoria, the first comprehensive study of primates in the wild ever attempted.

He was still working on the book in 1936, when (despairing at the wholescale plagiarism by the Belgian Nobel Literature laureate Maurice Maeterlinck of his earlier, groundbreaking work on termites, *The Soul of the White Ant*) he put a shotgun to his chest and blew out his own heart.

For thirty-three years after his death, the manuscript was lost. Then, in 1969, it was discovered by his son and published.

Marais describes how, at sunset, the baboon troop would become agitated, then morose. Darkness is the most dangerous time for diurnal primates like baboons. It's when they are most vulnerable to attacks by nocturnal predators—leopard, hyena, and the like. So, as sundown approaches, it's crucial to find safe, defensible roosts for the night.

He found Hesperian angst too in humans, fellow diurnal primates. For thousands of years, we retreated into caves at night to evade predators. And that instinct still lies strong within us, he believed, affecting one in twenty modern humans (based on his questioning under hypnosis).

• • •

When Marais's Hesperian melancholy strikes me, I'm cast into a netherworld, what the Scots call the gloaming. My French cousins call it, "entre chien et loup," *between dog and wolf*, a twilight landscape in which it is difficult to discern canine from lupine, to differentiate predator from pal, friend from foe.

The only logical way to react to such confusion, of course, is to treat both as wolves. Which is, by and large, what I do. But recognizing wolves is a skill you must relearn whenever you move countries. The coded clues, the poker-tells, the social signs—the shibboleths—they change.

The wolf as a paragon of evil, a merciless beast, symbol of unbridled savagery, is one of the most deeply entrenched tropes in northern mythology. Our metaphors are littered with wolves concealing their true identities, thirteen in the Bible alone, including the Gospel of Matthew warning against false prophets, "which come to you in sheep's clothing, but inwardly they are ravening wolves." Aesop and the Brothers Grimm both brim with big bad wolf fables, to say nothing of werewolves, first mentioned in the *Epic of Gilgamesh*, the world's oldest surviving epic poem.

I grew up in a world without wolves, but for their role in the northern literature I absorbed in Southern Africa. As a child, reading, for me, was like peering into the wrong end of a cultural telescope. The first chapter book I can remember reading did take place in Africa, but many thousands of miles to the north, in the Sahara. *The Little Prince*, that fable of loss and cosmic exile. Its author, Antoine de Saint-Exupéry, was an haute-born French aviator who had fled to New York from Nazi-occupied France and despaired of ever returning.

Having left his home asteroid (so small that the sun sets forty-three times there every twenty-four hours—a nightmare for Hesperian melancholics), the ermine-cloaked prince lands in the Sahara. And in search of humans, he climbs a needle-peaked mountain range and calls out, but only his echo answers.

"Just like Narcissus," Hugo remembered when I read it to the boys.

The abiding impression left by the book only became apparent to me much later, when I left university in England to go home to Zimbabwe. I decided to drive overland down the African continent with a group of college friends. We traveled in a 1957 Bedford RL truck we'd bought at a British army surplus auction, a truck so old we had to double de-clutch to shift gears. It was a mad, what-were-we-thinking, six-month (twelve-thousand-mile) odyssey, zigzagging across the African continent to avoid wars, but not always succeeding.

We drove the length of France, boarded a ferry from Marseilles to Algiers, crossed the Atlas Mountains, and on for days through the empty desert, until we reached an abandoned French Foreign Legion fort, perfectly preserved by the desiccated desert air, as if its kepi-clad, camel-borne, Beau Geste legionnaires had only just ridden away. Ahead were the peaks of the Hoggar Mountains, sky-piercing serrations just like the ones Saint-Exupéry had drawn.

The vista to the west was stark. Just the outline of two distant dunes, the right one at nearly forty-five degrees, the left one gentler, their arcs bisecting above the horizon. I had seen it before, that view, those precise angles. As the light faded into entre chien et loup, and Venus rose, it came back to me. That last illustration in *The Little Prince*: at his invitation, the snake has bitten the prince and his body has disappeared, leaving behind "the loveliest and saddest landscape in the world."

Saint-Exupéry had crashed in just such terrain when he had piloted a trans-Saharan mail plane and, in his epilogue, he exhorts the reader: if we ever encounter this desert landscape, not to hurry past it, but to linger.

That night, as a grown man, a college graduate, a war veteran, I did just that, in a fit of sentimentality. I walked away from our truck, over the rise, and lay down on the sand under the spray of stars. With no terrestrial light pollution to obscure them, the cosmos glittered powerfully, crowding closer than I had ever seen it, pulsing with energy like some gargantuan phosphorescent organism in an unfathomable ocean. And I felt the years peel away, transporting me back to my own childhood, to the boy I had been when I'd first stumbled through *The Little Prince*, before adulthood marched in and obscured the stars, polluting everything, urging me to see with my eyes instead of my heart.

As I looked up, I listened to the stars, listened for the chiming of their "five hundred million bells," and I found myself worrying that the muzzle had fallen off the asteroid's resident sheep, allowing it to eat the petulant rose and changing the chimes to tears.

My self-conscious sentimentality was mollified later by a line from Wordsworth, a line I saw hand-daubed on the wall of a hopeful mud-brick school in southeastern Zimbabwe. *The Child is Father to the Man*, it read. And I realized then that however hard I tried, there was no escaping my past. Wherever I went, it stalked me still.

"In the lost boyhood of Judas / Christ was betrayed," as the poet A.E. Russell put it.

• • •

So, after all these exile laments, why, then, don't I go back to Zimbabwe, back to where I came from, instead of caviling about America, a place that was generous enough to admit me? Why am I still here?

One reason I don't return to where I was born and raised, like some salmon to its native river, or Murphy's father driving back to Indian Orchard to die, is that I have something in common with James Joyce. His Irish compatriots would roll their eyes and say, there was nothing Joyce wouldn't do for his country, *nothing*—except live there.

I can deploy so many reasons for my African absence. I have been banned in my homeland, accused of spying, of being an enemy of the state, the subject of death threats. But in truth there is something even graver repelling me. It is my sojourner status, that sense that I don't really belong there anymore, and maybe I never really did. In *Mukiwa*, I wrote that I'm what Afrikaners—Africa's longest-resident whites, settling in the Cape from 1685, not long after the Puritans arrived at Plymouth Rock—like to dismiss as a "soutpiel." A salt penis. One foot in Africa and the other in Europe, with my genitalia marinading in the ocean. And now that I have a toehold on a third continent, and a second sea in which to pickle my penis, my hopes of a settled identity have further ebbed.

• • •

Much that is written about the dislocation of exiles alights upon the avian metaphor.

The Afghan filmmaker Burhan Qurbani, who fled his war-wrecked homeland to live in Germany, was warned by his visiting grandfather, "You are like a bird without legs; you cannot land. You will never be at home here and you will never be at home in Afghanistan."

A Japanese proverb puts it this way: "The crow that mimics a cormorant is drowned."

Some of us end up like Darwin's finches, as described in *On the Origin of the Species*; we have adapted in ways that make us just different enough from other finches that they no longer recognize us as one of their own. We are crucially altered.

All male songbirds need to sing the right calls to attract mates, to pair and propagate and prosper. Like the London birds forced to sing at night to be heard above the traffic roar. They learn these calls from listening to their fathers. But what if, like mine, your father is largely silent, secretive about his origins, refusing to sing? How then do you learn to sing yourself? What song, and to whom? Who will recognize it, recognize you? How do you find familiar finches?

I talk to my mother about how depressed my father was when we were growing up. "I seem to remember him taking Valium. Am I imagining that?" I ask.

"No, you're not," she says carefully. "He would have periods of deep depression. About the war and losing his family to the Holocaust. I tried talking to him, but he refused to discuss it. And there was nothing like therapy where we were in Africa."

"How did his depression manifest?"

"He would just stop talking," she says. "For weeks, sometimes months, at a time."

My father had cause to be confounded by life. Born in Warsaw to a wealthy, secular Jewish family, he was sent to England for a summer at fifteen years old, on an intensive English course. It was the summer of 1939. He was due to return on a Baltic steamer on September 6, but Hitler invaded Poland on the first. My father never saw his family again—most of them perished in Treblinka. He lied about his age and joined the Free Polish army, went on to fight in the Battle of the Bulge, the German counterattack after D-Day, and on to help liberate Holland and Belgium.

After the war he stayed on in England and met my mother at university in London, where she was studying medicine. Her father was dead by then, but her mother opposed the romance. We don't breed with these people, she told my mother. "These people" being Jews. My mother married him anyway, and they fled to the furthest place they could find, settling in the remote Chimanimani Mountains, in eastern Zimbabwe. Before leaving, my father expunged the last of his Jewish identity, taking my mother's family name as his own.

Growing up, we knew none of this. When war followed them to

Southern Africa, and I was sent away to boarding school, my father became a remote, brooding presence, torn by tumults of temper. It was only on his deathbed that he revealed his backstory, dropping his gentile guise and reintroducing himself to me. I was already in my forties by then. Already a father myself, already in America.

And then he was gone.

Anglican-born, Jesuit-educated, and now ethnically half-Jewish. I was not quite sure what to make of it, so I began to read about the Ashkenazi Jewish people. And what I found only amplified my sense of unsettlement. A Semitic people who fled the Levant, lived mostly in Europe for more than two thousand years, and yet were still regarded as such an alien threat that nearly 60 percent of them were killed in the Holocaust. In my father's homeland of Poland, that figure rises to 90 percent. As the old Yiddish warning goes, "When the bird alights too long upon the tree, it will have stones hurled upon it." Move on, move on.

Maybe I am genetically imbued with that self-defensive, nomadic quiddity, like a medieval Jew who has wandered beyond the pale into no man's land, a rough, wolf-ridden territory outside any laws (even iniquitous ones) where burly marauders may ambush you at any moment.

• • •

Georgina has had to navigate this late-onset Jewry with me. She compares it to finding out as an adult that you are adopted. Nothing about your *lived* life changes, but your perspective on it shifts.

My relationship with Georgina is an odd one. I am ten years older than her and as adults we have almost never lived on the same continent, yet we maintain a close bond. We check in with each other several times a week, through multiple moves, disruptions, and relationships.

Today we are amicably arguing about an incident when she was a toddler and I was carrying her through our neighbor's garden when their geese attacked us, pecking my bare legs. She claims I dropped her and ran.

"Oh, for fuck's sake," I object. "I would never have done that!"

"Well, I distinctly remember tumbling onto the ground," insists Georgina.

"You're *both* wrong," Her Grace pronounces. "Peter fell, and you *both* rolled down the hill."

We accept her adjudication.

She lowers her voice. "Also, I'd prefer if you didn't swear in Nema's earshot; she's proving to be a very quick learner and we have to set a good example."

I've noticed that Nema's English *has* improved enormously. And she is starting to pick up Her Grace's posh accent, started to happy tense herself. I worry that adopting a memsahib bark is not necessarily the best way for her to negotiate her presence in modern Britain.

"My swearing is a medical condition," I say.

"Tourette's?" Her Grace asks, her interest quickening as she switches into doctor mode.

"No, lalochezia—swearing to relieve stress and anxiety."

"Did you know that, on average, people who swear have a higher IQ?" says Georgina.

"Fuck, fuck, fuck," I say.

She rolls her eyes. "I *knew* you would do that—you're so fucking juvenile."

"Now, now, children," clucks Her Grace happily.

I sometimes wonder if our sibling rapport would survive extended proximity, whether it depends on geographic distance to work as well as it does. Georgina and I have an unspoken deal that we can't both be down at the same time. Whoever declares it first gets to inhabit it for the duration of that conversation, while the other must listen, sympathize, and—only if asked—counsel.

We connect through a shared sense of humor; it is literal, it is dark, and often, it is angry, especially as we have aged. Most of all, it is unmoderated. Neither of us has to edit, our dialogue is unfettered by its effect. Neither of us has to impress the other; we are way beyond that. And somehow this releases an extra energy, makes our conversation more fluent.

When I look at our affinity, it saddens me, because I realize how many historical friends I have lost to death, mostly childhood friends killed in the Rhodesian war and colleagues who have died covering conflicts (I cannot bear to expunge them from my contacts list, and simply add an RIP suffix to their surnames—a very lengthy category now). But also, just lost to distance, and to being on the road so much, as a reporter and moving continents three times. The one thing you can't make later in life is a historic friendship, those friends who know your bio, who knew you in your previous iterations, who are unimpressed with your schtick. Those friends who like you in spite of your faults.

For me, that ship has sailed.

Zephyrs
Among the Tamarack

It is still dawn in the city when Joanna nudges me awake. Phoebe is whining to go out, she says. True to her rescue dog origins, Phoebe has learned how to open the foot pedal garbage bin and scarf her way through its contents. Which, of course, gives her terrible diarrhea. So, whenever she is left alone, we must place an upturned kitchen stool on the bin lid. But sometimes, like yesterday, we forget. So, now I find myself, still half-asleep, stumbling out into the gloaming with her through Riverside Park towards the Hippo Playground, where a pod of rubberized iron hippos is buried to varying depths, as though emerging from an asphalt lake.

Although Phoebe is clearly bursting, she remains incredibly finickity about where she will take a shit. She shuffles this way and that, haunches quivering, looking for a perfect piece of rectal real estate. I've read somewhere that dogs align their asses with magnetic north, but I'm not sure that's true.

She waddles ahead of me like a furry seal. Every few paces, despite the taut leash, she turns to check that I'm still there, regarding me with an expression that manages to be both needy *and* reproachful.

Today Phoebe turns her snout up at spot after spot, adjudging them befouled by the odors of other dogs. Until, out of frustration, I venture into the Crab Apple Meadow, a fenced-off paddock with prominently displayed *No Dogs Allowed* signs, hence a greater chance of Phoebe finding a pristine poop port.

As soon as we enter, I spot something large hanging from the bough of a crab apple tree, gently swaying in the Hudson's morning breeze. At first, I think it is an effigy, an unseasonal Guy Fawkes, dressed in blue jeans, a beige blouson, and tan deck shoes. Its head hangs down, as though bowed in respect for a passing dignitary, its feet almost touch the ground. As it twists slowly on its rope, its face, topped by tousled salt-and-pepper hair, rounds into view; it is the face of a man, about my age. Phoebe cocks her head and raises her muzzle, catching his scent. She starts to howl.

The police arrive, alerted by other early-morning dog walkers who have gathered now at the fence; one of the cops starts rigging up yellow scene-of-crime tape. This is the third body they've found in a Manhattan Park in the last three days, he tells us. Not to mention the 12-9s—their radio code for person-under-train.

That afternoon, walking Phoebe as usual—her bowels still volatile—I find myself reflexively scouting for other hanging trees, ones with horizontal limbs within reach, strong enough to bear the weight of a man.

On the way back I see that a group of elfin preschoolers clutching the loops of their communal rope, towed by a teacher, have arrived in Crab Apple Meadow. The yellow police tape has gone now. Just a few remnants flutter from the tree branches, like the yellow ribbons tied to trunks by relatives of soldiers away at war, wishing them safe return.

The teachers release the kids to run among the carpet of fallen blossom. Shrieking, they kick it up into the air, clouds of pink and white confetti. The teachers give instructions, inaudible to me up here on the overlooking slope. I see the kids reach out and grasp one another's hands. They form a circle to dance around the hanging tree, unknowing of its recent cargo. Slowly at first, they dance, then faster and faster as they gain confidence. And they start to sing, their tiny, piping voices floating up the slope, until I recognize the song. *Ring-a-round the rosie, A pocket full of posies, Ashes! Ashes! We all fall down.* At the end they all collapse in a heap, laughing.

On my way home I find myself humming it, the tune lodged in my lobe.

I dream that night of the toddlers dancing around the hanging tree, singing "Ring-a-round the Rosie." The dead man jiggles in time to the beat, in surprisingly good humor for someone who has just taken his own life. Crab apple blossoms, magenta and burgundy and coral, fill the air, suspended.

• • •

That weekend up at Indian Orchard, as some sort of life-affirming antidote, I think, to the hanging man, I insist on taking the boys for a father-and-sons hike up the mountain. Hugo puts up a stream of excuses until I lose patience with him.

"You're being so *annoying*," I tell him.

"Yeah? Well, the feeling's neutral," he counters.

"I think you mean, mutual."

"Mutual? Yeah, well *that's* the feeling."

"Oh, come *on*, Hugo. You're just being *lazy* now," I huff.

"I am?" He grins. "Well, nature or nurture, either way it's *your* fault."

I try not to laugh.

Then he claims it's about to rain (it's not) and argues for the shorter route.

"We'd better make haste while the sun shines," he says.

"It's make *hay* while the sun shines."

But my correction is parried as less likely, and I can see why.

I have a long history of failing to convince him of mondegreens. It took me some time to prove to his satisfaction that the Pacific Ocean was not the Specific Ocean. Even then he fell back on the argument that it *was* a specific ocean, the Pacific one! I sometimes wonder if he has "oppositional defiant disorder," an instinct to defy authority. I kind of admire it, but I can't let him see that.

I have recently come across the Child Rearing Scale (CRS), where parents choose between the importance of four binaries in their children: independence *or* respect for elders, curiosity *or* good manners, self-reliance *or* obedience, and considerate *or* well behaved. I'm not sure I buy into these binaries, but if I did, I think I'd want my children to be the first of each binary. And irrespective of what I want, it's what they are.

Once we get up onto Bird Peak, their sullenness lifts. Nature and exercise work their dual magic, as they almost always do. The boys begin to pepper me with questions as we hike.

"Do you know that sharks pee through their skin?" asks Hugo.

I do not.

"Do you know why, at bar mitzvahs, you have to give money gifts in multiples of eighteen dollars?" asks Thomas.

I do not.

Apparently, it is part of gematria, an Assyro-Babylonian system of numerology used by Jews, which assigns letters with numerical values. Eighteen is the alphanumeric value of "chai" or "life."

"Do you think the voice in your head gets deeper as your own speaking voice does?" asks Hugo.

"Do you know the smell of a newly mown lawn is actually the grass's distress signal at being hurt?" asks Thomas.

Hugo agrees. "It's the smell of grass tears," he says.

Now he has found a little conclave of mushrooms. "Can we eat these, or are they poisonous?" He's been developing an interest in cooking.

I'm not sure, so I recite the old Croat proverb: "*All* mushrooms are edible. But some only once . . ."

It takes him a beat, and then he punches me lightly on the shoulder. "Da-*ad*!"

At the top we lie back on a warm flat rock. Phoebe sprawls among us, and both boys pet her. She is blissed at being in her pack.

"I think Phoebe is the frosting on the family cake," says Hugo. "She makes everything taste sweeter."

The dog sees a chipmunk and chases it into a small grove of saplings. Thanks to Murphy's tutelage, I now recognize them as young larches. Their bark is pink and flakey and, underneath, a darker, arterial red bleeds through.

"Do you know the difference between conifers and deciduous trees?" I ask the boys.

"Of course," Thomas says; this is elementary school stuff.

"And which are these?" I point at the larches.

"Conifers," he says confidently. "They have needles and cones."

He's right. But larches defy the usual arboreal taxonomy; like soutpiele, they straddle the divide. Their needles change color in the autumn—these ones are already turning yellow—and soon they will shed, just like deciduous trees. Larches are that rare genus, deciduous conifers.

I find myself wondering if this is what I need to become, a cultural larch, taxonomy-defying—deciduous *and* conifer, playing for both teams.

Just then, the slightest of breezes, a mere breath, rustles the saplings. And I find myself laughing out loud.

"What's so funny?" demand the boys.

"Zephyrs among the tamarack," I say. "It's something Grandma recited in a pronunciation audition for wannabe radio broadcasters. I never thought I would see it in real life. A zephyr is a gentle breeze, and tamarack is the Algonquin name for a larch; it means the wood used to make snowshoes."

When our hobbit house finally comes into sight at the end of the hike, I look at my watch. We have been out for nearly four hours.

"Dad, I want to inform you that I had a lot of fun with you today," Hugo says in a high, cartoon chipmunk voice.

"Yeah? Well, the feeling's mutual."

• • •

With the end of summer, the wauling chevrons of wild geese start to muster above Indian Orchard, readying to fly south to warmer climes. So many lakes are ladled into the Taconic dales that there's an abundance of migratory waterfowl here. I feel a melancholy descend; I want to flee with them from the frigid months that face us here.

"How do they know when it's time to leave?" Hugo had once asked.

I wasn't sure.

"And why do they fly in big Vs, and how do they decide who gets to be the leader? Is it a democracy of ducks?"

"They're geese," said Thomas.

"What's the difference?" asked Hugo.

"Geese have longer necks," Thomas told him. "And they mate for life."

By the time we next heard the squawking squadrons above us, and the boys reprised their chorus of queries, I'd mugged up on the mechanics of the migration. The lead goose, I was able to tell them, keeps rotating as it's exhausting work, piercing the air, while the others fold in behind, facing less wind resistance.

Later I hear Hugo earnestly explaining it to a friend. "The front goose has to open the sky for the other ones," he says. "It's the sky-breaker."

"Why do the geese keep honking like that?" Thomas asks me. "Shouldn't they save their energy for the long flight ahead of them?"

That was rather a good question.

It turns out they honk like that to cheer each other on, to boost their morale.

And after that, whenever I wanted to wish the boys good luck on some challenge they faced, some fresh section of sky they needed to pierce, I would say, honk, honk. And they would honk, honk back.

• • •

Hugo wanted to know where the wild geese went. I'd asked my own father the same question about the white storks that flocked to eastern Zimbabwe each November, our summer. He knew very well—the biggest population of white storks in the world comes from Poland, which, unbeknownst to me then, was the country from which my father too had migrated.

That question, in reverse—where so many birds disappeared to each autumn—was one that Europeans long puzzled over, before they'd set foot in what for them was the terra incognita of Africa.

They came up with various fantastical theories.

Aristotle believed the birds hibernated in hollow trees. Or burrowed into the bottoms of rivers. Or mutated into nonmigratory birds or even mice (as caterpillars morph into butterflies), just for the winter.

Christian luminaries, such as Swedish archbishop Olaus Magnus, were still riffing on Aristotle's explanation two thousand years later.

Magnus's *A Description of the Northern Peoples* (published in 1555) was illustrated with woodcuts of rookie fishermen mistakenly netting sleeping swallows from a winter riverbed.

In 1702 Charles Morton, another church minister, stepped into the migration mystery with a new hypothesis in his popular pamphlet "An Essay Towards the Probable Solution of this Question: Whence come the Stork and the Turtle, the Crane, and the Swallow, when they Know and Observe the Appointed Time of their Coming. Or where those Birds do probably make their Recess and Abode . . ."

Morton postulated, quite seriously, that the birds went to . . . the *moon*.

When I told the boys this, they fell about laughing. I know it sounds lunatic at first blush, I said, but is it *that* less likely than the moon's gravitational pull causing the ocean tides?

And Morton's wasn't even the first mention of moon migration. Around 1628, yet another churchman, my namesake, Bishop Francis Godwin, published *The Man in the Moone*, a short novel in which our hero, the plucky Domingo Gonsales, harnesses a wedge of swans to transport him across the sky. He is amazed when, instead, they pull him vertically into the firmament until gravity fades and, after a twelve-day journey, they land upon the moon. There Gonsales discovers (in addition to the Lunars, a race of carefree Christians who speak in song) various migratory birds enjoying a balmy lunar break from the grim Teutonic winter.

The pioneering ornithologist Francis Willughby did propound an alternative to the extraterrestrial theory. Birds migrated to warmer, southern climes, he sensibly suggested in 1676. But he was widely derided by the bien-pensant.

It wasn't until 1822 that Willughby was vindicated. That spring, in the German county of Klütz, near the Baltic Sea, staff on the estate of Count Christian Ludwig Reichsgraf von Bothmer spotted a white stork with a strange appendage. Lodged through its neck was an arrow.

The count ordered the bird shot. "Reason for shooting," he recorded as, "satisfaction of the generally aroused curiosity."

The stork's resident arrow was examined and found to be thirty-four inches long, the shaft made of tropical wood. Count von Bothmer sent the bird to the nearby estate of Grand Duke Friedrich Franz I, who had a taxidermy workshop.

This pfeilstorch—or arrow stork, as it became known—was one plucky, if unlucky, bird. But it flew into history, unlocking the millennia-old migration mystery. The arrow was recognized as an African artifact, and German naturalists finally had conclusive proof of the winter destination of migratory birds.

Two hundred years later, the arrow stork is still on display—its African weaponry intact—in a VIP vitrine at the Zoological Museum of the University of Rostock, one of twenty-five pfeilstorches since collected in various museum dioramas. I showed the boys a photo of it. The arrow is embedded vertically through the bird's neck, iron tip uppermost to give the impression that the stork is standing at attention, like a Tower of London beefeater holding a pike.

• • •

In ordering the killing of the arrow stork, Count von Bothmer broke an ancient taboo. Because they nest close to us, on our roofs, our chimneys, our church towers, we have always had an intimate view of storks' domestic life. We admire their altruistic allopreening, where one stork grooms another, which is rare among birds. And their assiduous childcare, the way they regurgitate food (insects and frogs, snakes, fish, and rodents) into their chicks' open beaks.

And when the ancient Greeks noticed that storks tend their young long after most other birds eject theirs from the nest, they formed the mistaken impression that young storks look after their parents, and so they revered them as a paragon of eldercare. The law of Pelargonia, which obliged human progeny to provide for their aging parents, was even named after the Greek word for stork, pelargos. If Count von Bothmer had pulled his stork shooting stunt in Aristotle's time, it would have earned him a death sentence.

The Greeks also contributed to storks' association with babies and fertility. Hera—remember her, the much cheated-upon wife of Zeus? She of the alabaster arms and cow eyes, who turned Antigone into a stork? She did the same to the comely Queen Gerana, whom she suspected of bearing Zeus's child. When, in stork form, Gerana flew back to retrieve her newborn human, flapping away with her beak-borne baby suspended in a blanket, she helped launch the image now ubiquitous on birth announcement cards.

The myth of storks delivering human babies was reinforced by the medieval European tradition of marrying on the summer solstice (June 21), with a bulge in births nine months later, in springtime, just as storks return to Europe from their African sojourn.

The Danish author Hans Christian Andersen cemented the various intersecting stork-baby-delivery myths for squeamish Victorian parents as a cover to avoid explicit sex education talks with their children. His anthology of fairy tales, first published in 1838, included "The Storks," an unsettling story I read as a boy.

In the story, a group of local yokels chant a threatening ditty at four stork chick siblings:

> *The first he will be hanged,*
> *The second will be stabbed,*
> *The third will be burned,*
> *And the fourth will be slapped.*

Only one lad refuses to join in.

The chicks' mother tries to reassure them that they will soon be relaxing in Africa, while "back here there isn't a green leaf left on the trees, and it's so cold that the clouds freeze to pieces and fall down in little white rags," and the boys "have to sit moping in a dark room."

When it comes time to learn to fly, the littlest chick is afraid and creeps back into the nest. His mother warns him that he will freeze to death if he stays in Europe, and that the boys will come, "and hang you and beat you and burn you."

So, the littlest chick learns how to fly, after all. And as they get ready to migrate to Africa, their mother agrees to take revenge on the taunting boys.

"I know a pond where all the human babies lie until the storks come to take them to their parents," she says. "The pretty little babies lie in that pond, dreaming more sweetly than they ever dream afterwards."

But, she says, the wicked boys won't get baby siblings. And for the ringleader, she has something even darker in mind.

"In that pond," said his mother slowly, "there is a little baby that has dreamed itself to death; we'll bring that to him. And then he'll cry because we've brought him a little dead brother. But don't forget that good little boy who said it was a shame to make fun of us! We'll take him both a brother *and* a sister! And since his name is Peter, you shall all be called Peter too!"

And so all the young storks were given the name Peter, and all storks have been called Peter ever since.

• • •

Reading Hans Christian Andersen's tale had a profound effect on me, a white boy in Zimbabwe, already cloaked in cultural confusion. A boy who had never been out of Africa, yet whose lineage was evidently elsewhere. I thought that I might be like a stork, a stork named Peter, white but with black tips upon his wings. And, by and by, when I was a young man, I too would migrate north like the white storks. And, like them, I would keep returning. Until such time as I could no longer tell which hemisphere was home.

But there was a difference. I was not part of a flock. I had no chevron to join, no sky-breaker in front of me to lessen the resistance of the cultural headwinds. And no fellow travelers to honk at, to boost morale, to cheer each other on.

I feel the echoes of that solitude still. Like some time-traveling Confederate soldier having fought on the wrong side of a losing war, marooned now far from home in an alien nation, shorn of context, ashamed and adrift, with few confrères who comprehend the convoluted course we have charted.

I feel too the disorientation of the first-generation immigrant parent, producing assimilated American children who are then somewhat embarrassed by us. It is, of course, a far greater issue for those navigating a new tongue. But it can still distance me from my own offspring. We have different cultural references; we speak in different argots.

And when I reread Hans Christian Andersen's tale—to my sons this time—I couldn't help seeing it as a fable of xenophobia, hostile whites threatening unwelcome African migrants.

Even the impaled pfeilstorch—the arrow stork—plays into that meme, laced with the implied savagery of African archers who felt no compunction trying to kill this widely venerated bird, this symbol of purity and new life, this bird who entertains no natural fear of man, who embraces our proximity, this eater of snakes, our legendary nemeses since Eden. Felling a stork, either on the ground or gracefully gliding, slow and stately—more than three feet from tail to bill, with a wingspan of around six feet—seems despicably unsporting.

Yet again, the news from Africa is unsettling, backing up the northern view of the "dark continent." Not simply Pliny's "ex Africa semper aliquid novi," *Always something new out of Africa*, which sounds almost neutral, but Rabelais's scarier gloss on it (the emphasis is mine): "It is the custom of Africa to always produce new *and monstrous* things."

The Roman symbol of Africa, memorialized on a silver coin struck by the emperor Hadrian, is a woman reclining on a throne, wearing an elephant headdress. In one hand she holds a cornucopia, symbol of plenty, but in the other hand squats a giant scorpion, its stinger swollen with venom, arched and ready to strike.

• • •

Radio presenters at the BBC World Service used to close each bulletin by announcing, "This is the end of the World News," an unintentional double entendre (seized on by Anthony Burgess in his book *The End of the World News*, a triptych on Freud, Trotsky, and planetary cataclysm—now unforgivably out of print). But after relating the African news—commonly a catalog of catastrophes—this sign-off can appear aptly apocalyptic. Africa serves as a screen upon which northerners project the shadow puppets of their own terrors.

I have contributed to this violent image in my years as an Africa correspondent covering civil wars, massacres, genocide, famine (according to that news editors' adage: if it bleeds, it leads). At least, I suppose, I've had continuity of contact. I was a "specialist," from Africa, if not of it (or is that vice versa?).

In *The Captive*, Proust points out that "the real voyage of discovery is not in seeking new landscapes but in having new eyes." Maybe we need to see Africa with new eyes. Take Nigeria: notoriously ill-governed, chaotic, corrupt, beset by Islamist insurgency in the north and oil spills in the south. News from Nigeria is relentlessly negative. Yet Nigerians regularly top "happiness" surveys, a paradox seized upon by Wole Soyinka in the title of his latest book, *Chronicles from the Land of the Happiest People on Earth*.

For me, the moment when those two Africas diverged most

jarringly, when my own cognitive dissonance was at its greatest, was when South Africa's first democratic elections were held in April 1994, ushering in the end of apartheid—just as the Rwandan genocide began. I chose to aim my gaze at the good news of the birth of the "rainbow nation." I so wanted a happy ending, and to cover that, rather than the Great Lakes massacres.

Maybe, somewhere inside my psyche, that choice was impelled by my own self-protection. I'm not sure I had room for any more darkness. My RAM of violence was full.

In any case, the fickle searchlight of the First World media seldom settles upon Africa for long. The north suffers from AADD: Africa attention deficit disorder. And when it does shine there, it concentrates on conveying Africa as a continent convulsed with conflict. A continent shaking a chipped enamel mug, begging for charity.

As more and more aid is left to charity, it has become a crapshoot, a souk of compassion, with various causes competing for philanthrodollars. Some diseases, issues, countries are easier to package, brand and sell than others. NGOs are forced to spend millions jockeying for advantage in the attention economy.

This is the complicated calculus of charity. This is the reality of the great alms bazaar. Personal experience is key, from Alzheimer's to Zika, from Angola to Zimbabwe. Northerners tend to support the eradication of the disease that has felled your parent, afflicted your child, the impoverished country in which you once went on safari, backpacked on your gap year, or volunteered for Peace Corps.

Is this really the best way to triage tragedy? It's become a Victorian freak show, a pageant of grotesques in which charities are cast as carnival barkers shilling for their causes: Roll up for river blindness! Join here for jailed journalists! This way for African amputees! Fix these harelips, clean that infected water, stop sex trafficking, end modern slavery, be a manumission-ary! Summon Jesus to the jungle, Our Savior to the savannah. Come see the girl malaria killed, open your wallet for the cholera child, check out the human skeletons in the famine parade.

In one humanitarian crisis I covered in southern Sudan, the conscience-goading image was a toddler with toast-rack ribs, kneeling with his forehead resting on the barren earth as a waiting vulture regarded him with hooded, hungry eyes. It was taken by Kevin Carter, a colleague from South Africa. The photo ran in the *New York Times* and won Carter a Pulitzer. Criticized for not helping the child, Carter said he had chased off the vulture, and that the plane he arrived on had been delivering UN food relief. The child, a boy named Kong Nyong, survived, but four months after receiving the Pulitzer, at thirty-three, Carter died by suicide.

All the King's Horses

Ernest Hemingway, I think it was, said you go broke, gradually, and then suddenly.

That's how my marriage ended.

It is July. A sunny Sunday, rising to eighty-four degrees. A light breeze out of the northeast. The boys are sleeping late. Joanna and I are playing tennis. Affable doubles down at the Lakeville public courts, where fingers of grass reach up through the cracked asphalt. Afterwards we pick up a copy of the *New York Times* at the retro Salisbury Pharmacy. We divide the sections up over breakfast at the White Hart Inn, reading aloud items we think will interest each other.

Page one leads with the "Unite the Right" march in Charlottesville.

On the op-ed page, Nuruddin Farah, the exiled Somali author, warns of famine there. He recounts the local folk tale of a woman who hears a cow lowing in the sky and beseeches God to pluck it from the heavens so she can feed her children. But when it descends to earth, the cow turns out to be a hyena.

Over on International, Grace Mugabe, Zimbabwe's First Lady, is accused of assaulting a young model she found in her grown sons' Johannesburg hotel room, lashing the girl across the face with an electrical extension cord while her bodyguards watched. The First Lady is now claiming diplomatic immunity.

Kristen R. Ghodsee has a piece on why women in the Soviet Bloc had better sex under socialism (more time, job security).

In the magazine, "Judge" John Hodgman deals with a case of animal-costume cruelty, to wit, whether dressing a chihuahua-cross-dachshund in a poncho and sombrero for a Mexican-themed dinner party is cruel and/or racist. Hodgman is indignant that the German side of the dog's ancestry is being ignored.

In the Vows section, Alvin Mann is marrying Gertrude Mokotoff. They met at the gym. Alvin is ninety-four. Gertrude is ninety-eight. There is a photo of Gertrude from the waist down. She's easing up the hem of her teal wedding gown to reveal a red-and-white garter around her thigh.

We drive back up the hill to Indian Orchard.

I switch off the ignition. The engine block clicks and creaks as it cools and contracts. We sit for a moment in silence, inhaling the Taconic view.

Then, still facing forward, Joanna begins to speak.

"I don't want to be married anymore," she says, apropos of nothing.

I think I have misheard her.

She repeats the line.

Only later do I realize there are two words missing: to you.

* * *

They say that man reacts to danger with a flight-or-fight response. But that's not quite true. There's a third choice: flight, fight *or freeze*. Many African antelope—impala, kudu, bushbuck, eland—do that when in danger; they hope to find safety by standing stock still. And so, apparently, do some humans. Our reaction to the stress hormone cortisol, produced in the face of danger, is to freeze, to become paralyzed.

Initially that's what happens to me.

I can't bring myself to tell anyone about my failing marriage. Once I start telling people, it will be real. If I hold off, it may yet prove to be a hallucination. A temporary midlife crisis.

Very reluctantly, Joanna concedes to couples counseling, on condition that I organize it, and it be conveniently close. Following recommendations, I find a therapist on Central Park West. We walk there together early one autumn morning for our first session.

The sidewalk is carpeted with golden ginkgo leaves shaped like tiny fans, mini punkah wallah fronds. I start to feel nauseous. It might be the ginkgo berries shed on the sidewalks. Crushed underfoot, they release their peculiar odor of vomit. New York's ginkgo trees were apparently a gift from the Japanese emperor. My working theory is that he did it to spite America for Japan's wartime defeat, as he included female trees whose fruit exclusively excrete this foul smell.

In the waiting room we sit in silence at opposite ends of a creaking claret Chesterfield, peering into our phones until the therapist opens the door. She and Joanna look each other up and down. They are wearing identical black, sleeveless Dior mini dresses, Manolo Blahnik pumps, and bright platinum bobs. It is all they can do to restrain themselves from high-fiving and shouting, "Snap!" To make matters worse, the therapist is British.

I am toast.

She asks us both for our "therapeutic goals," turning to me first. I say that I think we can reset and save our marriage, and that's what I want to do. Next up, Joanna. She's done, she says. Emphatically. She wants out. She dreams of lying on a white sofa, in a white loft, with white orchids on the table, just staring at the white ceiling.

• • •

It is during one of these counseling appointments (we give up after about five desultory sessions) that I first notice Joanna picking at her hairline absentmindedly. When I point it out, she continues unabashed. She has started feeling these little nodules poking up through her scalp, she says. She *must* get them out as they are driving her mad.

At first, she thinks they are blocked follicles, gummed up by hairspray, something she must apply to achieve that glossy platinum helmet. Or perhaps caused by too many encounters with hot Japanese tongs, to straighten it.

Then, she begins to suspect it is some ghastly form of seborrheic dermatitis, a late-onset acne she's read about that afflicts the middle-aged. But her research shows that mostly affects men.

One afternoon, during a meeting on Mahogany Row, the executive forty-third floor of Hearst Tower, she gets her answer. I try to imagine the scene: the frustration of it, like something caught in one's teeth, she almost has it between the pincer of her shiny black shellacked index and thumb nails. It must be distracting, maddening. Then, with an immensely satisfying pop, it would finally lift clean out. She would turn away from the interminable PowerPoint presentation to examine it. It would sit in her palm—a pink pod, a little Fabergé egg, but bigger than expected. She would press into it with her thumb nail, finding it surprisingly hard. Then, suddenly, it would give and there, inside the hard, glabrous capsule is a shard of glass.

Someone would call her name; she would look up to see the circle of white male executives staring at her. A trail of blood would have trickled down her temple, onto the collar of her crisp white Celine blouse.

There are several of them after that, glass splinters migrating upwards from her skull and out through her scalp. Only then does she realize their original source.

When she was seventeen years old, there'd been a car accident. Her boyfriend at the wheel of his mother's Hillman Avenger after a night at the pub. No other car involved, he'd reached down to tune the radio and lost control. Joanna's head crunched into the windscreen; she'd not been buckled up—people didn't back then.

Why are the remaining glass shards, this evidence of a former life, like the rusted turkey wire in the Indian Orchard earth, only emerging now? Why, after so many decades of remaining securely ensconced? Perhaps they are the biological bounty of the unclenching that comes with age.

It seems apt that this evidence of an antique wound is now reappearing, sharp and glittering and dangerous. I carry my own cargo of shrapnel. In my back, from a land mine in the Rhodesian war; and in my face, from an RPG blast in the Ugandan civil war.

I wonder if this has a bearing on my own reluctance to submit to the self-examination of therapy. That over the years I have managed to let the worst memories, the weightiest particles, slowly sink to the bottom of my mental pitcher. And therapy would only roil up all that settled sediment and send it swirling turbid to the surface.

Now, however, I have finally started solo therapy to help me cope with the end of my marriage. I am late to therapy, a middle-aged man struggling to talk about himself for the first time, self-conscious and embarrassed.

• • •

As a joke, I've taken to using the word Jexit to describe Joanna's withdrawal from our marital union. Like Brexit, Jexit, I maintain, is unnecessary, damaging, avoidable, self-inflicted, based on false information and prejudice and bogus ideas of independence in an interconnected world. And it has taken almost as long to bring about, since the first inklings. I hope it's reversible, but I fear not. Joanna's Article 50 is her midlife crisis—Article 55, in her case.

Jexit too is masterminded by an ambitious, tow-haired, charismatic leader. It's done without a prenegotiated exit deal. It flirts with financial collapse. It hurts those you have partnered with for a long time. And it jeopardizes the progeny of the Union, who may well end up seceding. It harks back to a fake nostalgia for a life never actually led. In short, it risks sacrificing everything in a bid for sovereignty . . .

We are walking the dog around the reservoir, on the bridle path (the aural pun is not lost on me). Walking the dog is the last thing we do together. To the south, the supertalls balance on basalt along West 57th Street. They puncture the clouds like giant asparagus spears, stunting the rest of the cityscape.

"The tragedy of life is not that we die," I find myself saying, "but that we stop loving."

Joanna thinks about this for a beat. "Who said that?"

"I did."

"Really?"

"No, not really," I sigh. "It's a paraphrase of Somerset Maugham."

We stand in silence, one of those elastic moments that stretch out as though the present will last forever, in all its particularity, mundane and intense and most of all, *now*. Finally, a helicopter clatters noisily overhead, ushering time on.

She turns to look up at me. "How did Maugham put it?"

I close my eyes for a second, trying to summon the exact words. "The great tragedy of life is not that men perish, but that they cease to love."

We walk in silence again for a while, and when she breaks it, her voice is different, harsher, decisive. "Well, whatever, we can't go on like this."

"Like what?" I say, playing dumb.

She explains how I "close her down." Nothing seems possible when she's at home, she says. At work, everything does. Without me, she can fly. Unfettered, apparently, by my earthly manacles.

"You can't park that car in my bay," I splutter. "I've been nothing but supportive of your career. I helped you launch it. I looked after the kids while you pursued your dreams."

Blah, blah, blah. I hear my voice as if at a distance. It has a weak, wheedling tone. I must stop. I'm only harming my suit. Just one more grappling hook, though, before I go, go.

"Day-to-day, we still seem to get along just fine," I say, but in a resigned way now, one that must accept what it does not fully understand. "We seldom fight. Don't you want to at least *try* to fix it? Don't we owe that much to the boys?"

I can't believe that I'm baiting and casting the for-the-sake-of-the-children cliché . . . This is not who I want to be, this supplicant, prostrating myself, begging her to stay.

I turn to her, realizing that up until now I've been looking into the middle distance while addressing her. And what I see in her eyes is deeply disconcerting. She feels *sorry* for me. Respect has gone. Pity has pulled into the platform. How did I become this poster boy for the beta male?

"Trying to figure out why you are doing this," I sigh, "is like trying to catch mist with a butterfly net."

"Nice image," she says, refusing to react to its substance.

That corny poster that teens used to Blu Tack to their walls when I was a teen comes unbidden to mind. Its Hallmark haiku—maybe it was from the book *Jonathan Livingston Seagull*—something like: "You love her? Then free her. If she returns, she's yours. If not, she never was."

In my heart of hearts, I know that once she walks out, even for a "trial separation," it's over, "we" are over. The clock resets. Our timelines will move apart, at first by small degrees. But small degrees turn into wide angles. As Frost would say, did say, "Two roads diverged in a yellow wood, / And sorry I could not travel both."

My surrender feels almost formal, after a long war of emotional attrition. I am the Japanese general on the deck of the USS *Missouri*, bobbing in Tokyo Bay, presenting my Samurai saber to the assembled American brass. Folding my flag into a plump triangle of patriotic pie and handing it to my erstwhile wife. Her will is implacable. I must bend to it. She wants this escape so badly I feel ashamed.

Another couplet from "The Road Not Taken" comes to me as we leave the bridle path and wait for the lights to change on Central Park West: "Yet knowing how way leads on to way, / I doubted if I should ever come back."

Joanna and I are not geese, after all.

We are ducks.

We do not mate for life.

. . .

At night we lie on opposite edges of our California king–sized bed, alone together. The bed, a bespoke one crafted by Tonga artisans in Zimbabwe, has a headboard made from a traditionally carved Tonga door. Its metalwork is fashioned into ndoro spirals, and our initials worked in so subtly that we didn't notice them for several years. It used to remind me of Odysseus and Penelope's conjugal bed, the one Odysseus built around an olive tree as one of its four posts, stable and rooted like their bond. Our Tonga bed now feels like a marital mockery.

Partners of twenty-five years, through all the drama of a life— emigration, children, the whole riotous roller-coaster ride of it. Now she has become a stranger to me, her mind a black box. I have no idea what she is thinking, no idea who she is. That mask that she used to don with an irony-aware eye roll each morning, to go to work as "Brand Joanna"—that mask now seems to have fused to her face.

I miss the red hair, and those old, imperfect teeth and that shy smile. I haven't seen that smile in some time, that special one you had to earn.

She has reinvented herself to such an extent that I'm beginning to think she is like Plutarch's thought experiment, the Ship of Theseus— repaired so extensively over the years that it is made up entirely of new parts, with nothing left of the original.

Unlike her, I feel largely unevolved and entirely scrutable. Like one of those transparent tropical fish, you can see right through into my emotional entrails. This puts me at a huge disadvantage.

In the morning she leaves for work. She shrugs on her Sgt. Pepper brocade coat, surveys herself in the gilt-framed hall mirror, pouts her mouth to touch up her lipstick.

I walk behind her to retrieve the newspaper from the front steps. Noticing that her collar is rucked up at the back, I reflexively reach to unsnag it.

As I touch the coat, she recoils. In the mirror I see her lips twist into a rictus of revulsion.

"I'm not a *baby*!" she snaps.

She wrenches open the front door and strides out, leaving me rocking in the vortex of her vehemence.

After work she tours apartments to rent, white downtown lofts with white sofas and white ceilings.

German has a word for the weight gained by a spouse after a split: Kummerspeck—grief bacon. But I don't plump for this; I do the opposite, losing weight: ten, twenty, thirty pounds, and counting. And it doesn't look good off me; it leaves me lined, gaunt, hollow-eyed.

At my annual dermatology checkup—crucial for pale-skinned Africans as the sun-stippled stigmata accumulate on our northern-designed rind—I fill out my personal details, but the receptionist slides the clipboard back to me across the counter.

"You forgot to fill in your emergency contact," she says.

My pen hovers over the box. I am stumped. Finally, I write Joanna's name. So much for moving on.

I complain to my newly acquired therapist that there is a humiliating asymmetry: I spend much more time thinking about Joanna than she spends thinking about me. She urges me to get over my codependency, to detach, focus on my own needs, to set boundaries. But I'm not sure who I am anymore, now I'm apart from Joanna. I seem to have lost sight of myself.

I worry that I'm suffering from limerence, the state of being obsessed with another person, desperate for them to reciprocate. Or athazagoraphobia, the fear of being forgotten (or ignored) by someone you were once close to.

The dermatologist's check reveals a crop of precancerous barnacles, basal cells growing in such profusion that they are too numerous to cut out individually. Instead, he proposes lasering my face and arms to slough off the outer layers of skin. Like a Taconic rattlesnake. He warns me to clear my diary for several weeks afterwards. You won't be able to go out in public, he says.

As the procedure begins, the nurse hands me a small red rubber ball.

"What's that for?" I ask.

"You'll see," she says.

By the end of the treatment, the doctor's room smells like fried Kummerspeck/grief bacon—mine. And the nurse must pry my lock-knuckled fingers off the ball.

•   •   •

An answer message awaits when I get home. It is from my mother, the only person other than spammers who still uses my landline. Her voice declaims as though to someone far away, which I suppose I am.

I have not yet informed her about my collapsing marriage. I tell myself this is because I don't want to worry her when she is in ill health, though really it is because I feel so humiliated.

When I call her back, she reports that she's now suffering from night terrors. David Attenborough, or at least, his doppelgänger—she can't be certain—emerges from her TV. He stands at her bedside and in the same hushed cadences he deploys when trying not to disturb foraging Virunga gorillas, he tells his audience that she is about to die. He conveys this news with faux solemnity, as he does when recounting efforts to save the elephants of Gorongosa. Attenborough is narrating her demise, just as he would an endangered pachyderm.

When she awakes from this unsettling quietus, she finds she has lost all sense of time, of place, of identity. She is floating, untethered, above herself, looking down upon her own prone body.

I remind her that she once saved my life in Gorongosa.

"I did?" she says, eager to claim the credit.

"Yes, but it was by accident."

"Oh, well, I'm sure I must have *meant* it; what did I do?"

"You know how, when you carried out those mass vaccinations in Chimanimani, you insisted on including the people over the border in Mozambique, even though it was against regulations; you said it was the only way to achieve 'herd immunity'?"

"Yes, of course."

"Years later, I was doing a story on the guerrilla war in northern Mozambique, and I was kidnapped by Renamo rebels; they accused me of being a spy and they took me south to their headquarters in Gorongosa. When their commandant looked at my passport, he recognized my surname. And he asked me if my mother was a doctor. And when I said you were, he rolled up his sleeve to show me the vaccination scar on his arm.

"'Your mother, she did this to me,' he said, 'when I was just a young boy. And look, I grew up strong!' And suddenly I was transformed from prisoner into honored guest."

My mother is gladdened by the serendipity.

"I wrote about it in *Mukiwa*," I remind her.

"Ah yes, of course," she says. "I remember now."

But she does not.

• • •

My therapist tells me she thinks that I may be suffering from PTSD. Of course, I am familiar with this condition and the danger it poses to me. (Some psychiatrists think it should be renamed post-traumatic stress injury, PTSI, to reduce its stigma.)

At the BBC hostile environments course, we had also been briefed by an expert on PTSD. Dr. Gordon Turnbull, a psychiatrist from the RAF, had debriefed hostages like Terry Waite, chained to a Beirut radiator for four years. Turnbull talked to us about war wounds not to the body, but to the mind. And somehow, I had found this more unsettling than the Jolly gore show.

Post-traumatic stress "disorder" is nothing newfangled. It's as old as history: there was evidence of it in Achilles in Homer's *Iliad*, in the 1666 volcano in Palermo, in Hotspur in *Henry IV Part II*, in the 1865 Staplehurst train disaster in which Charles Dickens was a passenger (afterwards he wrote a short story, "The Signalman," in which he accurately describes its symptoms), in First World War shell shock, in Second World War battle shock, in Korean War combat stress, and finally in Vietnam, where it was first called PTSD.

We all have different thresholds of disaster—the word means "falling star" in Latin. When a disaster happens to you, Turnbull explained, you try to block it out by detaching a bit of your psyche, pushing it away and holding it there at arm's length. It is pulled back by natural magnetism into your mind, so active avoidance is used to repel this intrusion.

PTSD sufferers can often suppress symptoms for years, for a life even. They avoid self-reflection, solitariness, and hurl themselves into careers, carving out greater success than most because they need to stay active, busy, engaged, to prevent that spring-loaded trapdoor from bursting open into the dark dungeon, the devil's boîte where they store their trauma.

In the 1980s, Turnbull said, an epidemic of PTSD broke out among British men going into retirement. It turned out that most were suppressing trauma suffered in the Second World War and only became symptomatic when they slowed down in old age and began to dwell on the past.

Of course, much that I heard I recognized. Especially the symptoms of hypervigilance—anything sounding remotely like a gunshot still makes my pulse race. I check the boxes for most of its symptoms but somehow, even now, I am reluctant to cop to it. Mainly because PTSD relates symptoms to a specific trigger event—mine don't flow from one event, but from many.

It was only later that I learned about moral injury. It has been described as a wound to the soul, and, unlike PTSD, it is not primarily fear related, but—in the way that it affects war correspondents—caused by bearing witness to, and failing to prevent, deeply transgressive behavior, resulting in shame and despair, anger and disgust. Check, check, check, and check.

I had wanted to believe that those of us covering conflicts, trained observers, who write and talk about the trauma we witness, could still detach it from our psyches, precisely because we dwell on it deliberately, amplifying it by purveying it to the public. But it turns out, that doesn't inoculate us at all.

Most war correspondents get slowly coarsened, ground down over time by exposure to conflict. (Trust the Germans to have a compound noun for this too: Weltschmerz—world weariness.) And few of us ask for help as there is an omertà among us, an omertà surrounding our own pain, an omertà enforced by the stigma associated with asking for help.

We often find it hard to keep a distance from the people we are covering, and when we come home, it finally catches up with us; we are altered and, just like returning soldiers, find it hard to fit back in.

All of us know the consequences that flow from that, the drinking and drugs, depression and divorce. And even so, few of us talk openly about it.

•   •   •

Martin Luther King Jr. Day dawns brutally cold. Even with all the apartment's ancient steam radiators full on, hissing and clanking, it is frigid. My derma wounds have matured into second-degree burns, gently suppurating. I need to wear a beanie to keep my hair off my sloughing, sloping forehead. The creases in the crooks of my elbows are wet with some kind of plasma; my hands are swollen puce. Shards of my skin flake off, revealing raw, red layers beneath, unready to be my uppermost line of defense, unfit to encase the moist mammal within.

I stumble out of my bedroom at 6:30 a.m. to make coffee, only to find that Phoebe has upended the garbage bin and spent the entire night trotting back and forth to plunder this cornucopia. Now there is wet garbage strewn across the parquet floor of the apartment, and on the kilims and the sofas and armchairs. Marinara pizza crusts, coffee grounds, jam-spread toast remnants, apple cores, orange peel, lettuce stems, burst tea bags . . .

Furious with the dog, I stomp back through to the bedroom to find her. She is on my bed, and she knows she's in trouble. As I approach, she loses control of her bladder, unloads her "night soil" all over the duvet, a large yellow bloom spreading around her.

I stomp back through to my study, barefoot. There, the dog, gorged with garbage, has laid a soft, tan turd, perfectly camouflaged on the Argentinian cowhide rug. The shit squishes between my toes. I hop to the bathroom on my unfouled foot to wash off, only to find once

I get there that I'm standing in three inches of icy water. I look up. A chunk of the ceiling has collapsed under the weight of a massive leak. It turns out that unlagged pipes three floors above have frozen and burst.

All this before 7 a.m. and uncaffeinated. The implausibility of these domestic mishaps converging—when I'm already a bleeding, oozing mess—is momentarily overwhelming. I flop down onto the kitchen floor amid the strewn garbage, sink my face into my palms, and begin to giggle uncontrollably.

This may be the low point of my domestic unraveling.

God, I hope so.

• • •

Hugo has dropped out of boarding school. He seems to have picked up on our marital discord. Later, I conclude that he didn't thrive there because he lacked the essential characteristic to do so: the desire to earn the favor of adult authority figures—teachers and coaches. To his credit, I think, Hugo doesn't care about *any* adult approval, not even mine. And, hopefully, this will free him from that pernicious cycle that has trapped so many children, including me, in the search for parental approval.

He spends a month mooching in his room, and when he emerges, he dons an apron and begins to cook. He has been watching back-to-back cooking shows.

Now he has started at Grace Church School in the East Village. He shows me the course options. For English he has chosen "Literature of the Soul." I worry that he has ignored the definite article and may be laboring under the apprehension that it is about soul music, given his penchant for rap. I suspect he once chose a course entitled "The Divine Comedy" because he thought it was about camp stand-up, rather than Dante. And once, when I'd noticed him avidly reading Voltaire's *Candide*, I'd asked him, casual as could be, how he was liking it.

"It's great!" he'd said.

A thrill of pride; my son transported by Voltaire! Who says this younger generation is intellectually stunted by digital devices?

He'd beckoned me. "When you're assigned three chapters you think it's going to be a whole lot of work, right?" he said. "But look at these chapters, they're *tiny!*"

He doesn't appear to have consulted the rubric of "Literature of the Soul," which would explain that it includes: "The best spiritual writing . . . from Jorge Luis Borges's *The Aleph* to Hermann Hesse's *Narcissus and Goldmund*, Myla Goldberg's *Bee Season*, C. S. Lewis's *Till We Have Faces*, David Maine's *The Preservationist*, Walter Wangerin's *The Book of the Dun Cow*, and James Baldwin's *Go Tell It on the Mountain*."

I'd better start reading and rereading these for the collaborative homework that lies ahead.

Hugo has also chosen a course called, simply, "Masculinity." It is taught by the school headmaster who uses, as a text, *Amateur: A True Story About What Makes a Man*, a memoir by Thomas Page McBee, a transgender man who took up boxing. It has taken millennia of masculine domination to get to this place, where the set book on a course called "Masculinity" is written by a transgender man. And who better to explain the spectrum of gender than one who has navigated across it?

• • •

Given that our family is disintegrating, Joanna wants to sell the Indian Orchard house. Part of me would like to keep it. It vouchsafes the boys' childhoods, memories of lazy summers on this hill and down at the warm, lapping lake. And it will be a wrench for me too, yet another exit, another parting. But a piece of me knows that to stay on (which we can't afford anyway) would be excruciating. Everywhere I look here will have associations of happier days, of an intact family, of our life before this dismemberment.

So, though heart-sore at the prospect, I agree, and we plunge into the glum business of selling the cottage and packing up its contents. Well, glum for me; Joanna can't seem to wait to scarper—she's ebullient. To me, it feels like we are packing up a life, embalming the domestic essence of our family, crating it, and burying it in storage.

Things I haven't really appreciated here are now imbued with an italicized intensity, acquiring an almost mystical aura just as they are taken away from me. For I know in my bones I will never come back here, a curtain will fall on this act of our lives, and it will retreat into that dim, labyrinthine theater, the theater of memory.

The local roads I have driven along for years now pass into lore, traced only on the parchment of my mind map. Like C. D. Wright, the Arkansas-bred poet who penned a poem consisting solely of abecedarian Ozark road names, I now try to martial mine: Belgo, Cream Hill, Deer Run, Depression Lake, Fire Tower, Mudge Pond, Pheasant Ridge, Pray Pond, Rodrigo Knolls, Salmon Kill, Sawchuck, Scribner, Shakshober, Silver Mountain, Sinpatch, Skunks Misery, Sunset Rock, Ten Mile River, Undermountain, Weed Mine, White Hollow, Yonderview . . .

In these last weeks, everywhere I go, I see with gimlet gaze, as though making mental photographs, impressions that will be left in the album of my mind to evoke this time. As though on a last-chance-to-see valedictory tour.

Last chance to see Saperstein's, "the store that time forgot," a retro one-stop-shop clothes emporium, with a sixty-inch-waisted pair of blue jeans hanging on the wall behind the cash register—an unclaimed prize for anyone who can fully fill them—and silver racks of stiff, canvas Carhartt and Dickies work pants, Duofold thermal long johns, plaid flannel shirts, rubber Crocs and soccer cleats, Scout uniforms, polyester prom shirts, and plastic ponchos.

Last chance to catch a movie in the Millerton movie house, which triggered the upswing of this once-desultory town, or Oblong Bookstore, named after the sixty-mile-long, two-mile-wide territory (including Millerton) that Connecticut shaved off its western border and gave to New York, in return for Greenwich.

Last chance to clang the front door cowbell of Terni's, purveyors of huntin' and fishin' equipment. To buy a newspaper there as an excuse to chat to the lugubrious Mr. Terni—"sir," to you and me— leaning on the worn marble counter of his old soda fountain in his shirtsleeves and braces, in front of his vintage, analog cash register, the one with a ka-ching handle, and behind him an array of tweeds, rods, shotguns, and cigars. Addressing me as "Capt'n Godwin," because he has read my books and knows I once served in the military. Telling me of the old days when he'd ordered his little house from a Sears catalog, and how it had arrived in sections, strapped onto a flatbed truck. And was hoisted up in only a week, just down the hill from us on Shagroy Road, where he and his wife, Ellen, live in it still, with fake candles in every window shining a real welcome behind jazz-hands-open, elf-green shutters.

Terni's, where Hugo purchased his first knife. Mr. Terni had slowly, seriously, steered him through the whole wall of options, from the huge machete-sized blades at the top, down to the modest pen-knife he finally convinced Hugo would be the "most fitting" for the tasks he had in mind. And when, to pay for it, Hugo had flourished a twenty-pound note—money he'd received from his Yorkshire grandparents for his birthday—Terni hadn't missed a beat; he'd held the note up to the light and squinted at the HRH watermark, and said, "Ah, from the old country; we don't see much of the Queen's coin here these days, young man—that'll do nicely." Even though it wasn't sufficient, and the Ternis didn't hail from England at all, but from Parma, in Northern Italy, home of the eponymous ham.

And on my last visit, when I tell him we are leaving, Terni hoarsely confides that he is too—he has terminal cancer and is just trying to eke out one more year to reach the centenary of the shop that was opened by his grandfather, before shuttering it for good. He stands smartly to attention, thrusts his hairy hand across the counter. "It's been grand knowing you, Capt'n," he says. We shake hands solemnly and I about-turn, open the cowbelled door one last time, and stumble out onto the sidewalk in tears.

While packing, Joanna asks me to get something from a tote bag. Inside, on a yellow, lined legal pad, I find her handwritten notes on how best to break up with your husband—how best to break up with me. I am unable to look away. It's a sort of mini manual for her marital manumission, a guide to uncoupling.

The phrases fall around me like incoming artillery shells: twenty-seven years long enough, good innings, moving on, she wants space, remain friends, people change, we're at different life stages. This last one is code for: she feels more successful than me, that she has left me behind, that she sees me as a drag on her wake. Her prow will cut more cleanly through the waters without me.

I fear she may be right.

• • •

Our final drive back to the city feels to me like a single-car funeral cortège. I silently register the landmarks one last time. Past Harney's tea factory, past the tiny town of Amenia, its name supposedly derived from the Latin amoenia—pleasant to the eye. Past the Metro-North railhead at Wassaic, once home to the Pequot people. Past the alpaca farm, where, during Hurricane Sandy, we were stopped by a state trooper in a Stetson, who, while attempting to catch an escaped alpaca, answered her cell phone and said, "I'm gonna be late home, honey, I'm just tryna lasso a llama." Past Wingdale and Big Ws, where

Wayne, the W of Big Ws, had walked away from his job as chef at the fancy Chanterelle in SoHo to start smoking the best BBQ ribs in the whole of Duchess County.

Past the sprawling, nine-hundred-acre, ivy-smothered, redbrick barracks of the Harlem Valley Psychiatric Center, "for the care and treatment of the insane" for three generations, home to five thousand inmates and a similar-sized staff—New York State's preeminent purveyor of electroshock therapy and frontal lobotomies, until it closed in 1994, run out of business by the rise of psychotropic drugs.

Now wreathed by barbed wire, its windows broken, its grounds choked with weeds, it supplies yet another eldritch arena for the boys to wonder at wide eyed as we drive by. Though a new sign has sprouted there, announcing that (once it is stripped of asbestos and refurbished) it is to become a campus of Olivet University, a controversial Korean-led Christian evangelical college on a mission "to preach the word of God to the ends of the earth."

Past the Mobil station from which sprouts a cell phone tower disguised as a giant conifer—the telephone tree, as the boys called it—over the Harlem Meer, and down the Henry Hudson to Riverside Drive and Joan of Arc, still brandishing her broadsword at the New Jersey Palisades. Our final retreat from our weekend retreat. Passed now into the past.

• • •

Looking back now, I think it's a tribute to the resilience of our marriage that it took so long to kill. It was like a conjugal cockroach. Having decided she wanted out, Joanna tried to put it out of its misery, stomped on it, leaving it for dead, only for it to twitch its whiskers and limp off under the stove.

Some say that the saddest thing in life is to find yourself alone. But sadder still is to find yourself with someone who makes you *feel* alone.

When I accepted this, that's when I finally tapped out and began dismantling the "us" into "she and I." Back to our component parts. Like the birthday Suzuki my father had taken apart and laid out on the garage floor. But this time, I cannot reassemble it as half of it is missing.

I think the reason I toughed it out for so long was that, by then, I defined myself more as a father than as a husband. That's what marriage ended up meaning to me, its essential gestalt. My family was my hinterland, my homeland.

I found the idea of divorce shocking because I'd had no experience of it; neither of us came from broken homes, the single most accurate predictor of divorce in the following generation. I still find that phrase frightening—broken home.

All the king's horses and all the king's men . . .

•   •   •

Georgina calls to say that Mum has had a relapse; her legs are swollen, and she is having trouble breathing. The doctor has been summoned, but London is wreathed in snow so everything there is jammed up. Apparently, the entire city has only three snowplows, because snow like this is so unusual. (New York City has 2,300 of them.)

A few hours later the doctor's verdict is in. Mum needs to be admitted to hospital. She has requested that I call her before she leaves home. Georgina thinks it is because she wants to say goodbye. So, while they wait for the ambulance to arrive, I FaceTime her. The line connects and I see her, sitting in her adjustable bed, propped up on her paisley pillows under her purple peony duvet, overlooked by the wall-mounted seascape.

Her hair, shoulder length and freshly brushed, radiates out in a static-crackling halo. She's finding it hard to hear and she's a little confused, mostly at how my voice and image are appearing from a little Gorilla Glass tablet in front of her.

An error message appears over her image. *Other user's connection is unstable*, it warns.

She chats brightly and inconsequently for a while, funny and acerbic. At one point I see myself in the little corner window of my phone and realize how rough I look—unkempt, with a grizzled winter beard and tousled hair.

"Bloody hell, I look like a suicide bomber," I joke.

"That's exactly what I was thinking," she shoots back.

I wonder aloud where my nose came from, her or dad.

"*My* nose," she says, "is not *long* as such, it's aquiline."

She pronounces it *ah*quiline.

"What does that word mean, exactly," I ask, "in the context of a proboscis? I thought it meant sort of beaky?"

"It's an aristocratic nose, my nose," she continues. "Classical, Grecian."

"Isn't an aquiline a mythical creature, a lion that swims?"

She looks at me blankly.

"Aquiline, aqua-lion, aquatic lion?"

Ignoring my lame attempt at a pun, she checks that I have the address of University College Hospital. As she is famously finickity, I warn her to be nice to the staff and not to complain about the food, or they might spit on it. She says they have proper waiters now, who come to your bedside to solicit your meal orders from an actual menu.

I explain to her that I'm single parenting because Joanna is away in LA on business, but I promise I'll get over to London as soon as I can, to read the *Times* (the *Tarms*) to her in my Zimbabwean accent.

"So don't go anywhere until I get there," I say.

This is code for "don't die yet."

"I won't," she promises.

My mother is an accomplished dissembler, but this is not one of her finer performances.

She's getting tired now, so I tell her that I love her and that I will see her soon. She nods but doesn't reciprocate.

"Tell him that you love him," suggests Georgina, off camera.

My mother looks up at me from her bed, confused.

"Tell him that you love him," she says.

The Saving Bullet

University College Hospital (UCH) is the biggest hospital in London, a bland white-clad tower-block that rises (with scant regard for its context) from the south side of the Euston Road. It is just up the road from the red-brick tiers of the British Library, once derided by King Charles as a "dim collection of sheds groping for some symbolic significance." UCH itself, when completed in 2005, was shortlisted for the inaugural Carbuncle Cup, presented to the ugliest British building erected that year. It was deprived of this dubious honor by the Drake Circus Shopping Centre in Plymouth, described by critics as a car crash of cladding, the nadir of bling brutalism, two cheeks of a monster's bum.

The hospital has a dozen operating theaters and the biggest critical care unit in the entire British National Health Service (NHS). Each year 120,000 emergency cases arrive at its Accident & Emergency unit. Those that need it are admitted to its complement of 782 beds. On a cold afternoon in early March, my mother was one of them.

———

When I arrive in London, a few days after her admission, my mother's condition seems to have stabilized. Georgina, who is about to fly out to Australia to moderate at the Adelaide Writers' Week, briefs me, officially handing over the baton in the relay of elder care.

As she leaves, Georgina asks me for tips on the Writers' Week, which I once attended as a guest author. The South African author J. M. Coetzee, who now lives in Adelaide, is the brooding literary eminence there. His wife, Dr. Dorothy Driver, an authority on African literature, moderated my session.

Years before, I'd reviewed Coetzee's book *Boyhood*. It was a rave review, or so I felt. The boy in *Boyhood*, which reads like a memoir though he calls it a novel, is one John Coetzee, referred to in the third person, which, I wrote, gives him a somewhat messianic feel.

Six years after the review, when he had just won the Nobel, I was reading Coetzee's latest novel, *Elizabeth Costello*, when I came to the character who teaches eighteenth-century English literature at a fictional university in Johannesburg. He is dull, defensive, ill-informed, and pompous, this Professor . . . Peter Godwin.

Revenge, a course best consumed congealed, and all that. But I was flattered. The Nobel-winning literary giant had actually noticed an albeit-imagined kick in the shins from a midlist midget. And deigned to *strike back*!

At the Writers' Week, I'd found myself sitting across from Coetzee at the opening dinner. He is a man without apparent vice, an austere, self-abnegating, monkish, contemplative, cycling, animal-loving, tee-totaling vegan. And it quickly became clear he had no patience for large dinners like this one, and the small talk they require. I, by contrast, was being generously topped up with fine South Australian Sauvignon Blanc—until I'd lost all reserve.

Finally, I pointed to my name card. "So, in *Elizabeth Costello*, Professor Peter Godwi—?"

"Complete coincidence!" he broke in before I could finish saying my name.

It was Coetzee who maintained that people can be in love with only one landscape in their lifetime. His was the Karoo, where his uncle had a farm. For Georgina and me it is still the Chimanimani Mountains, where we were born, the place that will always be home in my head.

One of the metaphors Coetzee uses to explain how growing up in segregated South Africa distorted white people is the avenue of pines (themselves exotic to Africa) planted by settlers to shield the Simon's Town golf course from the gale that blows relentlessly across the Cape of Good Hope (originally called the Cape of Storms, before "rebranding") from the South Atlantic. The trees grow at a forty-five-degree angle, bowed before the unrelenting gale.

I can't help thinking that my marriage has left me like that cowed avenue of Simon's Town trees. And that it will take some time for me to stand up straight again.

I finally tell Georgina that my marriage is failing, that Joanna has only delayed announcing it because Mum has been hospitalized and she realizes the optics would be "suboptimal."

"I guess she can't quite achieve escape velocity," I say ruefully.

• • •

The Empress Dowager seems downright perky, sitting up in her hospital bed reading when I arrive. The change of scenery seems to have revivified her.

I'm heartened at how well she looks. "You gave us all a big scare."

She grins back mischievously. "Well, it got you here, didn't it?"

For most people, hospitals are unfamiliar, scary places. For her, having worked in them for so long, they are commonplace and comforting, their rhythms, the sound and smell of them. She seems perfectly at home.

"Did you know," she says, "Agatha Christie once worked here, at UCH? So, I'm in good company."

"What did she do?"

"She was an assistant apothecary in the pharmacy. That's where she learned all about poisons for her crime thrillers."

I suppress my urge to namecheck George Orwell, who also spent time in the original UCH. When he was admitted as a patient, he fared less than well. Orwell died here of tuberculosis on January 21, 1950, at the age of forty-six.

The NHS is one of the few places that British classes are forced to mix intimately, in a nonhierarchical way. My mother lies in bed Z5, in a bay of four beds. Next to her, separated only by their nightstands, lies Vera. I peep at the chart hanging on her bed end. She is ninety-five and single, suffering from two broken arms and a broken pelvis. As I'm looking, she reappears, back from the loo, unfazed at my nosiness. Both her arms are in plaster from wrists to biceps.

"I fell over, trying to dust behind the TV set," she offers cheerily. "I live alone an' all, and so it took me some time to crawl to the phone."

Despite her injuries, Vera is as straight-backed as a household cavalry officer. Clearly in considerable pain, yet she is punctiliously polite to the staff.

Nobody visits Vera. She lies in her bed looking straight ahead; she doesn't watch her overhead TV or read. It soon becomes clear that Vera's main distraction is listening to us.

Kitty, the patient in the bed opposite, is an alcoholic who collapsed on the street outside her house, so neighbors called her an ambulance. She has an unnaturally orange, Trumpian tan, a helmet of dyed yellow hair, and crimson nails that curve like scimitars. A gold belcher chain encircles one ankle.

I find it impossible to estimate Kitty's age. Anywhere from a well-preserved seventy to a ravaged forty.

"My money's on the latter," says Mum. "Do you think she's a lady of the night?" She's intrigued rather than scandalized.

"No, she's just a bit frisky, that's all," I lie.

Later that evening, when I'm on my own at Mum's bedside, Kitty looks over and smiles broadly, then she runs the triangular tip of her surprisingly long tongue over her lips. She lets her pink hospital gown slide coquettishly down one shoulder, and out peeps an antique tattoo of Eros shooting an arrow, blurred and stretched now with the years.

• • •

I check into the Great Northern Hotel, the closest hotel to the hospital I could find within my budget. The Great Northern Hotel is neither great nor northern. It's a five-floor, mustard-brick building attached like a barnacle to the whale of Euston Station, where it was built as the terminus hotel for the Great Northern Railway, hence the apparent misnomer. Rooms face either south onto the Euston Road or, as mine does, north, over the retrofitted geodesic dome that encases the station like a giant glass golf ball.

I am in the cheapest category of room, a "couchette," based on an old-fashioned railway sleeper car. Had I been paying attention, the warnings were there to see in the online description, which asserts that "small has never been more luxurious" and that the bed fits "snugly." In reality, it has the proportions of a jail cell, with all the furniture similarly built-in or bolted down.

I usually find London comforting. Coming back here is like recalling a mother tongue, rusty but fluent again after a few days. This time, however, my mother lies ill in hospital and my wife is leaving me. The two most important women in my life, these twin pillars, now shaking simultaneously.

Unable to sleep in my tiny couchette, I turn to that old insomnia standby, the *New York Times* crossword. First clue: "Comic who said, 'if you want to read about love and marriage, you've got to buy two separate books'?" Who was Alan King, the Borscht Belt comedian?

• • •

This morning Kitty is being discharged; her orange spray tan is starting to fade, replaced by her natural livery, a medley of mottled pinks over a red trellis of burst capillaries.

The discharge nurse offers her spare clothes to wear for the ride home.

Kitty bridles. "Where's me own clothes?" she asks.

"I'm afraid they were soiled," says the nurse.

"Soiled?" Kitty looks nonplussed. "What do you mean, soiled?"

"Well," explains the nurse, lowering her voice, but not enough, "you'd vomited all over them, so the staff had to burn them."

"Oh," says Kitty, still confused.

"I can get you some clothes from the charity cupboard," offers the nurse. "They're all freshly laundered. You look about a size ten, I'd say. That right?"

"I'm an eight," protests Kitty implausibly. "But I don't need no dead folks' frocks. I'll just go home in this." She fingers her flimsy hospital gown, with its skin-revealing slit down the back. "Won't be the first time I've walked down the Caledonian Road in me nighty!"

At that she lets out a raucous laugh, like an anchor chain rattling through a hawsehole. This gives way to a liquid coughing fit. And, finally, she hawks fruitily into the silver kidney dish on her bedside table. She flicks her glance up, catches me looking at her, and favors me with a particularly lascivious wink.

I stay so long at my mother's bedside that night that the only café near the hospital still open is the McDonald's at the top of Tottenham

Court Road. This late at night it is the fast-food franchise at the end of the universe, like a *Star Wars* cantina, a canola-fumed demimonde populated by a mix of paramedics and cops, the drunk, the undomiciled, the derelict, the disturbed, the transient, the insomniac.

I feel strangely at home.

I punch in my order and pay at the bank of touch-screen terminals, and soon my packet appears at a pickup counter. There is no direct human contact.

The next day Kitty's bed is reoccupied, by Bessie, an elderly woman with a fiercely crackling chest and a temper to match. On her first morning, she is visited by her sons, burly men in their fifties; her "boys," she calls them. They speak with real Cockney accents, not the Mockney prevalent among posh Gen Z downward class-fakers. When the nurse pulls the privacy curtains around Bessie's bed, enclosing them within its soft sarcophagus, they forget, as is easily done, that they can still be overheard. Their talk is of protection payments and punishment hits. They are clearly hardcore members of the East End Mafia, and Bessie is not only in on it all; Bessie is the Godmother.

Her Grace and I listen, agog.

The trolley man arrives and pulls open Bessie's curtains. He sets up her breakfast tray and Bessie surveys it.

"I don't like marmalade," she tells him. "I want honey for my toast."

"We don't have honey, love," explains the waiter, speaking loudly and deliberately, as though to a slow child. "Only the fifteenth floor has honey. You've got to be on the fifteenth floor to get honey."

Bessie suddenly, shockingly, loses it. "I want some *fuckin'* honey!" she bellows at the waiter. The "fuckin'" ricochets around the ward like a gunshot.

"No, no, Mum," admonishes the older of her two lads. "You can't say 'fuck' in an 'ospital."

The waiter shrugs and trundles his trolley away to Oncology.

Vera leans across from the next bed. "The fifteenth floor is the private wing," she explains in a hushed tone, as though summoning up a distant deity. "You get your own room. With wall-to-wall carpet. And a big, flat-screen TV. And a duck-down duvet. The fifteenth floor has its own special lift, an' all. You don't have to queue up for it. And there's a man inside who presses the buttons for you. Imagine that?"

Vera beams into the middle distance at this paragon of luxury. A man to press the lift buttons. Imagine that.

Nema arrives to visit Mum, so I repair next door to the Wellcome Museum, slogan: "The Free Destination for the Incurably Curious." The new exhibition here is billed as "Somewhere in Between."

The first exhibit, *Refugee Astronaut*, by Yinka Shonibare, born in London of Nigerian heritage, fits the bill—a life-sized spaceman wearing a helmet with black-tinted visor attached to a pair of breathing tubes feeding off an oxygen tank. His moon boots are planted astride as he strains under the weight of his possessions, slung over his back in a twine mesh bag: paraffin lantern, kettle, pan, plate, books, family photos, pocket watch, butterfly net. His spacesuit is made of traditional African print fabric.

Who is he, this Afronaut? A Little Prince on a cosmic journey? A displaced, nomadic spaceman searching for somewhere habitable? Is he fleeing a toxic environmental apocalypse? Where will he find refuge?

The bright ethnic Ankara fabric of his spacesuit has its own identity odyssey. This style of wax batik textile was originally manufactured in Holland for Indonesians (then ruled by Amsterdam), who rejected it. So, the Dutch foisted the fabric on Africans—as ever, getting another continent's castoffs, but appropriating it, celebrating it, elevating it. Something originally made in Europe, rejected by Asia, accepted in Africa with all the brio of bricolage.

A bit like my father's family history. Made in the Middle East, rejected by Europe, settled in Africa. And, I suppose, by extension, me too: born in Africa, served time in England, washed up in America.

A film has just started, and I slump on the wooden bench to watch it, an audience of one; not a lot of "incurably curious" people this cold March morning. On-screen I find myself inside a perfectly ordinary McDonald's, circa 1980s. It is empty, if you don't count the clown, a life-sized inflated Ronald McDonald. A tentacle of water creeps under the door. The flow increases and the water level rises. The clown sways, starts to float. He stays upright for a few giddy seconds, as though making a triumphal tour of his aqua-circus, then slowly topples face-first onto the water.

The mundane becomes disturbing, dystopian, as cardboard fry pockets, Happy Meal boxes, wooden coffee stirrers, supersized soda cups, plastic forks, plates, all bob together on the rising tide, slick now with cooking oil. They are joined by trays and chairs. The oily water gurgles into the gullets of the garbage bins, through their hinged flaps. It reaches the illuminated sign urging us to "Eat like a Champ for just $1," which fizzles and dies. The cash registers stutter and short out. The neon golden arches flicker and go dark. Fast-food debris drifts by, fries, Chicken McNuggets, and a Big Mac—deconstructing into its constituent contents, diced lettuce, onion crescents, sesame-pocked buns, cheese-coated patties. The camera is underwater now, its POV like that of Jacques Cousteau peering at an ancient, submerged civilization, this Atlantis of fast food.

The screen fades to black and I sit there, suspended somewhere in between, in between the real McDonald's frying foods at the top of Tottenham Court Road for the late-night team of paramedics, cops, and tweakers, and this bespoke one, handmade in a studio by the Dutch collective Superflex and then deliberately dunked. In my tired, jet-lagged mind, the two scenes have merged into one establishment, a representative fast-food franchise, cleansed in the celestial wrath of an epicurean Noah's flood.

After this, whenever I return to the late-night Tottenham Court Road McDonald's, I find myself looking back at the front door for a finger of water reaching underneath it, a telltale harbinger of a flood foretold.

• • •

That night in hospital, after the waiter has cleared away Mum's tray, after the nurse has measured Mum's vitals and adjusted the drugs on her drip stand, smoothed her bedclothes, after the lights are dimmed, just as I think she is settling down to sleep and I can slip away to my couchette at the Great Northern Hotel, Mum suddenly bar-pulls herself upright. She adjusts the twin plastic cannulas that feed oxygen into her nostrils, like the Afronaut next door. They have already chafed angry red runnels on her upper lip despite the nurses' diligent slathering of Vaseline there.

"There's something I need to get off my chest, Peter," she announces.

Uh-oh. Nothing good ever comes of a sentence that begins with these words. It's like someone starting a sentence by saying, "With respect . . ." You know that whatever is coming down the pike at you, it's not respect.

"Go on," I say, swallowing my urge to flee.

When she continues, it's in an unpunctuated torrent, her words clearly pre-rehearsed.

"You were covering a war in East Africa; Sudan, Ethiopia, Eritrea, somewhere like that, I don't remember exactly where . . . ," she begins.

For the ten years or so that I covered conflicts across Africa and beyond, my parents never really knew what I was up to, in real time. It was a kind of Clintonian gays-in-the-military deal; don't ask, don't tell. They didn't ask and I didn't tell, at least until afterwards when I was out of the line of fire.

"It was a humanitarian disaster of some sort." She clenches her eyes in concentration, trying to unearth the memory. "At a refugee camp, Tug . . . something?"

"Tug Wajale?"

"Yes, that's it!"

Tug Wajale. I haven't heard that name for so long, I'd banished it from my head . . .

• • •

I park many of my important memories, memories like Tug Wajale, in a place reserved for the things I cannot bear to confront. That chamber in the back of my head, the one with the spring-loaded trapdoor that keeps threatening to burst open and release all those experiences too dark to disturb. It's a malign jack-in-the-box which, for good reason, the French call diable en boîte—devil in a box. My own devils are many and menacing.

"Smothered memories," Nabokov called them in *Lolita*, "now unfolding themselves into limbless monsters of pain." Larkin, in his poem "Sad Steps," calls them, "wolves of memory."

My memories of Tug Wajale remain raw and unmediated. A series of fragmented scenes, distorted, fairground mirror reflections, no doubt, images stacked steep upon each other.

• • •

It is 1986, and a humanitarian crisis is gathering in a remote, inaccessible part of northwestern Somalia. Ethnic Oromos from Ethiopia's Muslim minority are streaming south across the border, fleeing forced villagization and persecution by the Dergue, the communist junta led by Mengistu Haile Mariam, who oppressed Ethiopia at the time. The refugees are being prevented from leaving the border area, forced to congregate within a "temporary" refugee camp in the middle of the bush. Around a hundred thousand people. A thousand more every day, some with bullet wounds, arriving with only what they can carry.

A scene of biblical proportions, captured by Bryn Colton, the photographer on assignment with me, who then leaves to transmit his film and my initial copy. People packed into rows of low, lice-infested, olive-green tents, or under plastic sheeting, or goatskins laid over branches, or out in the open, stretching all the way to the ridgeline. They are being felled here. By cholera. Typhoid. Typhus. Hepatitis. Malaria. Blackwater fever. Malnutrition. Tuberculosis. Relapsing fever.

Dozens die every day. Mostly the very young. Parents bury their babies each morning at the foot of the hill. Bury them in shallow, unmarked graves, mere molehills. It is the season of Gu now, the rains, and when the clouds burst, they pour until the saturated ground can take no more and it regurgitates the freshly interred bodies. As they emerge, they are swept up in runoff streams and, once the storm abates, there are corpses strewn around, lying in the open. Hyenas come at night. They do what hyenas do.

Some images in the lockbox are startlingly fresh. A hyena padding away into the gloaming. It turns to look back with insolent eyes, unafraid. Its muzzle is dripping red. A baby's face staring up from the mud. Her open sightless eyes milky opals.

• • •

Then I too fall sick. Fever. Diarrhea. Vomiting. There are no drugs left here. And the rains have made the track impassable to vehicles. Camelback is the only way out. I follow behind another camel ridden by Haji, the fixer I have hired.

Hours pass, days perhaps. Haji unloading me gently onto the ground. He is smiling a wide smile. An apologetic, rust-red, khat-stained smile.

"Plane will come soon," he is saying. He points at the sky. With his arms he pantomimes its wings.

From where? I look around the desolate landscape.

"This is Garoonka," he says. "Aeroporto."

Clearly it is not.

Then I am alone in this desolate terrain with two plastic bottles of water. I am shivering in a fugue of fever. Nausea keeps my diaphragm in spasm. Every sip of the bitter, chlorinated water flows through me in minutes.

My pants are caked with shit. My crotch is stained with piss. My shirt is sodden with sweat. It has an unfamiliar, acrid odor. My stomach is cramping. My head pounds.

The sun beats down. Yet I am cold. So cold.

Hours pass.

The wind picks up. Dust eddies dance around me, playfully twirling. In my delirium I decide this is the khamsin wind that ravages much of the Middle East and North Africa at this time of year. Arabic for "fifty," the tally of days its season lasts, this wild southern sibling of the sirocco sends humans and animals scurrying for shelter, turning the sky ochre with choking columns of Saharan sand.

The gusts are tugging at the faded cotton kikoi I have wrapped around my head, whipping the knotted tassels against my face, luffing the luggage label on my backpack.

Disparagers of "foreign firemen," as conflict correspondents used to be called in the trade, sometimes call us "return ticket heroes": parachuting in to cover a story only when it comes to the boil, then leaving as suddenly as we arrive for the next, and the next, with no continuity of contact, no real context, no cultural depth. Now, it seems, my return ticket may remain unused.

My breathing is labored, shallow; the scorched air seems stripped of oxygen. My water is nearly finished now. I realize I may die in this place, at twenty-seven years old, waiting on the edge of a nonexistent airfield for a plane that will never come, in a country that most people couldn't find on a map.

I think of the random strands of my life that have led to this moment; this stupid, avoidable, terminal moment.

I search in my khaki camera jacket, pat its array of pockets, the cartridge loops ranged across its chest like a civilian bandolier. I am trying to find my notebook and pen, to write a letter to my parents. I labor over the sweat-stained page.

The ink blotches.

I grow confused. I am starting to hallucinate.

A line of poetry shimmers into sight.

So we, whose life was all before us . . .

But the rest of the verse eludes me. As does the poet.

I close my eyes.

• • •

I am awakened by the chatter of distant machine-gun fire, staccato bursts of it. Maybe the combat has crossed the porous border and I can catch the attention of the soldiers. I raise myself up onto my elbows. I can make out a cluster of white-robed figures, quite close by, arrayed in a semicircle, their backs to the gale. Tall and thin, they remind me of those hybrid creatures, half-human, half-avian, that populate Hieronymus Bosch's surrealist painting *The Last Judgment.* These figures have impossibly thin legs and narrow faces with long, red, aquiline proboscises. I wonder if I have died and gone to hell. I fall back to the earth and into the gentle arms of oblivion.

———

When I come to, the sun has swung across the faded, wind-picked sky towards the Gulf of Aden. The Hieronymus Bosch figures have disappeared and with them the chatter of distant gunfire, replaced now by a low rumble off to the north.

I sit up and try to shake myself alert. The sound is swelling. Its timbre altering.

A dot on the skyline, growing. A plane lumbers into view. I recognize it from the Airfix models I made as a little boy and suspended with fishing line from my bedroom ceiling, a Dakota DC-3. It circles low, tilting so the pilot can check the condition of the "airfield."

The plane's aluminum fuselage peeps through its peeling white livery, flashing in the sun, heliographing its antiquity and poor repair. I wave, try to stand up, but I have no strength left. Then, daunted no doubt by the brush-choked field, the plane rumbles away and I subside, lying back in my own shit, slipping out of consciousness.

In my sleep, I dream that death comes to me. Smiling and nubile and coquettish, she raises herself up on high-arched feet, onto the tips of her toes, her alabaster arms like Hera's, gleaming from her sleeveless, raven robe, her face a ghostly, geisha white. She plants a kiss full upon my mouth. Her plump lips are cracked and cold. They taste of blood. Of blood and carrion. When I recoil, she laughs. Her teeth are rusty, the color of khat.

I am awake now.

That sound again, shriller now, aircraft engines, and suddenly the plane is upon me, wings wobbling wildly in the crosswind, approaching almost sideways, crablike, yawing. It touches down, skittish, hurtling through the undergrowth, saplings slapping its wheel struts, propellers desperately feathering to lose speed, bounces up again, down, up, until it heaves to a halt several hundred yards away.

With a surge of adrenaline, I haul myself up, drag myself towards

it. The fuselage door swings open, and a spindly, sectional ladder unfolds until it makes landfall. Leather-sandaled feet appear; ethereal,
indigo-robed figures descend. I bellow at them, but only a dry croak
emerges. I am waving, waving as I stagger forward.

At last, I am seen.

A cry goes up.

Then all fades.

"Anyway," my mother continues briskly, "I got a phone call, I think
from a doctor in the intensive care unit of a hospital in Nairobi, saying you'd been admitted there. They'd got my number from your
passport—you'd listed me as your emergency contact. They said that
you were in bad shape, your liver was failing, you were unlikely to, to
survive, that I should come"—she pauses, and when she resumes, her
voice has a slight tremor—"to say goodbye."

She pulls herself together and continues in even more of a rush
now, wanting to get it all out, to purge herself of this toxin that has
poisoned her for decades. "I was terribly busy at the hospital, and it
was a long flight from Harare to Nairobi, expensive too. Long story
short, I never came. And I never told your father anything about it,
about . . . the call."

I sit quietly, trying to process my mother's words.

What I want to say to her is this: "'Long story short'? WTF?
Where do you want me to file this? In the mental manila folder labeled
Own mother doesn't give enough of a shit to come to your deathbed?"

What I want to say is that there are two quite separate sins
here: the original one, of it being too *inconvenient* to come to say
goodbye—and that's all it was, inconvenience; at the time there were
daily direct flights from Harare to Nairobi, they were not that expensive, the flight time is only three hours, and there is barely a time
difference.

What I want to say is, the penance for failing to attend my impending death is that you should have to continue to bear that burden *alone*—just as I was left alone; the burden of that knowledge is its own punishment.

But now you have committed this second, discrete sin, all these years later, in wanting to unburden yourself on me and have me grant you absolution. In asking me for this absolution, you have made me aware—for the first time—of your original sin. You have transferred that burden to me. And now *I* must live with it. The knowledge that my own mother, the person who gave birth to me, couldn't be bothered to say goodbye. I cannot unknow this now. It unfurls in my brain like a malignant flag.

You want forgiveness at the expense of my suffering.

That's what I want to say.

I realize that she is looking at me expectantly, waiting for my reaction. She reaches out her frail, freckled hand. The skin is stretched taut over her metacarpals like the muslin over the wooden wing struts of the Wright Flyer I once saw in the Smithsonian when I took the boys there.

I close my eyes and begin to speak, not really knowing what will emerge.

"That's okay, Mum, it's fine," I say, patting her cold, dry hand. "Never mind."

But my voice sounds like the voice of someone else. Someone far away.

• • •

I sit alone at the beveled pewter bar of the Great Northern Hotel. I need to drink my way past my mother's confessional.

The bartender is dressed all in black, a Roma apparition. Black tulle blouse, black lace mittens, black fingernails and lipstick, black tats of Celtic knots and Chinese ideograms, black hair whipped up into a wild, waxed beehive, and kind, kohled eyes. She solicits my order.

My liquor of choice tonight is Bushmills Irish whiskey. I acquired a taste for it in Northern Ireland covering the Troubles for the BBC and staying at Belfast's Europa Hotel, famous for being the world's most bombed hostelry, attacked thirty-six times. Its shattered windows were so often boarded up that journalists, riffing off Elvis's "Heartbreak Hotel," called it "Hardboard Hotel."

Soon the Roma Queen is refilling me unasked, with liberal measures. She senses I will be a generous drunk.

Somerset Maugham reckoned that "what makes old age hard to bear is not the failing of one's faculties, mental and physical, but the burden of one's memories."

That's what preys on me.

Sometimes, when the weight of my own memories gets too much, I have thought about killing myself. My rapture at being alive, the extraordinary privilege of existence, blinded by an epiphany of despair. Shrinks now archly label this "suicidal ideation." But when push comes to jump, I am too scared to. My "courage" in the field, I realize, isn't real. It is fueled mostly by a fear of *appearing* cowardly.

I have flirted with the war correspondent's equivalent of suicide by cop, what Graham Greene called "the saving bullet," the merciful one . . . not self-inflicted but from an unseen enemy on some distant battlefield. Instead, when the burden of my past gets too much, I seek solace in spirits. Bertrand Russell described drunkenness as temporary suicide. I guess it is a sort of reversible suicide. Suicide for sissies. Sissies like me.

The bartender tops me up again. Her extensive array of ear-piercings catches the light from the crystal chandelier. I am transported back to one sunny student summer in the Côte d'Azur, lying on a nudist beach when a young, naked ice-cream vendor knelt on the warm, blond sand to open her cold box, displaying her genital jewelry at my head height, most memorably a line of lapis lazuli studs along her plump, plucked lips.

I compliment the Roma Queen on her ear studs. She takes this as a cue to guide me around her auricular topography, inclining her head close so that I can examine the cartilage ridges and valleys. They gleam softly pink, like the interior of a seashell. Her hair smells of apples.

"Here and here," she says, in the manner of a flight attendant indicating emergency exits, "are the upper and lower helix. This is the orbital. This is the daith. This is the snug. This here is the tragus. And this little nub in the middle is called the conch."

In my whiskey welter, her recitation follows the cadence of *this little piggy*. This little piggy went to market, this little piggy stayed home, this little piggy had roast beef, this little piggy had none. And *this* little piggy cried "wee, wee, wee" all the way home . . .

At the end of the ear tour, I half expect her to tickle my armpits.

Hitherto my otic lexicon has been limited to lobe, the one part my own ears lack, a lack inherited from my mother. Such earlobes as mine, the bartender informs me, are called "adherent" lobes, rather than "free" ones, of which my father sported a rather prominent pair.

• • •

I'm the last person at the bar now. The Roma Queen is shutting up shop. She hands me the rest of the Bushmills bottle to take back to my couchette and helps me to my feet. When I stand, I feel lightheaded, as though I might pass out. A phrase swims into sight, and then another. Words I recalled when I was waiting on that bush strip in Somalia. Words that return to me when I'm in danger. Words written prophetically in 1940 by the young poet Frank Thompson, Iris Murdoch's Oxford beau, before he was cut down at twenty-three years old while helping Bulgarian partisans fight the Nazis.

The Roma Queen escorts me to the elevator.

I can make out more phrases now. They are assembling into sentences, like soldiers taking up their marks on a literary parade ground.

The elevator arrives and I step into it unsteadily. You can preserve many things in alcohol, it is said. But dignity is not one of them.

Now I can see a whole stanza, swimming before me.

I turn to face the Roma Queen through the open door. She smiles at me, a kindly, crooked smile. Her rows of earrings twinkle, beckoning like runway landing lights. She reaches inside the door and with a fingernail of bitumen black taps the button for my floor.

"Sleep well," she says, and the doors sough shut.

In the middle of the night I wake, still fully clothed, on my couchette bunk. Frank Thompson's valedictory poem "An Epitaph for My Friends" has finally forced its way to the forefront of my brain.

> *So we, whose life was all before us,*
> *Our hearts with sunlight filled,*
> *Left in the hills our books and flowers,*
> *Descended, and were killed.*

And I remember now, the origin of my rescue plane, the old DC-3 that improbably arrived that afternoon in Somalia, in that corner of some foreign field, just as my fixer said it would. Every year, in the last month of the Islamic lunar calendar, millions of Muslim pilgrims converge on Mecca from around the world on the Hajj. And afterwards they disperse back to their homelands, able to use the honorific Haji. Back then, most flew on special Hajj charter planes, many of which didn't conform to international safety standards, policed by IATA. They were mostly segregated from international air corridors and airports. The pilgrims didn't much mind that many of the planes were old and battered—if you die making the Hajj, most believe, you are fast-tracked to heaven.

It was one of those planes carrying pilgrims back from the Hajj that plucked me out of Somalia, just as Haji, my fixer, knew it would, having taken it himself.

• • •

At the next hospital visiting hours, I find my mother sitting up in bed, reading the paper. She is very exercised about news from Zimbabwe, where pellagra and scurvy have broken out in the prison system—again. When I was a human rights lawyer there, I often visited political prisoners incarcerated in Zimbabwe's Chikurubi Prison, where the conditions are infamously awful. Pellagra and kwashiorkor and scabies, I knew all about, but scurvy is a new one to me.

"I thought scurvy was a sailors' disease, and was wiped out hundreds of years ago?"

It appears we have both decided to ignore her Somalia confessional, doing what we always do in this family, avoiding the painful rather than discussing it.

Scurvy, Her Grace explains, back in full doctor mode, is one of the oldest nutritional maladies in history. It is brought on by a diet lacking in vitamin C, which crashes red blood cell production. Half of a ship's crew in the Age of Discovery could expect to die of scurvy—two million sailors perished from it, far more than all the deaths from all their wars.

The Spanish knew as early as 1579 that citrus prevented scurvy, but because no one understood *why*, the Royal Navy's "Sick and Hurt Board" took another couple of centuries to supply their ships with Rose's lime cordial, a cure that earned British seamen the nickname "limeys." (It was only in 1932 that the scientists figured out *how* the vitamin C in citrus prevented scurvy.)

Although scurvy had long been conquered by the time my grand-father served aboard His Majesty's warships, the memory of this sea-farers' scourge lived on among the ranks, in their sea shanties. For the way you die of scurvy is unusually ghastly.

My mother remembers him describing the dreadfulness of it to her as a young girl.

After about a month without vitamin C, you begin to feel le-thargic, irritable, depressed. Your limbs ache and your joints swell. Your mouth dries and you lose control of your bowels. You become jaundiced, feverish. You suffer shortness of breath. Your hair follicles, clogged by keratin, swell into angry red pustules. New body hair that does manage to emerge grows in bent and corkscrewed. Your nails thin, becoming brittle and spoon-shaped. Your eyes sink into your cheeks and your vision blurs. Your gums bleed, your teeth loosen and fall out.

So far, so bad.

But it's in the last stages of scurvy that something quite astonish-ing happens to you. Fractured bones that healed years ago begin to rebreak. And finally, the scars on your body reopen. Even the oldest ones, the merest dermal landmarks, plaques commemorating previous pain, split asunder and bleed anew.

Some of our wounds, it seems, never really heal.

Is it possible, I wonder, to suffer from a kind of spiritual scurvy, when you undertake long-distance voyages across oceans, ending up far from home, the place and people that once nourished you? The vitamin C you lack would be the C of Culture, the C of Community. Deprived of that, your spirit sickens and eventually you tear along your incipient fault lines, the perforations of your psyche. Your old scars open and you begin to bleed.

In some parts of rural Africa, even today, teenagers acquire facial scar-ring after puberty as a badge of maturity. An elder will carve a pattern into your face with a razor and rub the lacerations with ash to ensure that as they heal, the wounds will ridge into hypertrophic scars. Sometimes these can develop into growths called keloids—Greek for crab-claw—that rise out of the wound. Such secular stigmata prove your bravery; it's a matter of honor that you bear the slicing stoically, without flinching or crying out.

These three-dimensional tattoos make you appear fierce too. The facial scarring seeks to scare your enemies and allure potential mates. Such scars are indelible displays of identity. They signify status and bloodline. They secure your position among your clan, your people.

They prove that you *belong*.

When I was a boy, I so envied those ritual scars and wished that when I grew up, I could claim clan markings of my own. That would endow me with my own cultural GPS, identify me to one and all. But of course, my parents nixed the idea.

Africans captured and shipped to the Americas as slaves fell victim to scurvy at a terrible rate. And as they lay dying in packed holds of transatlantic sailing ships plying the Middle Passage, their clan scars reopened, and they bled out along the very markings that etched their identities.

And those who did survive the voyage with their clan scars intact had these identities stripped from them upon landing in the New World. They were fattened up, greased with palm oil, and auctioned off to the highest bidder. In a process that has been called soul murder, their new owners allocated them English names and forbade them from using their real ones or speaking in their mother tongues. And they never found their way home again.

• • •

Georgina is back from Adelaide, jet-lagged and tired. She listens patiently while I vent about Mum's "confessional." Finally, I'm done.

"Duh," she says.

Not the reaction I was expecting.

"Duh? Duh, what?"

She rolls her eyes. "Duh, you're missing the point."

"And what's that?"

"How old were you when you were there, at Tug Wajale?"

I think for a moment, calculating. "Twenty-seven? Why, what's that got to do with it?"

"Exactly the same age as Jain was when *she* was killed. Nothing shatters your heart like losing a child. Mum was at the hospital when Jain's body was brought in. To have been at your death too, I don't think she could have borne it."

Chicken Little

ELLAH (WHO WON THE PRIMARY SCHOOL EISTEDDFOD WITH GEORgina) is visiting Her Grace tonight, so we have bought Japanese takeout. We lay it out on the ward windowsill, the sushi platters and bento boxes, with all their accoutrements, neon-green blobs of wasabi and pink parings of ginger and tiny tubs of soy sauce, and we arrange ourselves around Her Grace for supper. Hospital regulations prohibit all of this, but the nurses look the other way.

We have also smuggled in that most hospital haram of substances—alcohol—a crisp Kumusha Chenin Blanc with citrus notes (produced in South Africa by a Black Zimbabwean refugee, Tinashe Nyumudoka) to which Her Grace is particularly partial. I've decanted it from a thermos into paper McCafé cups filched from the McDonald's at the end of our current known universe, i.e., the end of Tottenham Court Road. Vera joins us too for this furtive feast.

Ellah and Georgina have been best friends since elementary school, when Ellah was the first Black girl admitted to the previously segregated school. She has lived in London longer than Georgina. Yet another member of the Zimbabwean diaspora.

Kwasarwa ani? *Who is left?*

She is explaining to Vera that her clan's traditional totem is the eland. She likes that, Ellah says, because unlike many female antelope, the female eland has horns. It is armed and dangerous. And because you shouldn't eat your own totem, and few eat eland (as it's protected), it's not much of a sacrifice.

"What would our family totem be?" wonders Her Grace. "What animal would best symbolize us Godwins?"

Some kind of migratory bird, we decide, one that travels between south and north. The Ndebele already have an avian avatar for white Africans, one of their nicknames for us is inkonjane—the swallow—a bird that comes to Africa from Europe, where one swallow does not a summer make.

Maybe a swift (*Apus apus*), which can stay airborne for ten months, grooming and sleeping on the wing? And whose little, ungainly legs make it vulnerable to predators whenever it remains earthbound for too long?

Or what about the legendary bird of paradise, which was believed *never* to land at all? The Greeks called them "apodes"—*without feet*—what Burhan Qurbani's grandfather had warned him he would become in Germany. The Greeks thought birds of paradise survived on a diet of dew harvested from the clouds, and nectar from sunlight, and that they never needed to crap. Gorgeously plumed, ethereal creatures that floated aloft like avian angels and only fell to earth upon their deaths.

"Point of order, Ellah," I say. "Can one have a mythical totem?"

"Hmm, I'll allow it."

"How about the Oozlum bird, which flies around in ever-diminishing circles, like an ndoro, until finally, it flies up its own arse?"

Her Grace chortles. "That reminds me of your father's description of a pedantic academic friend of ours, who, your father said, knew more and more about less and less until he knew absolutely everything about fuck all."

Fuck emerges as *fark*. Georgina and I are taken aback. Her Grace never swears.

"What's an ndoro?" Vera would like to know.

"It's a spiral seashell that was used as a currency in Zimbabwe in precolonial times and is still a common motif in art there," Ellah tells her.

"Ah, I see," says Vera, who is clearly still somewhat mystified by the turn of this conversation.

Or what of a nearly mythical bird, the endangered blue macaw? A talented mimic, these days its calls often parrot the snarling chainsaws that are felling its native rainforests. The macaw will likely go extinct mimicking the soundtrack of its own destruction. Like the last cave art of the aboriginal Khoikhoi people of the Cape. The images were of sails in the offing of the sea. Then there were no more paintings. The ships bore the white men who would destroy the Khoikhoi way of life forever.

Maybe our totem should be the chicken? Not just any chicken, but the fabled Chicken Licken—or Chicken Little as she became once Ellis Island clerks adjusted her name on migration to the US. She's the ground-bound hen who scurries around the farmyard spreading "alarm and despondency" (an imprisonable crime in wartime Rhodesia when I was a boy) by warning, "The sky is falling! The sky is falling!" when really it is only an acorn. She is a catastrophizing chicken. A fear-mongering fowl. Just like Chicken Little's fairy-tale cousin, Peter, who falsely cried wolf so often that when a wolf *did* attack, no one believed him, and the wolf killed him.

Chicken Little has an ancient precursor too, Menedemus, in Terence's play, *The Self-Tormentor*, who similarly railed, *Quid si nunc caelum ruat?* What if the sky should fall now?

It seems to me that both Terence's Self-Tormentor and Chicken

Little had a point, if only in a stopped-clock-is-right-twice-a-day way. In the end the sky *will* fall upon each of our heads, in the shape of our mortality, in the shape of death.

Most of us live our lives as if death is only a rumor. We are all accessories to this big lie. But isn't the foreknowledge of our own death the thing that really makes us different from other species, that mandates our melancholy? Our punishment for eating Eden's apple of knowledge?

Oh, to live above it all, in the air, like the bird of paradise, to drink nothing but dew from the clouds and to eat nothing but sunlight and to breathe the sky. To be part of it; that way the sky could *never* fall upon our heads.

"How about a white stork?" suggests Georgina.

"Yes. Very suitable," declares Her Grace.

Ellah approves. In Shona, the white stork is called shuramurove, she says.

And so, our totem is decided.

• • •

Perhaps there is a lesson to be found in the white stork's binary existence. That you *can* live in two worlds, belonging equally in both hemispheres without becoming culturally bipolar. I mean, who can say if the stork is a creature of the north or of the south? Where does it feel more at home? Where is it domiciled? Where would it pay tax? It breeds in the north, in Europe, so its chicks are anchor babies, yet it spends more of its time in the warm south, in Africa.

But no, even white storks have a tough time migrating between their worlds. Every April they set off from Southern Africa for Europe on a journey that takes around fifty days (the southern trip back to Africa in autumn takes around a month, nudged by tailwinds). For most of the trip the storks glide along the top of thermals at four thousand to five thousand feet. But if disrupted by dangerous weather, they descend and stand on the ground facing into the wind until conditions improve—latibulating.

They bypass the Sahara by flying along the Nile and then they overfly the Levant, avoiding the Mediterranean because thermals don't form over the sea. But to do so means the birds are forced to funnel into narrow flyways through Lebanon. There, local hunters exact a terrible toll on them. Large, soaring birds like storks make ludicrously easy targets.

Although shooting migratory birds is illegal in Lebanon, the Committee Against Bird Slaughter has cataloged the many, malign ways Lebanese hunters kill them, mostly for sport. They blast away with shotguns and AK-47s and then proudly post photos of their bags on Facebook. One online post is a macabre photo of a dozen dead storks a hunter has pinned to a washing line in a parody of a birth announcement card. He has jammed a cigarette in the beak of the closest one.

The Lebanese hunt even in their towns and cities, shooting from balconies and rooftops. They erect fake trees on the roofs of housing blocks to entice exhausted birds looking to roost for the night. They draw outlines of trees on walls and illuminate them after dark to trick the birds, so they crash into the walls and kill themselves (like the Indian Orchard turkeys). They paint the branches of trees with superglue so that the feet of alighting birds will stick fast to them (no matter how furiously they flap to be free). They erect fine mesh nets invisible from the air, to trap smaller birds. They play recordings of birdsong to attract other birds of the same species, then capture them or kill them.

Little wonder, then, that some white storks have stopped making this perilous journey. Starting about thirty years ago, the biggest single European colony of white storks, in Portugal, stopped migrating south. Attracted by garbage dumps rich with fast-food remnants (and the somewhat milder winters brought on by climate change), they are now remaining in the north.

But the McScraps will soon run out as the EU bans open landfills. Will the white storks then be able to survive in the north? And if not, can they find their way back south, to their other home?

The last of the birds who have made the journey are now dying. And no one really knows if navigating the migration route is learned behavior, or if it is held in their phyletic, inherited memory, the part that Eugène Marais believed held our deepest, unconscious instincts.

Monarch butterflies migrating south over Lake Superior turn due east when they reach the water, but halfway across the lake they execute a right-angle turn to fly south again. Scientists think the butterflies make the turn to avoid a mountain that disappeared millennia ago. Now *that's* phyletic memory for you . . .

Maybe we are all avoiding ancient mountains that have long vanished, following primordial mind maps of places that no longer exist, obeying instincts that no longer serve us.

While tracking down the stork memory question, I come across an audio recording of white storks communicating. They do so by clattering their long red bills. I press the link to listen. It is a sharp, stuttering staccato. A sound I have heard before. A sound that I have held sequestered deep in my devil's boîte, the sound I heard on a deserted Somali airfield, which I took to be machine-gun fire. And now it all falls into place. The honor guard of white Hieronymous Bosch figures with their aquiline proboscises, arranged in a line with their backs to the early khamsin winds. They were white storks, my totem birds, my north–south comrades. My wingmen, grounded by adversity—just as I was.

The chatter of gunfire was their beak talk.

• • •

Nema is at the hospital again to visit Her Grace—she comes diligently, almost daily, on her own time, unpaid. Georgina and I leave them to chat, and we adjourn to the Wellcome Café for tea, and then wander through the museum again. A pristine white ceramic vase by Tamsin van Essen is cloven by a jagged wound, sutured with crow-black staples. Like the Japanese art of wabi-sabi, van Essen finds broken things, once repaired, to be more beautiful than their originals. Her other pots portray psoriasis, acne, osteoporosis, cancer, syphilis, and scars.

In the *Medicine Man* exhibit, we view Napoleon's monogrammed silver toothbrush. The bristles are made of horsehair. Georgina has googled it, unearthing some classic Bonapartisms.

"Glory is fleeting, but obscurity is forever," she says he said. And, "Never interrupt your enemy when he is making a mistake."

"Pretty sage. But how did that pan out for the genius Général at Waterloo? Respectfully, there he didn't know his ass from his Elba."

Georgina is still consulting her phone. "Hah, did you know that Napoleon was buried sans pénis?"

"Non," I say. "I did not. A bone apart?"

"Arf, arf. Évidemment his doctor coupéd it during the autopsy."

"What happened to it?"

"Well, it changéd hands a few fois. And in 1927 it was put on display in New York, laid out in a shoe box on a wad of cotton wool. It was an inch and a half long and was variously described as a shriveled eel, a piece of jerky, a bébé's finger . . ."

"No wonder Napoleon said, 'Not tonight, Joséphine . . .'"

"It was purchased by a New Jersey urologist for three thousand dollars. He kept it under his bed until he died."

"That seems un peu loin-fetched. Votre source, madame?"

"Un livre, *Napoleon's Privates: 2,500 Years of History Unzipped*."

We move on to Darwin's walking stick. The tapered white shaft is made of whale bone topped by an ivory pommel carved into the shape of a small human skull with glittering green glass eyes—a morituri (we who are about to die) Darwin used to remind himself how little time we have upon this earth.

———

Georgina calls me over to another glass vitrine. It features a dainty pair of wooden bellows riveted to a metal nozzle. "Apparently, in the eighteenth century, doctors believed that injecting tobacco smoke into the rectum could revive victims of drowning." She rolls the r of rrrrectum, for effect.

From the wall plaque she reads, "This is one of the resuscitation kits placed along the Thames for use on people dragged out of the water."

"Just what you really need as you lie gasping for air," I say. "People trying to blow smoke up your ass."

"You keep getting that word wrong; it's up your *arse*," Georgina corrects. "An ass is a donkey. You've been in America too long."

"You're starting to channel the Empress Dowager," I warn.

• • •

On our return there is a new admission to Her Grace's four-bed bay. Sofia is Southern European, Greek perhaps, and she soon makes Cosa Nostra Bessie look like a pussycat. Sofia too has serious respiratory issues, wheezing heavily like a punctured accordion. But this has not curbed her copious cigarette habit. Smoking is prohibited inside the hospital, so she spends most of her time wheedling the staff to wheel her down to the sad little courtyard on the ground floor where the smokers huddle. But the hospital is short-staffed and cannot oblige as often as Sofia would like, which is very often indeed. Soon she becomes abusive, pulling off her oxygen mask to shout at passing nurses and orderlies.

On her first night I hear her rummaging in the drawer of her nightstand, then the telltale *click, click* of a lighter, a flame flickering next to her hissing oxygen tank.

"Jesus," says Georgina. "She's gonna blow us all up," and she slides out past her to the nurses' station. The night nurse comes running over. She snatches Sofia's lit cigarette from her lips before Sofia can take a real drag and confiscates her pack of Camels and her lighter. Sofia emits an outraged bellow; she swings round, surprisingly fast for someone who can barely breathe, and slaps the night nurse across the face. The nurse stumbles back, more shocked than hurt.

Sofia reaches into her drawer again and produces a small knife. She brandishes it at the nurse.

"I'll cut ya!" she wheezes.

"Now, now, Sofia. Calm down. No one's getting cut tonight," says the night nurse, slowly approaching. "Why don't you give me the knife for safekeeping, and everyone can get back to bed?"

She puts her hand out and Sofia feints at it with her blade. The night nurse retreats and calls for backup. More nurses arrive and a couple of security guards. Outnumbered, Sofia switches tactics. She puts the knife to her own throat.

"Anyone touches me an' I'll cut meself," she shouts. "Gimme back my fags."

No one moves.

"Hmm, a Mexican standoff," observes Vera from the next bed.

"Yes," says Her Grace. "Interesting."

They speak like soccer commentators pondering rival teams' tactics. Neither seems particularly perturbed.

"My husband used to smoke," Her Grace tells Vera. "He also found it very hard to give up."

"Never touch 'em meself," says Vera.

The staff order us to stay back. Sofia's bed is nearest the corridor, so it blocks our escape. We are trapped.

It takes half an hour to negotiate a truce. Sofia will be allowed one out-of-hours smoke break in the courtyard if she hands over the knife. Her Grace is fast asleep by the time we slip away.

The Quick and the Dead

THE DOCTORS WOULD LIKE TO HAVE A CONFERENCE WITH US TO DIS-cuss Her Grace's treatment plan. The challenge they face is that she is caught in a vise of two medical issues that require rival remedies. She has congestive heart failure, which is causing liquid to build up in her lungs, making it difficult to breathe. To clear this, they need her heart to work harder. But she also has hypertension and a racing pulse, so it is dangerous to make her heart pump faster. They will continue to monitor her closely, and for the time being she seems stable. At one point they mention that she may be released in a couple of weeks once they have titrated her meds. We leave the session feeling optimistic.

"Would you find it . . . um, *helpful*, to see a priest," I ask my mother after the consult, "for a pastoral visit?"

I think she might find ecclesiastical contact comforting, given that her father was a Royal Navy chaplain for more than twenty years.

She considers my suggestion while munching slowly on her breakfast toast. She chews now like a ruminant, in a circular motion.

"Yes," she says, finally swallowing. "I think I'd like that."

Nurse Mutambo, another member of the Zimbabwe diaspora, gives me the number for the hospital chaplain service and when I call, a recording greets me in a Slavic accent. I leave a message that my mother, Helen Godwin, would like to talk to a chaplain, and ask him to call me back to discuss.

• • •

We are sitting on a bench in Paddington Street Gardens, next to the Monocle studios, so Georgina can have an illicit smoke. She's supposed to have given up, and for a long while we believed her, until she was busted by the Google Maps Street View. There she was, captured by a passing Google camera car and preserved in digital amber sitting on the low wall outside her house, sneaking a fag.

Georgina has just interviewed Judith Kerr, the German Jewish writer, one of the only other visitors who makes it past Her Grace's velvet rope.

Kerr wrote *The Tiger Who Came to Tea* and *When Hitler Stole Pink Rabbit*. Her family fled Germany just before the Second World War, to escape the Nazis. And in her interview, she talks of attending an exhibition of paintings done by Jewish children at Theresienstadt, the concentration camp in the Czech Republic.

I visited Theresienstadt when I was making a documentary for the BBC on "lustration" after the Velvet Revolution. It was the only concentration camp that the Red Cross ever got access to. For the inspection, the Nazis pulled off a despicable deceit. They set-dressed the camp, had the inmates perform plays and concerts for visiting Red Cross inspectors.

There were two kinds of drawings in Theresienstadt, Kerr tells

Georgina. The younger children drew nostalgically, typical family tableaux of parents and kids, cats and dogs. But the older kids painted much darker images, reflecting what they were seeing in the camp: people being beaten, tortured, people with nooses around their necks.

In preparation for the interview, Georgina had unearthed her own copy of *When Hitler Stole Pink Rabbit*, inherited from our sister, Jain. It is inscribed by our aunt Honor: "To Jain, on her 21st birthday." An odd gift to someone entering adulthood, until you realize Honor is surreptitiously trying to prepare Jain for her own Jewish heritage, hidden then by our father. Jain met her death seven years later still unknowing of her Jewish origins.

Kerr dedicates her latest book, *Creatures,* to "the one and half million Jewish children who didn't have my luck, and all the pictures they would have painted." She is measuring out unlived lives in unmade art.

"We're sitting on top of eighty thousand dead people," Georgina says. "This used to be St. George's Burial Ground. It was converted into a park in 1885 by London's first female professional landscape gardener, Fanny Rollo Wilkinson. Not a lot of people know that; you won't see her mentioned on any of the plaques here. The patriarchy made sure of that."

She punches me lightly on the shoulder.

I look around at the park properly. It is handsome, orderly, lined with London plane trees, hawthorns, lime, cherry, and laburnum.

"Over her career she transformed seventy-five parcels of disused land into public parks," says Georgina. "Then she retired to Suffolk to breed goats."

"As one does."

"Yes, as one does."

• • •

There is a stranger at Mum's bedside when we return. He has long, dark hair and a clerical dog collar the color of tobacco.

"Uh-oh, Rasputin in the house," I say.

Georgina begins to sing the lyrics to "Rasputin," her voice dropping an octave.

"Abba?"

"No, you cretin, Boney M." She pinches her trousers out at the hips to mimic Sharovary pants and attempts a Cossack hop.

As we approach, I see that Rasputin is holding a Communion wafer aloft. Mum has her mouth open wide, a baby bird waiting for her holy worm.

"Body of Christ," he announces solemnly, and he pops the wafer onto her outstretched tongue. The pale, unleavened disc sits there for a moment. It is embossed with a Maltese cross and, in its lee, a gamboling lamb. Then Her Grace recoils her tongue, surprisingly fast, like a lizard.

He offers her a small silver goblet of red wine. "Blood of Christ?" he inquires.

She nods enthusiastically, and he pours it down her gullet.

He reaches into his scuffed leather satchel and takes out a small glass cruet, like a mini salad dressing decanter, and a little ceramic crucible. To my horror I realize that this is his last rites kit. He intends to carry out the whole religious rigamarole, the anointing with oil, the laying of hands, the sacrament of extreme unction reserved for the dying.

If he reads her the last rites, it feels like she won't recover, can't recover. We are consigning her to the hereafter.

I look over at Georgina. She is as appalled as I am at the messaging of this last rites ambush.

From his worn black missal, the priest begins to recite the Apostles' Creed. I try to make eye contact with him, to signal: Abort! Abort! It's too soon for last rites. Come back later, Padre.

Mum has recognized the Creed now and joins in with growing gusto. She has presided over many such deathbed rituals in her decades as a doctor, and now she is presiding over her own. Hers is soon the dominant voice, booming its Empress Dowager's *heppy* vowels across the ward.

"He descended into Hell," she declaims. "The third day He arose again from the dead; He ascended into Heaven and sitteth on the right hand of God the Father Almighty, from thence He shall come to judge the quick and the dead."

The ward has come to a standstill as staff and patients alike pause to listen to her ex-*straw*-dinary voice.

I finally catch the priest's attention and shake my head vigorously to indicate he shouldn't administer the last rites. He looks confused. I draw my forefinger across my throat in the gesticulatory Esperanto for "Stop!" But this only makes him speed up, and so does Mum, until they are fairly cantering through the Creed.

The priest is now holding his hands out over Mum in the final prayer for the dying.

"This is the Lamb of God who takes away the sins of the world," he intones. "Happy are those who are called to his supper."

At this, Vera in the next bed awakes with a start. "Is it suppertime already?" she asks no one in particular.

The priest uncorks his cruet. He drizzles holy unguent into the crucible, dips his thumb in it, and, leaning over Her Grace, he draws on her brow and stands back to admire his handiwork. The shape of a crucifix is marked there in oil, glistening in the strip lights.

"Helen, be sealed with the gift of the Holy Spirit," he says.

"Mmm, smells like Christmas," Her Grace says, beaming.

"Matron, she tells me you're doctor to the destitute in Africa, so I use special holy oil for you," says the priest. "Is called 'chrism.' Olive oil and balsam. Mixed together, consecrated by bishop. Is aroma of Christ."

His cell burbles the opening bars of "O Come, All Ye Faithful" and he reaches inside his cassock to take the call.

"Sorry, very busy today. Lots of people . . ." He catches himself before finishing the sentence. Busy with other patients popping their clogs, one presumes . . .

"Of course," says Georgina, once the priest strides away to douse more of the dying, "Christ *would* smell of Christmas trees. Makes perfect sense."

"Maybe we should make a balsam-based perfume," I suggest. "We could call it Omnisc[i]ent. The *i* could hover just above the other letters, its dot could be a halo. There'd be a huge market for it among the faithful. The catchline could be, 'You've eaten His body, you've drunk His blood, now wear His scent.'"

"I'd buy it," says Mum.

She seems oddly unperturbed at having just received the last rites.

• • •

We are waiting for the elevator—again. For a modern institution catering to a predominantly immobile clientele, UCH is unforgivably light on lifts. This one seems permanently stuck on the twenty-fifth floor.

Georgina dances with impatience. "Who are the quick anyway?" she says.

"The quick?"

"Yes, you know, 'He shall come to judge the *quick* and the dead . . .'"

"The living."

"I know *that*. But why quick? Did they outrun the grim reaper?"

I imagine the black-hooded reaper lifting his long coal cloak, the better to dash after those miscreants who hope to dodge the lethal sweep of his scythe.

The elevator finally arrives; its doors open onto a throng of the infirm, a scene straight out of a Hogarth painting. Most are armed with accessories—crutches and canes, walkers and wheelchairs, IV drip stands, even a gurney. But we have been waiting too long to be denied entry, so we press our way in, to a chorus of complaining tsks and tuts and groans as the sick subside before us. I busy myself on my phone.

"I've looked up 'the quick,'" I say as we are decanted onto the ground floor. "It's from Old English, *cwic*, which means 'alive, alert,' and it's of Germanic origin. In Dutch, *kwiek* means 'sprightly.' Tolkien would have approved. You know how he hated words of Latinate and Greek origin."

"Another one to drive Nema mad," says Georgina. And suddenly she grins. "Do you lecture at uni-*verr*-sity?" she asks, imitating Her Grace.

"Oh, just fuck off already."

The Mountain Has Fallen

WITH HER GRACE IN HOSPITAL, GEORGINA HAS BEEN TIDYING HER room and has found the records sent by our cousin Christen of the clash that ended our grandfather's liturgical career. Mum has told us the broad outline of it, but here is the blow-by-blow correspondence. And it is way worse than I realized.

After twenty years' service, Christopher retired from the navy and was given a parish, a "living" in Cobham, Kent, by the local gentry, Lord Darnley, who had heard him preach and been sore impressed. He was a popular choice, revamping the church, ending collections during service, launching a parish magazine. The village of Cobham had no other churches, so the Reverend Godwin Rose placed this notice on the church door:

Christian Hospitality in Worship

All are cordially invited to join in the public worship of God.
Those who are baptized communicants of a Nonconformist

Church, but who are out of reach of its ministrations, are wel-
come to Communion.

This area of Kent was a center of hop-growing, and in August, trains would arrive from the less salubrious parts of London
bearing seasonal workers to harvest the hops. Many were so-called
nonconformists—Baptists, Methodists, Presbyterians, Quakers—
and my grandfather went among them inviting them to attend his
church.

When they came, in their working clothes, sweaty from their labor
in the summer fields, lacking the facilities to bathe, their presence irked
some of the posher members of the congregation, who complained
anonymously to his boss, the Bishop of Rochester. The bishop com-
manded my grandfather to remove the notice.

My grandfather refused.

The bishop reminded him of his oath of canonical obedience.

My grandfather pointed out:

The Bishop in conversation appears to regard the admission of
Nonconformists as in itself unobjectionable. But he is rigidly op-
posed to any public avowal of these sentiments.

My own view is that the time has come when not to avow
such sentiments is, as far as practical issues are concerned, to deny
them . . . [S]o to withdraw the notice without some more weighty
reason than a mere question of order would be pusillanimous and
tantamount to accepting the Bishop of the diocese as keeper of his
clergy's conscience.

Furious at this accusation of hypocrisy and the direct theological challenge, the bishop accused him of perjuring himself, having
"offended against Church discipline and common morality." And he

brought an action against my grandfather in ecclesiastical court, to have him "defrocked"—expelled from office.

The judgment was clearly going against the Reverend Godwin Rose because of his breach of the oath of obedience—the clerical equivalent of that abject parental "because I said so" argument. But he died before judgment could be officially handed down.

I now see where Hugo gets his "oppositional defiant" trait.

• • •

In the last few days, Her Grace has asked me to read to her from *Mukiwa*, my coming-of-age memoir, in which she plays a prominent role. Every few pages she interjects with footnotes and reminiscences. Vera listens too, and from time to time she has questions. She would like to know from me, for example, whether I found it disturbing to witness autopsies as such a young child.

"He was a very curious little boy, always asking questions," my mother answers on my behalf. "It didn't adversely affect him at all."

I just shrug.

Later, when we get to the part where I went to war, Vera asks me baldly if I killed anyone.

"In that kind of combat," I hedge, "it is often difficult to tell who killed whom."

She is polite enough not to press me.

I've been reading for hours now and I'm hoarse. But every time my mother's eyes close and I think she's fallen asleep, and I stop, she orders me to continue. It reminds me of reading bedtime stories to the boys as toddlers, desperate for them to drop off.

Eventually she does sleep.

I gather up my things, smooth her counterpane. But as I turn to leave, she suddenly lurches. Her back arches and her legs thrash out, her arms flail, and her head shakes from side to side so violently that I think she will injure herself. I can understand why people believed for so long in spirit possession—the ferocity of her convulsions seems more than the strength of her body alone; it feels like some other force, some demon, must be doing this. She doesn't even *look* like Mum anymore.

I run for the nurse, and she quickly injects a sedative.

The spasms slowly subside.

The next morning, we are there when Mum awakes.

"I don't think I'm going to make it," she says. "I'd better go to hospital."

"You're already in hospital," I say.

"I am? How did I get here?"

She becomes agitated and distressed and another seizure takes hold. Her limbs thrash so violently that I think she may break a bone. Georgina brings the nurse, who sedates her again.

"Horrible rabbits," says Her Grace. "They were bound to get me in the end." And with that she falls asleep.

Georgina and I are both shaken by the convulsions. It is heartbreaking to see Mum suffer like this. Georgina tries to blame herself for Mum's sudden downturn.

"I think she overheard me talking to the social worker about moving her into a home when she's discharged from hospital," she says. "And that may have undermined her will to live."

I tell her that of course she didn't induce Mum's convulsions, that this is strictly medical. But I can see that she is unconvinced.

Mum's attending doctors call us into a small, private consulting room off the main ward. The junior doctor twizzles the wand to close the Venetian blinds.

The prognosis is not good, they say. Her Grace has developed cascading symptoms of pulmonary heart failure. They have run out of treatment options. They think it is time to move her onto a palliative care regime.

"Palliative care?" I say.

"Yes," says the senior doctor. "It's when we make her comfortable— "

"We *understand* what palliative care is," says Georgina brusquely. "It means you're giving up on treating her. You're no longer trying to cure her, just managing her death from now on."

The doctors exchange glances.

"Well, given her age and condition—"

"No!" says Georgina. "*We're* not ready to write her off, even if *you* are!"

She looks at me for support and I nod.

"Well, yes, of course, this is something we do in consultation with the family."

After the doctors leave, we sit in the stifling little room on our own.

"How could she have deteriorated so quickly?" asks Georgina. "They were just talking about releasing her from hospital in a few weeks. And now they're dismissing her."

• • •

We sit with Her Grace all that morning, taking turns reading to her. By lunchtime she has had two more convulsions. And they are getting even stronger. The privacy curtains stay closed around her as she is scaring the other patients. We have to hold her down as she flails. The convulsions leave her exhausted, her eyes glassy, her breathing increasingly labored. She tries and fails to eat lunch. Her fourth convulsion of the day starts soon afterwards. I hold her shoulders while Georgina lies over her legs. They are getting longer too; this one lasts ten minutes. It feels like an hour. When it finally fades, Georgina bursts into tears.

"I can't stand to see her suffer like this," she says. "It's just too horrible."

I agree.

The palliative care doctor meets us in the same stifling little "conference" room. She waddles in, massively pregnant, and eases herself gingerly onto the hard-back chair, squatting on the edge of it with her knees splayed so her baby bulge can fit between them. The juxtaposition of new life and new death is not lost on us.

She talks us through what happens next. Basically, they will put Her Grace on an adjustable sedative drip and titrate it to a dose where she doesn't have convulsions. This will lower her pulse rate, which will probably flood her lungs and ultimately kill her, but she will be "comfortable" as she goes. The doctor hands us a pamphlet entitled *End of Life Care.*

"How long will it take?" I hear myself asking. The pronoun is doing some heavy lifting.

"A few days, maybe a week or so," she says.

The meeting over, she struggles to get up from her chair, and I offer her my hand to help hoist her. She takes it and, as she pulls herself up, she emits a resounding fart.

"I'm *so* sorry about that," she says, coloring.

"That's all right," says Georgina. "I farted all the time when I was pregnant. How far gone are you?"

"I'm due next week," she says, and she waddles slowly away.

Nema is sitting at Mum's bedside when we come out of the palliative consult, holding Mum's hand in both of hers, chatting quietly. We give them time together before returning. Then Nema draws me to one side.

"Why is your mother saying goodbye to me?" she asks. "I thought she was getting better. That she was . . . recuperating." Her vocabulary is increasing exponentially.

"We thought so too," I say. "But the doctors now tell us she won't recover. I'm so sorry—we just found out."

"So, you mean she will *never* come home?"

"I'm afraid not."

Nema puts her face into her hands and starts to sob. Then, embarrassed by this display of emotion, she turns and runs out of the ward.

• • •

Through the window, heavy, contused clouds skirr past, shedding rain and sleet, but allowing gludders of sunlight to dapple through in between. We wake Her Grace to see it.

"Oh, will you *look* at that," she croaks excitedly. "A monkey's wedding, just like home." By which she means Zimbabwe, which is what we call it there when it's somehow sunny and rainy simultaneously.

"How are you feeling?" I ask and, in my question, I hear the echo of tabloid reporters shoving mics in the faces of some recent victim. *How do you think I'm feeling, numbnuts?* I imagine her thinking. *I'm dying here.* But she indulges me.

"Well, I'm inhabiting a fascinating wormhole between this world and the next. I can tell you the rules, and then you can write about it." Her voice is weak but clear, clearer than it's been for a while. "I am about to leave this world."

She seems unafraid at the prospect of death, excited even.

"What's the view like from the bridge of the good ship mortality?" I ask.

She pauses.

"From up here you cannot tell islands from clouds," she says finally.

Vera pads slowly over, back from the loo.

"Allo, 'Elen," she says. "How we feelin' this afternoon?"

"Couldn't be better," says Mum.

"Same 'ere," says Vera, and they both laugh and clasp hands; the solidarity of a departing cohort preparing to die.

The meal man has arrived with his trolley.

"We gotta choice between cod an' chicken," announces Vera. "What's it gonna be?"

"Hmm. I think I fancy a little fish this evening," says Mum.

We plump her pillows and sit her up so that she can eat. It's clear she's not hungry but she doesn't want to disappoint us, so she forks a morsel of cod into her mouth, followed by a tiny torn crust of bread.

"Loaves and fishes," she says. "Just like the Last Supper."

I exchange glances with Georgina. "Don't get any ideas!" she laughs.

But her laugh is hollow.

After dinner, there is a commotion across the ward, nurses scurrying, tidying. An instinctive movement like iron filings rising when a magnet passes overhead. Presently the cause becomes clear when a departmental matron, who is a Black Zimbabwean, arrives, surrounded by underlings clutching clipboards. Matron's authority here is absolute; even the doctors defer to her.

She strides straight over to Mum's bed. "Good evening, Dr. Godwin," she says.

Georgina and I fall back. Matron looks briefly at Mum's chart, then she sits at her bedside and takes Mum's wrist in her hand. Looking at her watch, she measures Mum's pulse. They both know that medically, this is utterly unnecessary—she just wants to give Mum some physical contact, to comfort her. She wants to say goodbye. The two of them chat in a low murmur for a while, then Matron squeezes her hand and departs, her clipboard retinue scurrying behind her.

Mum drifts off to sleep, and I sit there thinking of this extraordinary ellipsis. At how my mother helped train and tend to these nurses for so many years in Zimbabwe, where they would still like to be now.

Yet here they all are, brought together again, thousands of miles away, on a different continent, in the European cold, like storks stranded in northern climes.

• • •

Another convulsion.

Nurse Mutambo arrives to turn up the IV sedative and slowly Mum subsides. As she passes through a brief window of alertness, she says, "I think I'll get up now, and take it from there."

Then she falls unconscious.

A rainbow appears, sharp and vivid. I try to photograph it with my phone. The broad swathe of the spectrum arcing above the IV drip stand. When I look at the photo later, I see that in the lower left corner I have inadvertently captured my mother asleep in her hospital bed, her pink plastic hospital ID bracelet in the foreground.

"You two look exhausted. Go get some rest," orders Nurse Mutambo. "Your mother's stable now, she's comfortable. Come back in the morning."

Georgina and I head out; she peels off to the Underground and I trudge back to the Great Northern Hotel in a stupor, staggering with fatigue.

Once in my little couchette, I strip off and step into the hot shower. I turn my face up to welcome the stinging pellets of water.

My cell rings.

"I was wrong," says Nurse Mutambo.

There are no cabs or buses, so I sprint along the Euston Road, crossing the traffic against the lights, cavalier among the cars. It seems contrary to the laws of nature that I be killed on the way to my mother's death.

All the hospital lifts are loitering on other floors—of course—so I run up the ten flights of stairs. By the time I burst through the curtains surrounding bed Z5, I am wet with sweat and having difficulty breathing. But not as much difficulty as my mother. Each inhale produces a terrible crackle.

Nurse Mutambo materializes. She adjusts the IV drip and flicks off the beeping alarm of the heart monitor.

I hold my mother's hand in mine. Her pulse is faint. After a while, her eyes flicker open. They look at me blankly. Then they focus and she sees me. She squeezes my hand weakly and tries a smile.

"I wish to pay you a compliment," she announces.

This is a highly unusual occurrence.

"I find that . . ." She pauses, choosing her words carefully. "I find you don't *annoy* me." She adds, "Most people do."

I grin and squeeze her hand back.

I notice the terrible crackle has stopped. *That's a relief,* I think, *she's breathing easier now.*

It takes me a beat to grasp that the crackle has stopped because she is no longer breathing at all.

Although I have expected this for days now, I can't quite believe it. I sit there dry-eyed, holding her hand as the warmth slowly ebbs from it.

After a while, Georgina comes flying in, flings off her scarf and coat.

"Is she . . . ?"

My expression must have answered because she doesn't finish the question. Instead, she climbs onto the bed and lies alongside Mum, hugging the full length of her body.

Presently Nurse Mutambo rustles through the gap in the curtains. She makes the sign of the cross, carefully detaches the oxygen cannula from Mum's nostrils and unsheathes the IV needle from the blue vein in her arm. A ruby bulb of blood bulges from the puncture there, and gently bursts. Nurse Mutambo swabs it away and stretches a Band-Aid across the wound.

"Gomo riya rakoromoka," she says. The mountain has fallen.

It's what you say in Shona when someone substantial dies. Then she withdraws, the curtains swish shut behind her, and we are left alone with our death.

Georgina busies herself gathering up Mum's personal items from her bedside locker, her silver-backed hairbrush and her battered copy of *Mukiwa* and her purse. I lean over the bed to take off her gold briolette necklace, the one with the little silver safe key hanging from it. I'm having trouble getting the chain over her head, so I gently lift it and reach behind her neck to pinch open the tiny lobster clip. It takes a few tries, and while my face is close to hers, I can smell her very particular scent, a blend of Pond's Cold Cream and rosewater spray. And I think to myself, *this is the last time I will ever smell my mother. And this is the last time I will ever touch her.* When I turn around with the chain, Georgina inclines her head and flips her hair up off her nape, and I place the chain around her neck and reclasp it.

Never Say Die

THE NIGHT MY MOTHER DIES, I CHECK OUT OF MY ROOM AT THE GREAT Northern. A light snow has fallen over London and the southeast, only an inch or so, but enough to throw the English rail system into chaos. Stranded passengers seeking emergency lodging must have triggered the hotel's "dynamic pricing," I suppose. So, that first night after my mother dies, I sleep in her room at Georgina's, in her bed, her high hydraulic bed.

I lie under her peony-festooned duvet, my head resting on her paisley pillows, thinking of her view from above us, of not being able to tell islands from clouds. Of what the world below will be like without her in it. Of what *my* world will be like without any parents, "an ordinary orphan," as my grandfather had put it in his "To Be Opened in the Event of My Death" letter. There is no longer even a *notional* cavalry—neither parents nor spouse—to ride to my rescue when I lie wounded on some foreign field. What I had hoped were pillars have turned out to be pilasters.

My mental topography is tectonically altered. Her Grace, this strange, madding, brave, eccentric, imperious, tough old dame; this pioneering doctor; this happy tensing Empress Dowager who found in the end that I did not annoy her, is dead.

Gomo riya rakoromoka.

Sleep is beyond reach. I lie there bathed in the red light of the digital clock's giant numerals. They cast an eerie glow on the breaking waves of the seascape above Mum's bed, the waves which reminded her of the systole and diastole of a heartbeat, clenching and unclenching. I think of her own heart at the end, beating so fast, unable to keep up, overwhelmed. Finally, I kick aside the duvet, pull on my clothes, and go into the kitchen to make tea as quietly as I can so as not to wake anyone.

But Georgina is already there.

"You too?" she says.

We both need to get out of the house, so we leash the delighted Bella for a predawn walk through the dark streets of South Hampstead, across to Primrose Hill.

We climb to the top of the hill and sit on the dew-damp bench there as the dawn slowly infuses the new day into being.

Below us, in one of the few views that present a coherent skyline of this venerable city, the landmarks of London are appearing now in the early eastern light. The London Eye, the Gherkin, the Shard, the Cheesegrater, the Walkie-Talkie, the Egg, the Armadillo—all the Boaty McBoatfaces of new London architecture. The dome of the Regent's Park mosque gleams golden, and far, far beyond it, tiny in the distance, the flag over the Tower of London ripples in the breeze that sweeps down the sinuous Thames and through Traitors' Gate.

The flag abruptly folds, hangs flaccid for a minute, then changes direction as the wind shifts to the southeast.

Bella sits suddenly still and cocks an ear.

Georgina stands and puts her finger to her lips. "Listen," she says.

I can hear nothing. Then, faintly at first, slowly swelling, a sound we both recognize. One that reminds us of home, though it is utterly improbable here. The roar of a lion. It comes in short, percussive, bass bursts, up the slope from Regent's Park zoo.

I reach over and put my hand on Georgina's arm.

She dabs impatiently at her wet eyes with her other sleeve. "How can we *still* be homesick?" she says.

I nod, not trusting myself to speak.

"I mean, what are we even homesick *for*?" Her tone is angry now. "I've lived in England for fifteen fucking years."

"It's the . . . dislocation," I say inadequately.

"Mum was as out of place here as that lion," says Georgina. "Sequestering herself in her bedroom like it was her cage. Remembering other places and other times. Anything but here and now."

"That was her choice."

"I sometimes think she was just trying to stay out of my way, so I wouldn't send her away. I wish I'd been nicer to her, talked to her more. I should have been a better daughter. And now she's dead. And I'll never be able to make it up to her."

"You were a *great* daughter," I say. "You and Nema looked after her so well. No boiled cabbage and disinfectant-fumed institutions for the Empress Dowager."

"And yet she was still so *lonely*," says Georgina.

And for the first time since our mother died, she begins to weep openly, which sets me off too.

The vaunted Godwin armor of stoicism lies in pieces.

Bella dances around us, upset by our grief, unused to this public display of emotion.

I hug Georgina into my chest and feel her muffled sobbing there, and her shoulders heaving.

And there we stand together. Two newly minted, middle-aged

orphans, up on Primrose Hill, blubbing into the dawn as the lion roars in Regent's Park.

• • •

As seems the custom now, Georgina posts a death announcement on social media, with a photo of Mum in her thirties. She wears her doctor's white coat, a stethoscope slung round her neck, a newly delivered baby patient swaddled in her arms. Next to her is her matron, Margaret Gray, my godmother, the person who had helped convince Mum to risk carrying me to term.

"Have you told Nema?" I ask.

"Yes," says Georgina. "Well, I left a voicemail and texted her. But I haven't heard back."

Likes and comments flow in from Mum's ex-patients, now a diaspora scattered around the world. People whose children she vaccinated, whose diseases she diagnosed and treated, whose lives she saved. As we harvest the condolences, we notice how no one can bear to use the dreaded D-word.

"Never say die," I tell Georgina. "Say anything else. Say passed. Say perished. Say departed. Say left us. Say slipped away. Say called to the Lord. Say gone. Say moved on."

And it becomes a game between us, a duel fought with dying euphemisms. Whoever runs out first, loses that round. It's sudden death.

I think it was Mark Twain who realized that the secret source of humor is not joy but sorrow. Our family has always deployed humor as a defensive perimeter, an emotional Maginot Line, and about as effective, which is to say not at all. But that doesn't stop us from industriously digging these wry trenches and jocular bunkers, raising high these humorous berms, hoping that we will not be outflanked by the tanks of tragedy, even as we hear the sinister clanking of metal tracks and the Maybach engine growl of imminent Panzers.

• • •

"We need to tell the Canfield bees about Mum," says Georgina. "According to ancient English tradition, the bees need to be informed of human deaths. It's called 'telling it to the bees.'"

"Or what?" I ask.

"Tell it to the bees, lest they / Umbrage take and fly away," she recites. It's a line from a poem she has found called, appropriately, "Telling the Bees," by the Irish writer Katharine Tynan.

She can't quite recall why we're supposed to tell them.

"It may be because bees carry our souls into the afterlife," I suggest.

"Makes sense," she says, even though it makes no such thing.

I realize we're just as superstitious as the Ndau people I grew up among. With our St. Christopher medals when we travel and our "bless you"s when we sneeze, our throwing spilt salt over our shoulders, our touching wood, our fingers crossed, our not walking under ladders, our number thirteens and our seven years' bad luck for breaking a mirror, our black cats and four-leafed clovers, our rabbits' feet talismans, and all the rest of it.

When we reach the apiary at the top of the communal garden, the one Mum used to visit from time to time, Georgina reaches into her pocket and retrieves her keys. They hang on a little gecko key ring made in Zimbabwe of wire threaded with tiny, shiny amber beads. She taps the keys gently on the top of the pine box housing the hive.

"Helen Godwin is dead," she announces. "Her Grace is gone."

We stand, silent for a moment, listening to the low murmur of the bees as they flow in and out of the hive.

"Did you know they change the key of their buzz—from E to A— when they are distressed?" Georgina says.

I did not.

• • •

A call comes in from the hospital. It is Nurse Mutambo.

"We have one last item here, left behind, belonging to your mother," she says. "It is Kutu."

Black and brown, a sort of beagle, with hugging, pipe-cleaner legs that can be easily bent into new shapes, Kutu—it means "puppy" in Shona—was part of Xanthe's toy pet collection that she would bring "on visits" to Mum in her downstairs bedroom. Mum declared this one her favorite, so Xanthe had gifted it to her, and the puppy took up residence downstairs.

When Mum went to hospital, Xanthe brought Kutu to visit her there and let Kutu sleep over. She posed the puppy on the pillow near Her Grace's head, then we started to move Kutu around for fun, and the nurses joined in. Mum's job was to find her, like a game of Where's Waldo?. Kutu clung, koala-like, to her bedside bars, or on the window handle, or to the rail of the privacy curtains, or on the rim of her bedside water glass, or even hugging the steel stem of the IV drip stand. And that is where they had found the puppy, abandoned, still at her post, valiantly holding the plastic tube of Mum's disconnected IV.

When we arrive in the ward, it feels eerie. I somehow expect to find Mum in bed Z5, where we had left her. So it is a jolt to see it now occupied by someone else, a tiny, silent sparrow of a woman with large, liquid eyes.

Vera is still in the next-door bed, looking off into the middle distance. She perks up when she recognizes us.

"'Allo, there! Fancy seeing you back 'ere. It's been so boring since you lot left." She holds out her plastercast arms to be hugged. "I bet you miss yer mum. I do. I miss 'er terribly."

Vera tells us that the night before she died, when she was on high dosages of morphia, Mum had a long, imaginary conversation with her father, and sang a nursery rhyme for him, "Ring-a-round the Rosie." He was dead some eighty years, and yet there she was, on her own deathbed, still trying to get his attention, still trying to perform for him, impress him, earn his approval, make him proud. Still in pursuit of the lost object, her absent, seaborne father. Just as I had, in my way, pursued her, my largely absent mother.

And now, finally, I understand the importance of her static seascape painting, and why she had hung it over her bed in home after landlocked home. Her father had worked at sea, so she kept this little bit of the sea, these waves, next to her. It must have been her way of staying close to him.

• • •

After reclaiming Kutu the puppy, we report to room 101, the "bereavement room," as we have been instructed to do. It is appropriately subterranean. Inside, all is artificial arcadia. There is a triptych of a lily pond on the wall, and wood veneer garden benches from which to view it.

"Very *Soylent Green*," mutters Georgina.

Two of the several dozen ceiling panels have been replaced with backlit photos of a sky, periwinkle blue, punctuated by cheerful little puffs of white cloud. The effect is that of the bifurcated view from a car's sunroof.

As we wait, we discuss burial options.

"I once schlepped out to Cypress Hills Cemetery in Brooklyn to find a graveyard reserved for 'friendless journalists,'" I say. "I hope I don't end up there."

Georgina pantomime-plays the world's smallest violin.

"In Holland," she says, "if you die friendless, they send a government official and a poet to read a poem at your graveside, so that you aren't buried all alone. It's called 'The Lonely Funeral Project.'"

The bereavement counselor arrives. We know it's her because it says so on her breast badge. That and her attire. She wears standard-issue Greek widow's garb: a frock of Stygian black with rounded bib of white lace filigree, a neck doily like Ruth Bader Ginsburg's dissenting collar. This is her work outfit, as though in permanent mourning, like those professional mourners you hire for funerals in many African societies, immortalized in Zakes Mda's book *Ways of Dying*.

She is so sorry for our loss, the bereavement counselor announces in a voice infused with routine dolor, before diving into the bureaucratic details of death, though she is careful to avoid the D-word itself, employing a stream of euphemisms instead, a late entrant and clear winner in our contest.

We need time to arrange for our mother's funeral, says Georgina, because her friends are scattered across the world.

"There's no rush," explains the counselor. "Your mother can be stored in the mortuary on the floor below us while you make all the necessary arrangements."

"For how long?" I ask.

"Up to a year."

"A year!"

"Yes, and at little extra cost," she says, in an upselling tone.

"Maybe we should get her cryogenically preserved while we're at it," Georgina suggests.

"I'm afraid we don't offer that service here yet," the bereavement counselor says, failing to recognize the attempt at gallows humor. "Sign here to allow Mum to be frozen."

I find myself bridling at her use of "Mum."

She's not *your* mum, I want to say. It's a family relationship, not an honorific.

But, of course, I don't. I'm still English enough that the unholy trinity of conflict-aversion, emotional repression, and fear-of-embarrassment remains my cultural default, my axis of angst. The Venerable Bede would approve.

"You'll need to get the death registered," the bereavement counselor is saying now. "The registry is in Camden Town Hall, just down the Euston Road. It's opposite O'Neill's Irish pub. You can't miss O'Neill's."

Indeed, you can't. O'Neill's iconography is a portmanteau of every Hibernian cliché, pure "heritage Éire." The pub name is emblazoned in jolly Gaelic font, the frontage populated by leprechauns frolicking among shamrocks to pan pipes and harps. And green, everything in competing shades of Emerald Isle green. Except the pots of gold at the end of the rainbow. And the rainbow itself, of course, which seems apt, now that Ireland improbably has had a gay taoiseach, Leo Varadkar, the son of an Indian immigrant.

"Lost her battle, resting in peace, in a better place, gone home, succumbed, taken, with God, crossed over, released," Georgina lists as we walk.

"That's not fair, you're just citing all the ones used by the bereavement counselor."

"Nothing in the rules prohibits that," she says.

• • •

Finding the pub is the easy bit, getting into Camden Town Hall, not so much. The GMB workers' union is protesting raucously outside. The pavement is thronged with demonstrators jostling their placards on poles. They chant and jeer, urging us not to cross their picket line but instead to join their boycott of Camden Town Hall. Tricky, given that Camden Council has a monopoly on issuing death certificates in this part of London.

A retro robot approaches—a protester wearing a cardboard box body with various dials and knobs drawn on it in black Sharpie, and another, smaller box as a head, with little square eye holes and a chevron of frown. Its mouth is an Amazon arrow logo, downturned like a sad-face emoji, an inverted smile. It carries a placard which declares, *Workers Not Robots*.

"Where. Is. Your. Solid. Arity?" it says in a metallic, robotic voice and waves its arms around in short, stiff, jerkily robotic gestures.

It's quite funny, really. We smile in what we hope is an encouraging way and keep walking. But retro robot has no peripheral vision through its cardboard eye holes and, misjudging the distance between us, it glances off me, loses its balance and topples to the ground, where it lies, immobilized like an upended beetle.

"He pushed me!" yells retro robot through its upside-down Amazon mouth. And it points at me.

Its comrades rush over to hoist it upright.

"Scab!" accuses the robot, through its cardboard mouth hole.

"Scab! Scab! Scab!" they all shout.

Georgina turns to face them. "We're just trying to register our mother's death, for Christ's sake," she says. "Not bust the union."

"Give us a break," I add. "We're in mourning here."

"So are we, mate," shouts the robot. He has removed his head box to reveal a flushed red face and a sweat-beaded ginger beard. "We're in mourning for a living wage."

Inside Camden Town Hall we sit for an hour in the vestibule, on sticky sofas of cracked black plastic. All of life, and death, passes through while we wait. Several tiny, bawling babies have their births registered. And we watch through a smeared glass partition as three union-busting weddings take place in the next-door registry office, all of them Western men exchanging vows with taffeta-frocked Chinese women towing airline wheelie bags.

Finally, the registrar invites us into her cubicle. With no advance small talk, she fires an opening fusillade of questions. Above the grumble of Euston Road congestion and the background of protesters' chants, the only sound is the clatter of her shellacked nails on the eroded keyboard as she enters the rudiments of Mum's life—and death—officially clocking her out of existence, "shuffling off this mortal coil," as Mum's father put it, quoting from *Hamlet*.

According to the certificate the registrar is tapping out, the "Disease or condition directly leading to death" is "community-acquired pneumonia." The community in question being the other patients in University College Hospital, who had infected her. Georgina and I sit there, stewing in our unspoken guilt at the notion that Mum would probably still be alive had she stayed at home. That we sentenced her to death by allowing her to be hospitalized.

While the printer chugs out copies of the death certificate, I look blankly through the dirty window at the redbrick turrets of St. Pancras station, where the Paris Eurostar trains pull in and out. Georgina idly fiddles with the spider plant that sits on the corner safe. Its tentacles reach down the safe's gunmetal flank, ending in baby plantlets. They congregate there, around a bright yellow sticker warning of the dire consequences of perjury.

"Could you desist, please?" the registrar says sharply.

Georgina desists.

She sits quietly for a bit, then turns to me. "Did you know, St. Pancras has the 'longest champagne bar' in Europe?" she says, using air quotes. "They're very proud of that."

• • •

In the following days, whenever I go down Euston Road, I'm unsettled by the image of our mother lying in a freezer drawer in the basement of UCH, her eyelashes frosted together, a luggage label tied to her toe. When I tell Georgina, she has been plagued with the same thoughts.

She reminds me that our maternal grandmother, Cecilia, left her body to science in her will, to be dissected by medical students learning anatomy.

"How laudable," I say. But really, I'm remembering how my medic friends at university gave their autopsy cadavers nicknames and made jokes about them as they slowly sliced them up in a yearlong autopsy, peeling the flesh back, bit by bit, to see how the human body functions, and returning them to the fridge each night. I'm haunted by a vision of our grandmother splayed out on a stone slab like some laboratory frog with her entrails exposed.

Georgina makes a booking to have Mum cremated.

We start the sad business of packing up Mum's room. It turns out her Empress Dowager throne, the heavy, hydraulic bed, is only leased and needs to be returned. Her other intimate equipment—including her stool commode—we place on the pavement on the day that recycled garbage is collected. Prim-lipped, rosacea-cheeked denizens of South Hampstead brisk past muttering about the obstruction. One chats blithely on his phone while his brindle pit bull lifts its leg and squirts several bursts onto the aluminium legs of Mum's worn walker.

Then we get to work sorting through her papers and files. They are meticulous until about five years ago, when she suddenly gives up trying to get well. I feel like an archaeologist of her state of mind, sifting through the sediment of her preoccupations: pamphlets on how to prevent falling, how to keep your short-term memory.

I open her wardrobe. Most of the "outside clothes" hanging there she hasn't worn for years. Many are tropical outfits, flimsy, faded, floral, fifteen years old, brought with her from Zimbabwe.

"What shall we do with these?" I ask Georgina. She feels the fabric, worn thin.

"Toss them, I guess. No one will want them." She brings several big black garbage bags, and we get to work. I notice that neither of us can just stuff the clothes into the bags; we are folding them fastidiously before placing them inside, as though we are packing for Mum to go on holiday somewhere warm.

Georgina reminds me that after Jain died, Mum couldn't bear to get rid of her clothes. Instead, she had laundered and ironed them, then she sat at her sewing machine and made bags out of Jain's old sheets and packed the clothes in them. She sprinkled the clothes with cedarwood shavings, to keep them fresh, and stored the bags in the top of her bedroom cupboard. After three or four years, when Georgina grew to comparable size, they would get a ladder and climb up there and rummage around for outfits. That was the primary source of Georgina's wardrobe.

"I sometimes wonder what it must have been like for Mum seeing a living daughter walking around in the clothes of a dead one," says Georgina. "It never occurred to me at the time. It must have been a constant reminder of the loss."

"What about you?"

"I think it helped me to feel close to Jain. Instead of her helping me to choose outfits, like she used to do, I wore hers. Most of them were clearly out of fashion by the time they fit me. Other girls would tease me, but I didn't care."

• • •

Georgina and I drag the black bin bags of Mum's clothes up to the big green Goodwill bins at the top of Canfield Gardens. It takes us several trips and by the end the bins are overflowing, and we are unable to stuff the last bag—Mum's peony-covered duvet—inside it, so we leave it on top.

We return to Mum's room, now eerily empty. There are dust bunnies on the floor where her bed and desk used to be. Behind the radiator, where it must have slipped from Mum's bed some considerable time ago, Georgina spots one last item, a book. I retrieve it with a clothes hanger. *Birds of Sadness*, by Margot Arnold, is stiff and warped. It's a prize presented in February 1942 to Mum's high school class for their participation in "Warship Week," when towns around England were raising money to refurbish the Royal Navy's fighting ships. Her school district of Bushy, Hertfordshire, had adopted HMS *Woodpecker*, a Black Swan Class sloop that went on to sink six German U-boats before itself being sunk by a torpedo.

On the flyleaf is a Chinese proverb: "You cannot prevent the birds of sadness from flying over your head, but you can stop them from building nests in your hair."

Georgina looks at the partition wall, which is designed in such a way that it can be unclipped by hand at the ceiling and easily dismantled. She tasks me to do this, but after an hour on the ladder with a screwdriver and pliers, I am defeated. Georgina disappears for a while and returns with a pair of plastic safety goggles and a sledgehammer; she hands them to me.

"Seriously?"

"I want the light back," she shrugs.

It is getting dark now, the Hesperian hour, but I work into the evening heaving the hammer at the wall, smashing and smashing, until the floor is littered with splintered wood and shattered Plexiglass. We sweep it all up into big industrial-strength black bags, then vacuum and mop the floor.

"It feels like we are expunging the last physical signs of Mum," I say, surveying the empty space where she lived the last ten years of her life.

I sleep that night on the Zanzibari daybed, with Bella at my feet, and I am awoken at dawn by the sun streaming in.

Georgina appears with coffee. She looks up at the shafts of sunlight dancing on the suspended motes of dust.

"Holy shit, that's amazing." She takes a swig from her mug. "But I feel so guilty. Like I'm celebrating Mum's death."

———

Later that day, I'm looking blankly out of the window of the number 13 bus going south down Finchley Road, when I spot something
familiar on the pavement outside Swiss Cottage Post Office. It looks
oddly like Mum's peony duvet. I lift my phone and take a quick shot.
It's blurred, but when I enlarge it, there's no doubt. It *is* Mum's duvet
and, snuggled underneath it, is a prone figure. I send the photo to
Georgina.

We see the duvet often after that. Its new owner is a man, clearly
sleeping rough. We call him Peony Man and send each other Goo-
gle pins of our sightings. Sometimes he stores the duvet opposite the
Manhattan Dry Cleaner, in the retro red phone box at the end of
Canfield Gardens, which mostly serves now as an emergency pissoir.
Georgina spots it peeping through the windowpanes.

Peony Man doesn't stray far. Mostly he migrates up and down the
Finchley Road. He favors the area under the art deco ledge of Waitrose
supermarket, and the entrance to the O2 Centre. Each time I catch
sight of the heap of distinctive purple peony print, I feel a little jolt in
my chest. As though, in some bizarro alternate universe, it might be
Mum snuggling under there, latibulating, and I could bring her tea in
the World's Best Grandma mug, and she would declaim poetry and
criticize my accent.

I find I want to talk to the duvet's new occupant, or at least ask
him his name. That he might somehow serve as a conduit to her—
communing through shared bedding. But I can't test this absurd hypothesis because he's always asleep, a navy woollen beanie pulled down
over his eyes, his weather-beaten cheeks livid with burst capillaries.
Once I notice his feet protruding from the bottom of the duvet, his
gnarled toenails have torn through the elasticated ribs of his thread-
bare compression socks, bidding bonjour to the good burghers of
South Hampstead.

"What would you say to him if he *did* wake up?" asks Georgina, rolling her eyes. "Tell him he's kipping under our dead mother's duvet, Her Grace's livery?"

Then, on a trip to Waitrose for emergency supplies of Montrachet, Georgina holding a leashed Bella, we turn the corner onto Finchley Road and see that peripatetic Peony Man is back under the art deco overhang.

Bella sees the duvet too, clearly smells Mum and, tugging Georgina behind her, scampers towards it, barking with excitement. The duvet lifts and its occupant's head emerges to see the dog bearing down on him. Understandably, he thinks he's under canine attack.

"Gerroff! Gerroff!" he shouts.

I grab the leash and yank Bella away while Georgina gushes placating apologies and a £10 note. I pull Bella home. She howls the whole way.

"By the way, you know that lion we heard roaring at the dawn just after Mum died?" Georgina lights up a cigarette—she's started openly smoking again since Mum's death.

We are walking Bella on Primrose Hill once more; there's something about the altitude, here in low-lying London, that we find comforting. The park is full of gulls that have ventured inland because of a storm out at sea, and Bella is chasing them.

"Well, I looked them up, and guess what? The Regent's Park lions aren't even *African*. They're Asiatic. Who knew that was even a thing? I thought Asia had tigers instead." She exhales and the tendrils of smoke hang briefly in the chill before dispersing. "Honestly, we're such fucking frauds."

I suppose we are all frauds, to some extent. We cherry-pick and manipulate the stories we tell ourselves, the versions we can handle. As Viet Thanh Nguyen put it in his book *Just Memory: War and the Ethics of*

Remembrance, "All wars are fought twice, the first time on the battle-field, the second time in memory."

Omissions and differences of emphasis can end up shaping a narrative that ossifies into orthodoxy, airbrushed of inconvenient truths. In the way it distorts reality, bias is like bad breath—you never really smell your own.

Ordinary Orphans

"YOU KNOW THAT FAMILY CURSE THAT MUM WAS ALWAYS GOING ON about?" I ask Georgina that night, as we make serious inroads into our second bottle of wine. "Well, I think it may be true."

Mum used to blame our family's bad luck on an old curse cast upon her Rose ancestors, and like most of her superstitions, we had dismissed it. But going through Mum's stuff, I have now found a reference to it in the parish register of Pen Selwood, the little south Somerset village near Wincanton, where generations of our Rose ancestors lived. The ill will goes back to the renovation of the church there in 1805, and the allegation that, much to "local indignation," our great-great-great-grandfather, a local landowner, also called Christopher, made off with old tombstones and other consecrated masonry and (with other culprits) used them "for vile purposes," namely, to repair walls and outbuildings, including a pigsty and a lavatory. The complaint is anonymous.

———

Later, we would embark on a journey to Somerset, in search of these forebears, excavating the archaeology of our identity and seeking to undo the curse Mum believed they had triggered. Of course, we don't *really* believe it, we tell ourselves, but why not try to reverse it anyway, just to be on the safe side? And I realize then that we are just like her, a vein of superstition runs deep in the caverns of our subconsciousness where the light of logic never shines.

"We'll just be covering our bets," insists Georgina.

According to her research, we must apply an apotropaic remedy. It's from the Greek, apotro—averting; and paios—evil. And in our case (after false forays into salt baths and satanism, voodoo and psychics), it seems relatively simple: we must find the destinations of the consecrated stones and return symbolic pieces of them to the graveyard and the church. And as we make restitution, we must pray (there is no specific incantation) to be forgiven for our ancestral crimes. This should be sufficient, given that the original cursers are unknown to us, so we cannot trace their successors to apologize directly.

"I do harbor an eleventh-hour doubt," I say. "That in one sense, our ancestors were just early eco-warriors, doing something rather enlightened—they were recycling."

"If you think like that, you will render this *entire* exercise futile," warns Georgina, "to say nothing of re-upping the curse."

I don't mention it again.

Pen Selwood sits in the next valley over from Stonehenge, among a patchwork of meadows on a low ridge, studded with beech and ash trees. Friendly horses canter up to the hedgerows to have their muzzles scratched. Sheep graze in the pastures, newborn lambs butting at their bagpipe udders. It's more of a hamlet than a village, though its strategic position at the crossroads of three counties meant that the English fought two historic battles here, against the Saxons (in 658), and the Vikings (in 1016); the Brits were beaten in both.

St. Michael and All Angels, the scene of our ancestral crime, is a small stone church built mostly in the fifteenth century. Its squat, gray tower is topped by battlements with gargoyles glowering from their gutters. The church sits within a well-tended, walled graveyard, populated by pink zimdodendrons and cherry trees and, of course, that staple of English churchyards, the yew tree, which can live for more than six hundred years.

When a yew tree was recently felled here, we are told, the arborist discovered a locked chain around the trunk that the bark had grown over and concealed. People used to do that to yew trees to lock in evil spirits. The trees are heart-stoppingly poisonous to man and beast alike, and the theory is that yews were planted on sacred sites like cemeteries to stop farmers from grazing their animals there. But their branches were also prized for longbows, the artillery of the medieval era, so churchyard yews also served as arboreal armories.

To anyone else, St. Michael and All Angels would be just another quaint, unremarkable English country church. But to us it is made significant by what we find prominently guarding its front door. Two tall headstones with botonée crosses, and a third, coffin-shaped tombstone. These are the graves of our direct ancestors. Twelve Roses in all, the first one buried here in 1769, the last in 1887, their lifespans ranging from eighty-eight years to three months. In all, Roses lived here for more than two hundred years.

To effect Operation Curse Reverse, we visit Pear Ash Farm, home to multiple generations of Roses. The farmhouse is higgledy-piggledy, added onto over the centuries, with terra-cotta tile roofs and thick stone walls. Living here now is Charles Buckler. He's in his seventies but looks a wiry twenty years younger than that from vigorous farm labor, with white muttonchop sideburns and square jaw and twinkling blue eyes, his trousers held up with a belt of baling twine, his boots mismatched. As he shows us around, we select small rocks and pebbles from the old garden walls and lintels, steps, and pathways.

In the barn, which had once been the piggery, he explains, several orphaned lambs are bleating for their bottles. Georgina goes over to chuck their chins and, as she does so, two swallows swoop in through the open stall door and up into the rough-hewn rafters, where they settle into a modest mud nest.

"It's amazing," says Charles. "They fly back from Southern Africa at this time of the year, and they are able to find their exact nest."

"Inkonjane," I say to Georgina.

• • •

Back at the churchyard, we place our stones in crevices under the headstones, at the base of the yew trees and the walls, and we mutter prayers as we do so.

"What did you pray?" Georgina asks.

I prayed for forgiveness for all the things I have done wrong, for all the people I have hurt, and for the people our family has offended. And then, just in case there *is* an afterlife, I prayed that all the Roses are enjoying themselves there, and that they approve of us atoning for their recycling overreach.

Our ancestors were baptized in the scalloped limestone font of St. Michael's. Our flesh is buried under the yew trees in the earth of Pen Selwood graveyard. Our name is carved again and again into its weathered headstones.

This, here, is what Zimbabweans would call our musha, the place we are originally *from*, though we may travel the world. If we were First People anywhere, it would be here. This is where we could have the right of return, to jambanja the land, like Zimbabwean guerrilla veterans chasing away white settler farmers from formerly Black-owned land, claiming, as Doris Lessing acknowledged in the title of her first short story collection, *This Was the Old Chief's Country*.

This, here, I suppose, is the cultural continuity we have been seeking. But when we discuss it, we realize that though we may be *from* here, we are no longer *of* here. Instead, it feels more like a US president's ethnic excursion, an Old Country drive-by: Kennedy or Reagan or Biden going to Ireland. Beautiful as it is here, it no longer resonates for us the way that Southern Africa does. That is where our formative *lived* life has been, whether we like it or not. And as Lessing noticed:

> *The chief gift from Africa to writers, white and black, is the continent itself, its presence which for some people is like an old fever, latent always in their blood, or like an old wound throbbing in the bones as the air changes. That is not a place to visit unless one chooses to be an exile ever afterwards.*

• • •

We get word from Golders Green Crematorium that Mum, in ash form, is ready to be collected. Georgina insists I drive us there. I hate driving her car. It's a thirty-five-year-old, ivory VW Golf cabriolet with a sharp-angled fuselage of 1980s design, before cars became curvaceous. It has no power steering and must be hauled around corners with considerable muscle. The gear stick has primitive synchromesh, and the clutch groans in protest every time it's depressed. The black canvas top is latticed with rips held together with duct tape. Three of the four old-fashioned wind-up windows don't open, the arms just rotate impotently. In short, it's a mess. But barely a week passes without some admirer tucking a note under the windscreen wiper offering to buy the car.

Northbound traffic up the Finchley Road is heavy, commuters funneling out of the city, straining for the North Circular like horses heading back to their stables at day's end. To reach Golders Green, we are following a route devised by Waze, which promises that we are "outsmarting the traffic together." Unable to get her phone audio to work, Georgina calls out the turns like a play-by-play commentator. But today Waze is too smart for its own good.

"At the next intersection, turn right," she instructs, leading us out of the traffic jam.

But we soon find ourselves blocked by a raised curb that turns our shortcut into a cul-de-sac. Cement dust is still evident on the fresh stonework.

"No Waze!" says Georgina, emphasising the zzz. "This must be brand-new, this median."

Ahead we can see a sign for the crematorium. We are so close, but all the alternative routes involve doubling back to rejoin the crawling caravan of commuters on the Finchley Road.

"Or?" says Georgina, leaning out the one working window to get a measure of the concrete curb that surrounds the median. "We could take the direct route."

. I look at her inquiringly.

"Just Do It," she says, in a Nike slogan sort of way.

I ease the car gingerly, diagonally, one wheel at a time, up onto the traffic island. The moment the last wheel mounts the median, we are bathed in flashing blue light. Its source is a police car cunningly concealed behind a hedge.

"What are the odds?" says Georgina mildly.

The cop walks over. He is Sikh, wears a smart, black, oil-glistened beard and a navy turban which has a silver Metropolitan Police badge pinned to it. Though the Met has long since dropped the Royal from its title, the badge still features ER (Elizabeth Regina) II at its heart and is still topped by a crown.

He taps on my window and mimes for me to roll it down.

"I can't!" I shout from inside. "The handle doesn't work."

But he doesn't seem able to catch what I'm saying. The turban is wound tightly over his ears, and I find myself wondering if it affects his hearing. I have recently read that the Metropolitan Police is experimenting with Kevlar turbans so that Sikhs can join tactical firearms units from which they were excluded because Charhdi Kala Sikhism mandates a turban for adult males, and regulation helmets cannot fit over them.

He taps again, harder, getting annoyed now, raising his voice. "Open the window!"

Instead, I open the door and he leaps back, clearly suspecting I harbor hostile intent.

"Stay in your car, *sir*!" he orders.

Over the years, I've noticed that English cops tend to get more polite just before they lose their tempers.

"The window's jammed," I explain, with my hands held up and out, like in the movies.

Georgina leans over to defuse the situation. "We're on our way to cremate our mother, Officer."

"Licence and registration," he says, regaining his composure and ignoring her.

I produce my ancient UK license. It's a paper one in faded claret from the days before they even had a photo. It hasn't ventured out of its plastic carnet in a decade. As he unfolds it, the leaves begin to crumble. He looks at it in disgust, holding it in the pinch of thumb and finger, away from his pristine uniform, as if it might infect him.

"This is *prehistoric*," he says. "This type of license isn't even *legal* anymore."

I affect surprise.

"Besides which, it expired. Years ago."

"Hang on, I've got an American one here somewhere," I remember, and I start rifling through my backpack.

For several years after I arrived in America, I continued to drive on my UK license, until a lawyer friend pointed out that once I was a resident there, I would no longer be covered by insurance if I had an accident. New York state refuses to exchange a British license for one of its own, so, despite having driven for decades I found myself in the humiliating position of having to do my driving test from scratch. Writing the Q&A exam at the DMV, sitting with a group of sullen teenagers in a driver's ed class over a Broadway smoke shop. And then taking a refresher lesson with an instructor because a driving test is different to real-world driving.

A friend recommended her instructor, Attila. He was Turkish, she said, but once he arrived in his gray Hyundai, well, you can see where it had to go, Attila the Hyun(dai).

Attila had inherited some of his namesake's legendary manner, barking orders in a cheroot-scratched bass and taking unkindly to backchat.

"What you doing?" he demanded crossly, soon after we began. "Why you looking in mirror all the time?"

I explained that in the UK test you must check your rearview mirror every seven seconds.

"Well, in England you may worry about what is behind you, about where you coming from," he said. "But you in *America* now. We look ahead only, at what is in front. Not what is behind us. Okay?"

It struck me then as a pretty good summary of the main difference between the two cultures. One seems fixated on the past, dwells on it, the other barely consults it.

I finally find my hard-won New York driving license and hand it over to the officer. He gives it a cursory glance and hands it back, walks away, and climbs back into his patrol car. Georgina and I look at each other, uncertain what we are supposed to do. Then from the loudspeaker on the police car roof, we hear his amplified voice.

"Follow me," he says, and he escorts us to the crematorium, blue lightbar strobing, siren yowling.

. . .

The suburb of Golders Green has more than forty synagogues. It is home to the city's biggest concentration of Orthodox Jews, the Williamsburg of London. It is also home to Golders Green Crematorium, the oldest crematorium in London, built in 1900.

Many of London's illustrious creatives are interred in the mausoleum here. Not so much a Who's Who, as a Who was Who: Bram Stoker, Sigmund Freud, Enid Blyton, Kingsley Amis, Peter Sellers, Joe Orton, Doris Lessing. Others—Rudyard Kipling, H. G. Wells, Vivien Leigh, Vaughan Williams, Amy Winehouse—were incinerated here but interred or scattered elsewhere.

The last time I was here was to film a documentary about the funeral industry for the BBC. And how a big North American multinational had quietly snuck in and taken over many of the mum-and-dad co-op high street funeral parlors in England and, with only one slight change, boosted their profit. That change? They reprinted the casket catalog and in the new version simply renamed the bestselling, bottom-of-the range, pine veneer coffin. It had been called "The Classic." In the revised catalog they called it "The Economy." In a single month, the next model up ("The Traditional," at nearly twice the price) became the new bestseller. No one wanted to bury Grandma in a coffin called "The Economy."

In the crematorium office we sign for Mum's ashes, which they have scooped into a plastic urn of Harrod's green, embossed with a gold GG logo.

"How considerate," says Georgina. "My initials."

With an air of routine reverence, the receptionist loads the urn into a green plastic shopping bag and hands it over.

As we are leaving, it begins to rain. Not the usual, dreary drizzle but a brisk, decisive shower. Georgina reaches in and gently withdraws

Mum from her plastic bag. She hands me the urn and eases the empty bag over her head.

"What?" she demands as I look askance. "I've just had my hair blown out. Mum would understand."

We get to the car and Georgina brushes aside the blue-stemmed Chuckit! ball throwers and the beslobbered tennis balls from the back seat and nestles the urn in Bella's shed fur. She clips the safety belt around it, and we head home.

The single wiper swabs a smeary arc across the passenger side. The driver's-side wiper rotates in perfect duet with its rubber-threaded twin, dutifully describing the arc it would clear, but cannot, its empty metal claw making no contact with the glass, which quickly becomes mottled and opaque with raindrops. I must crane across to see the road ahead.

Georgina sighs. "Like so much in my life, it's worn out. I keep meaning to replace it."

• • •

When we bring the urn into the house, Bella noses at it, wagging her tail. Georgina sits cross-legged on the floor. She twists open the top to examine the powdered ashes, and Bella sniffs them assiduously.

"I wonder if she can pick up Mum's scent?" she says, recapping it and placing it onto the mantelpiece, where she decorates it with fairy lights and drapes Mum's old stethoscope around it.

We plan to divide and mix Mum's ashes, so half of hers can be interred with Dad, back in Zimbabwe, and half of his can be intermingled with hers, here in London. The idea is that there will be a place to remember them on both continents. Georgina has a portion of Dad's remains—from the pyre—saved in her top cupboard in a shopping bag from Bon Marché, his local supermarket in Harare.

"This may prove problematic at the end of the world, if the Rapture turns out to be true," she says from the top of the ladder. "But, on balance, I think it's worth the risk."

She lifts the Bon Marché bag out and hands it down. While I gingerly unknot it, Georgina gets Mum's urn from the mantel and opens it. She delicately decants some of Mum's ashes into a mason jar, handling it as carefully as if it were cocaine, to make room for Dad. Then she places a funnel into the urn.

As I carry the Bon Marché bag over, I can feel some hard pellets in it. I know, from having tended his pyre, that Dad's detritus is not finely powdered like the Golders Green product. When I upend the bag and pour, I see what the pellets are. They are Dad's teeth. They clatter onto the plastic funnel and unite with Mum's ashes.

• • •

Going through Mum's stuff, I come across a little memento album of her parents. With its olive-green hardback cover, it has been mislaid among her medical books, so I've never seen it before. I call Georgina in, and together we pore over it.

Under the headline "Fashionable Wedding" is a yellowed clipping of the local paper's write-up of our grandparents' nuptials. Cecilia wore a trained bridal gown of ivory silk, made "en Princesse," her veil fastened with a wreath of orange blossom, and a bouquet composed of lilies of the valley, white tulips, narcissi, and asparagus fern, tied with ivory ribbon, it reports. "The bridegroom's gift to the bride was a set of silver-backed brushes and mirror, whilst the bride's gift to the bridegroom consisted of a complete set of Shakespeare's works."

Georgina gets on her hands and knees and rummages in the box of Mum's toiletry items and there they are. More than 120 years old now, the mirror is cracked, and the tufts of the brushes are discolored and worn, but still she took them everywhere with her, still she used them to the very end.

There is also a letter written in my grandfather's copperplate cursive on stationery headed "HMS *Colossus*, 1st Battle Squadron." The letter is sheathed in a Royal Navy envelope, addressed to Cecilia, and marked, according to naval protocol, "To Be Opened in the Event of My Death." It is dated July 28, 1914, the first day of WWI. He is about to go into battle, a little over a year after their wedding, writing to his pregnant wife, writing in the knowledge that he will be dead if she reads it. This is his voice from beyond the grave.

My Darling Cecilia,

> *This is a task which I have already performed once too often, namely, to settle up arrangements in the event of my "pegging out."*
> *As regards money: You will have, if I am killed in action: Admiralty Pension of £80 a year, and £14–16 for the child.*
> *NB. The child, tho' posthumous, is eligible for the pension, and treated like an ordinary orphan.*

"God, what a phrase," says Georgina. "'An ordinary orphan.'"
He goes on to give his wife details of their modest life insurance and bank accounts. Then this:

> *If you meet the right man, do marry again, my Precious . . .*
> *And if you feel inclined, think of me at midday and 10 p.m. about.*
> *We may not be more separated from each other than we are at this moment anyhow, tho' I shall have "shuffled off this mortal coil" a few years before you.*
> *I have confidence that nothing can prevent our spiritual*

*communion from carrying on again, tho' first you may have to
do a job of work here in looking after our child . . .*

*It might be a while before we can actually pick up the
old threads. Goodbye till then, darling. Try to make the best
of the intervening time and bear up now for our child's sake.
You'll find life more sufferable in two months' time. Be a stoic.
Remember, to see you happy is always my greatest happiness. So
try to be happy, my love.*

*We're told that the present is not worthy to be compared
with the glory that shall be revealed. So what will Heaven be
like if here our life has been so ideal?*

*I shall meet you and our little child when you've finished
your life's work here and follow.*

Au revoir my precious Cecilia. God be with you.

*Always, your adoring,
Christopher.*

He survived the war and died in 1936 at fifty-one. Cecilia lived another twenty-seven years after that, but despite his urging, she never
remarried.

There are copies of his obituary here too, headlined "A Beloved
Broad-Minded Priest." It turns out that he had died very suddenly.
On Sunday, according to the local paper, he had conducted a service,
preached a sermon on religious snobbery, advocating for divorced people to be allowed to take communion. "If we were to follow Christ's
practice and teaching, surely the church would not consider itself too
holy to eat and drink with divorced persons," he preached, "for Christ
ate and drank with publicans and sinners."

After the service, as was his habit, he swam in the headwaters
of the Thames. He had nicked himself shaving and the cut became

infected. The following Thursday he was taken to the Royal Naval Hospital with septicemia and pleurisy. "More than once on Friday night he expressed regret at going too soon and tried hard to live," the paper reported. But by Saturday morning he was dead. Antibiotics, which would have saved his life, became commercially available a few months later."

The obituary goes on to say, "The mortal remains of the deceased vicar were placed in the chancel. The sunlight of a lovely June evening shone softly through the stained-glass windows onto the plainest of coffins, draped with a Union Jack."

In the congregation was the Earl of Darnley (patron of the parish living) and the Dowager Countess of Darnley, and Sir Herbert (and Lady) Baker, architect of empire.

Not in attendance was my grandfather's nemesis, the Bishop of Rochester.

"Buglers sounded the reveille. A few days later his ashes were scattered in a quiet glade near Cobham."

The album holds photos too. Outside an ivy-mantled manse, the young chaplain at the handlebars of a large motorcycle with his six-year-old daughter, Helen, and her older sister, Honor, grinning in the sidecar.

"Mum told me that he used to drive her the five miles to school each day," says Georgina. "And he would walk her around the garden and explain all the plants to her, and their genus, and what their names were in Latin. And how she missed him so, when he was at sea for months and months, and she would go on strike, refusing to go to school, and just staying at home, waiting for him to return."

At the back of the album are some folded condolence letters. Here we find mention of something about him we had not known, something that gives a new meaning to the entire trajectory of my mother's life. At the time of his death, Christopher Godwin Rose was studying medicine. He'd already passed the first set of exams and was attending night school for the next ones.

So, at eleven years old (the age Georgina was when Jain died, the age my aunt, Janina, was when she was gassed in Treblinka), Helen dedicated herself to becoming the doctor her father never lived to be. She would fulfill his dream.

• • •

Because we miss Mum, Georgina and I have started talking to each other in her late-onset ext*raw*dinary, happy tensing, Empress Dowager voice. And we wonder afresh where it came from.

I start reading up about that happy tensing accent, and I come across an analysis of the Queen's successive Christmas broadcasts, which shows how she modified her accent over the years, becoming more, well, *common* . . .

At the end of the analysis, I find a link to a recently unearthed audio recording of the Queen, the first recording of her ever made. It is from the spring of 1940; the Battle of Britain is about to begin. Elizabeth is fourteen years old and still a princess, broadcasting on the BBC's *Children's Hour* to the kids who have been evacuated from British cities to the Commonwealth, beyond the reach of German bombs, over the seas to Canada, South Africa, New Zealand, Australia, and lodged there with strangers.

Georgina walks in just as the recording begins to play. It is uncanny. Australia is *Awe*stralia. Having is *he*ving. There is th*ar*. Home is *hi*ome. And, of course, happy is *heppy*.

"Oh my God," she says, when the princess signs *aw*ff. "That's it. That's *exactly* Mum's new voice."

And we realize then that Mum's new voice was actually her old one, the voice she'd used as a little girl. In her final year she had reverted to the way she had spoken when her father was still alive, gone back to the prelapsarian voice she used when she was eleven, to the last time she was truly happy. Before her father died and she was sent away and war came, and "everything went to hell."

Her original voice, her memsahib bark, was a shibboleth to a place and to a class that no longer existed. A secret password to a club that has long since closed its doors.

Godwin, Party of One

We decide to delay Mum's funeral for a couple of months, to give time for her friends to make travel arrangements, as many of them live far away. I return to New York, back to the ashes of my own life.

Once back I find myself instinctively reaching for my phone to call London, to share some experience with Her Grace. I miss our teasing banter.

I am trying to write her obituary for the *British Medical Journal*, the UK's professional publication for doctors. It insists on a very particular formula, so I find myself trying to track down the details of Mum's job titles and professional qualifications. She had trained at St. Bartholomew's Hospital, the oldest medical school in Britain, started in 1123. Mum had vaguely insinuated that she was among the early women students to enroll in this all-male bastion. But when I contact St. Bart's, they inform me that she wasn't among the early women students, she was in fact in *the* very first female class of Bart's 824-year history, the six female students admitted to the class of 1947.

———

From London I have brought a sheaf of letters I'd found in a box under Mum's bed. I hadn't felt ready to look at them before, but now I take them out. The first one is a typed blue carbon copy of a letter from my mother to the headmaster of my first school. It is dated July 11, 1964, when I was six years old. The early phase of the civil war has just begun.

Dear Mr. Simpson,

I wish to apologise for my son Peter's infrequent attendance at school during the last week, and to request that due to most unusual circumstances you take him into the Hostel as a boarder immediately.

As you know my family have been deeply involved in the murder of Mr. Oberholzer who was my husband's subordinate and a near neighbour. We were among the first at the scene of the crime and since then as G.M.O. for this district I have had numerous and erratic calls on my time by the Police, and my husband has been fully occupied with Police Reserve duties.

The security situation has been such that on the two occasions I have been able to bring Peter the 25 miles to school we have had to have long delays at Police check points waiting for suitable escort, and Peter has become very apprehensive about traveling, having seen and heard altogether too much during the last few days. It would now appear that the present situation is liable to last for quite a while yet, and that I will not be able to keep to my regular schedule of daily journeys to Melsetter, and that as a consequence Peter's education will suffer if he continues as a day scholar.

Thus, both to ensure continuity of schooling and to let the child have the benefit of regular hours and congenial

companionship in the school hostel after his traumatic
experiences, I would most earnestly request you to accept him as
a boarder without delay.

                                        Yours sincerely,
                                        Helen Godwin.

I arrange the rest of the envelopes on my desk in date order. Affixed to each is a three-penny "Rhodesia" stamp featuring a curly-horned kudu and, in the top right-hand corner, the Queen. The correspondence consists mostly of my compulsory weekly letters home from boarding school. With all the intended recipients now dead, they read like letters from my boyhood self, across the years, to my adult self.

The letters start out in wobbly, penciled print. The first one, written shortly after the violent events my mother describes above, reads, *Dear Mummy and Daddy, I hope you are very well . . . How are the dogs? . . . I'm glad Jain is doing well. Nothing has happened at school . . . Please bring me a gun. Love from Peter.*

Eventually the letters change into tightly looped cursive ink. But they remain remarkably consistent. A bland recitation of school activities—sports played, movies seen, the weather, Young Farmers' Club outings, exam results, hikes.

Then there are the missed visits: *Dear Mum and Dad, there will be a film show here at school Sat 26th at 6.45 p.m., please try and come.*

They didn't make it.

Again, and again: *How come you did not come on Thursday? I was expecting you.*

When are you coming next?

One letter signs off, *Anyway there are only about 29 days until I am home again. Longing till then.*

In the bundle there are a few replies from them. They are bland, vague, generic, telling him of dogs and horses and the weather.

After a while, Peter gives up asking them when they are coming to see him, and he starts signing off his letters with *See you sometime.*

. . .

Starting when Peter is about eight or nine, there are references to pills. At first I don't pay them much heed, and then comes this letter:

Dear Mum and Dad,

Thanks for taking the trouble to come all the way here to see me. I think Malawi will be a super holiday, and a restful one for Mum and Dad.

For that French poem we had to learn, I got 10/10 for knowing it but only 4 and a half out of 10 for pronunciation. Oh well, I did my best.

Please in your next letter could you send me some Valium as I have practically none left. Some days I go without them, other days I take a half tablet in the morning and see how it goes.

I am glad to hear that Jain is working hard, it should be good for her.

I do not mind coming home for the Easter weekend by bus.

We beat Plumtree in cricket for the first time in 20 years, so all Prefects lines were let off. I didn't have any, though.

I have joined Art Club. It is a little disorganized, but I will go there in my spare time and paint something.

I think I will go to town soon, maybe even today, just for the good of getting away.

Please remember my Valium, write soon,

Lots of love, Peter xx.

At the end of the letter, Peter has drawn a peace sign and written *Peace (of mind)* underneath it.

But I had no peace of mind. For the most part I was miserable at boarding school. I realize now that I have tried to block the fact that the only way I could get through that time was to be dosed up on Valium. And it wasn't some short-term thing; I took Valium for years. Just as my father had.

I can't help comparing my reaction to Hugo's boarding school malaise. The moment he said, "Enough!" late one winter's evening, I jumped into the Volvo and sped up the Taconic luge to Lakeville to get him out of there. I think somewhere deep inside I was trying to rescue him in the way that I so wish my parents had rescued me.

Repeat after me: parent the child you have, not the child you were.

Also in the bundle of letters, I find a memorandum of a wager. It is in Jain's writing and reads:

> *Bet between P Godwin and J Godwin*
> *P Godwin bets J Godwin that she will not have set a*
> *wedding date before May 1979. The sum of Z$30 will be paid*
> *to the winner of this bet by the loser.*
> *Signed: Jain Godwin*
> *Peter Godwin.*
> *Witness: Wendy Webb* [Jain's best friend]
> *Witness: Helen Godwin.*

The note is undated, but I remember we'd made the wager in 1976, before I left the army to go to university. Jain won it—her wedding was set for May 1978—but she was killed before she could collect her winnings. And before she could be married.

• • •

I suppose the boy really is father to the man. The die is cast in child-hood. The grooves of adulthood scored early. And for my family, identity has always been an unstable entity. It is in constant motion—kinetic and frequently needing to be renegotiated. Down through the generations, it seems, our loyalty to authority has always been suspect. We are not team players. Algernon Sydney turned on his king and was rowed down the Thames in a prison barge and into Traitors' Gate and hanged there. My grandfather, instead of kissing his bishop's ring, bit his hand, and was cast out of the clergy. My father turned away from his country, his ethnicity, and his name.

And I grew up in a colony that rebelled against the Queen; I fought on the wrong side of a losing war. My eldest boy, Thomas, was always on the verge of getting expelled from boarding school—only a year in China saved him—and Hugo is already showing a Quixotic defiance of anyone who dares try to trammel him.

Once, when Hugo was still a toddler, in the early days of satnav, he had refused to get out of the car when we reached our destination.

"Why not?" I'd asked, getting frustrated.

"Because I'm scared."

"Scared? Of what?"

"Of the bears," he had said, looking around fearfully. "The woman in the dashboard kept saying, 'Bear left, bear right.' Too many bears."

And in a sense, he'd been right. There be bears all around. You just can't see them clearly, at first. Bears and wolves, dragons—all manner of monsters at the margins of the map, lurking in the terra incognita, lurking both in palm and pine, lurking beyond the pale.

Modern navigation is like keyhole surgery; with GPS you see only the organ you're operating on, seldom the whole atlas of anatomy. Physical maps—the artifacts of actual atlases—are growing rare now, and I miss them, the comprehensiveness of their compendium.

The art of map-reading is an atrophying one; a whole language is being lost, the cryptology of cartography, the arcane symbols of our terrain: contours, colors, crenelations. And the constant reorienting, the way you must figure out for yourself where on the map you are and which direction you're facing, without a blinking blue arrow continually fed by celestial bat squeaks, triangulating your position. Thriller writers of book and screen must now conspire to render protagonists' phones inoperable for their plots to work.

But not all of us are securely triangulated, echo-located by satellite wherever we go. Not all of us are fed the shortest route, the obstacles ahead, the car crashes and roadkill, breakdowns on the hard shoulder, police speed traps. Oh, were it so in real life! Oh, that we could instantly be diverted whenever we took a wrong turn, that our inner GPS would simply announce that it was "recalculating" and beckon us back on course.

My own psychological map is still an analog one, a physical one, folded, faded, frayed, one without a "you are here" arrow blinking blue. On an analog map, if you cannot locate *yourself* precisely then you are already lost, even if you know your destination (and I don't).

There's an old Irish joke: A tourist stops to ask a farmer for directions. The farmer ponders, then shakes his head. You're starting from the wrong place, he says.

That's how it feels to me; I've started from the wrong place.

Maps exude a false sense of security anyway. Just because you can see a destination, doesn't mean you can reach it. Those warnings on car rearview mirrors: "Objects may be closer than they appear." With maps, those warnings should be read in reverse; your object may be further than you think.

There is much too that is still unmapped, that remains terra incognita. The course of true love, for one. And the one journey I can never quite navigate: my way home. Even if I could find it, like the Afghan apodes, I no longer have the feet with which to land there; all I could do is swoop overhead, glancing enviously at the twinkling of the cooking fires below, the minarets and the chapels, the synagogues and the temples and stupas, the olive groves and the fig trees and the fields of golden wheat swaying in the downdraft of my wings.

And so long as we remain aloft, we can easily veer into perilous parts. We might end up like the skein of stubborn swans who haul the Reverend Godwin to the moon. Or the migrant birds trapped in nets by Lebanese hunters as we try to fly across the Levant. We might be pierced through the neck with an arrow like the pfeilstorch or be shot on the orders of Count von Bothmer and end up stuffed in a German museum vitrine. Hans Christian Andersen's boys might come at us, to slap and to stab, to hang and to burn. The European Union might order the closing of the landfills on which we feed. Or, like the Canfield bees, we might lose our way at nightfall or get ripped apart by killer hornets.

Oh, that we could stay permanently above the fray like birds of paradise, subsisting in the sky solely on sunshine and dew, dropping only when we die of old age. Instead, like Icarus, the wax that binds our man-made wings might melt, plummeting us to earth, our bodies crumpled and unrecognizable, a mangle of foreign cultures, a bouil-labaisse of bricolage in which constituent parts can be identified here and there, but not the whole. Like Emin Pasha, who no one recognized, so no one claimed as their own. Until he became famous, when everyone did. And I realize now that Emin doesn't just remind me of my father, he reminds me of my syncretic self too, with my mélange, mash-up, Franken-accent, a cultural centaur. Godwin, party of one, a man without a nation, without a tribe.

• • •

I remember now the place we first lived when we arrived in New York: Manhattan's Meatpacking District. Back then it still had several working abattoirs. The whine of band saws filled the air and dumpsters of bones lined the streets. In summer they stank. This was long before it became a tourist hub. Before the High Line was reimagined as an elevated park. Back when it was still a desolate, disused rail track, cordoned off by coils of razor wire. Sometimes I would sneak up there with friends and walk along its diagonal route, two stories up, wending our way between empty warehouses that have since become art galleries.

The High Line had been a freight rail spur, the end of the route bringing livestock from the Midwest to be slaughtered. On smelling the cattle carnage in the abattoirs below, and realizing they were riding to their own deaths, the steers emptied their bowels in terror. And in their dung were the seeds of the pink, Midwestern grasses from the home ranges they had grazed.

The invention of commercial refrigeration made it cheaper for the livestock to be slaughtered where they were raised and trucked into New York as deadstock. By the early 1980s there were no more cattle trains, and the last of the fear dung grasses sprouted and grew on the High Line rails, undisturbed.

In the design of the High Line park as a postindustrial tourist attraction, the landscape architects made a feature of preserving the midwestern flora they had found up there, calling it a "self-seeded landscape that grew wild for 25 years after the trains stopped running," but they left out the bit that the soft pink grasses had grown in the dung of terrified cattle on their way to be killed.

Back then, before the tourism revamp, the Belgian cobblestones of Gansevoort Street were still the glistening preserve of a thriving trans sex trade, and there were few places to eat locally. My regular was Florent, a twenty-four-hour café, presided over by a gay Frenchman, Florent Morellet, who gave it his name and styled it not so much as a New York diner, but as a parody of a New York diner, an ironic, camp diner. It was long and narrow, with red leatherette bench seats, quilted aluminium walls, and a pink ceiling from which hung a slowly revolving disco ball. Every Bastille Day, a bewigged, powdered, and bustled Florent emceed a Marie Antoinette lookalike competition.

Florent was a benign version of Mos Eisley Cantina, the *Star Wars* bar, where anyone could "fit in": abattoir butchers, sanitation workers from the garbage-barge dock, trans working girls, clientele from a cluster of nearby sex clubs—the Anvil, Manhole, the Mineshaft, Pandora's Box, the Clit Club, and the Nutcracker Suite—artists from the Westbeth building, "resting" actors, and me. No matter how late you arrived, you were always welcome, because Florent never closed. Until one day, of course, it did. Forever.

Florent had decorated one wall of his diner with framed artwork drawn by his father. They were intricate maps of cities, not actual ones, but wholly imaginary. Now, it strikes me that maybe this is what we should all do, draw our own maps of imaginary cities, city-states of mind that we can inhabit, that we can call home. And when we go there, they will grant us asylum. They are the ultimate sanctuary cities. They meet Robert Frost's definition of home, the place where, when you have to go there, they have to take you in.

• • •

Who the hell really belongs *where* anyway?

All this moving around, back and forth, so much fauna and flora "out of place." Asian bittersweet vines and multi-flora roses in the Taconics. Tamaracks, which are neither deciduous nor conifer but both. Japanese ginkgoes in New York. Asian hornets and urban foxes and night-singing robins in London. Darwin's altered finches and Kalahari ass-eyed cows staring down lions. Migrating swifts and swallows and wild geese and storks. Murphy living in her longboat Volvo, and her Sunshine State father driving home to Indian Orchard to die in his camping chair. Burhan Qurbani now without feet to land in Germany.

Gina the Baltic Russian and Nema from Sudan trying to escape her country and her marriage. Solitary Vera and alcoholic Kitty and Mafia madam Bessie and knife-wielding Sofia. The "kwasarwa ani?" squadrons of Zimbabweans thousands of miles from home. Yinka Shonibare's Afronaut in his ethnic, made-in-Holland jumpsuit. The pierced Roma Queen bartender and the Great Northern Hotel, which is neither. Jexit Joanna. Her Grace, the Empress Dowager, she of variable voice, and my Ashkenazi, Polish, Anglo-African, Valium-dosed father. Georgina, surrounded by her African artifacts in South Hampstead and Bella her bouncing English springer spaniel. My American-born boys blowing their vuvuzelas on the Upper West Side, and Phoebe, the sad-eyed Georgian rescue mutt. And me, now on my third continent, leaping onto the rigging of yet another passing ship.

The distinction between exotic and indigenous, between native and foreign, is blurred. The urge for vanilla purity and pious pedigree is pernicious, born of prejudice and fueled by fear. It is suffocating and limiting and most of all, bloody *boring*.

E pluribus unum, baby.

We're messy and mixed up. But isn't it that very mélange that makes us mighty? A resilience that rests upon manifold, substantial columns, real Parthenon pillars, not cosmetic plaster pilasters?

Maybe the origins of our many migrations, of our restless exile, can be found in Genesis 11:8–9. "So the Lord scattered them abroad from thence upon the face of all the earth: and they left off to build the city. Therefore, is the name of it called Babel; because the Lord did there confound the language of all the earth: and from thence did the Lord scatter them abroad upon the face of all the earth."

By confounding language, God had sown enmity among peoples where amity once reigned.

At my primary school in Zimbabwe, the class bully, Slabbert, would collect red ants and black ants and store them together in a mason jar, with holes punched in the lid. Though both were armed with menacing mandibles, they coexisted there perfectly peaceably. Then we would gather round to watch Slabbert shake the jar. Whereupon the ants would rip each other apart, both colors wrongly assuming they'd been attacked by the other.

But does not New York confound Babel? A place of many tongues and cultures that manages, for the most part, to live at peace even when many of its residents are antagonists back in their places of origin. Crowded into our mason jar, we are amicable ants.

A Holiday from My Head

I AM NOW LIMPING AWAY FROM THE WRECKAGE OF MY MARRIAGE LIKE the dazed survivor of an air crash. But as acute fades into chronic, I seem stuck, monochromatic.

My therapist thinks that I'm afraid to disappoint women, to let them down or to confront them. And that this is a long-lasting consequence of my unrequited childhood need for affection from a busy, distracted mother. A mother who played an emotional sleight of hand—convincing me that, to earn her attention, her love, I had to be independent, mature, autonomous, a mini-adult—and therefore not require her attention.

The therapist thinks that I may be suffering from something she calls "the defense of the loyal child," where the angry but dutiful child, not knowing what to do with his anger, enacts a kind of "fuck you" that becomes a sadomasochistic "fuck me," because the child inadvertently cuts off his own abilities—his own voice—which wants to speak his own separate truth.

She calls this auto-castration.

It is true that I am a man who is drawn to strong women. And I have now lost three of the strongest women in my life: my older sister, Jain—who was my substitute mother—my actual mother, and, now, my wife.

As well as PTSD both from fighting in one war and reporting on many others, the therapist suspects I may be suffering from something called hyper-independence, a response to childhood trauma, which discourages me from asking for help, and from making new friendships because I have no faith in their duration, having felt abandoned and alone as a boy.

Whatever the cause, I seem to have lost confidence in my own ability. And if I can no longer write, what utility do I have left? This, then, is my challenge, the challenge of trying to start again, of finding a new place in the world at sixty years old.

In an effort to dislodge myself from this Hesperian headlock, I have been considering psychedelic treatment. Early pilot studies have shown that ketamine has some success in ameliorating PTSD, depression, and addiction. My primary care doctor has joined one of the first legal ketamine start-ups as medical director, and he talks me through the procedure.

His facility administers ketamine intravenously—just sub-anesthetic. This higher dose he describes as ego-dissolving, mind-manifesting, increasing neural plasticity, and tapping into your inner healer. I feel the need for something strong, dissociative, to help my train of thought jump its tracks, to take a holiday from my head, to go on a real trip.

I lean back into the La-Z-Boy and listen to the gentle roar of the traffic on Madison Avenue below. An IV needle is inserted into the ridge of vein at the crook of my elbow. It reminds me of the weeks I have just spent sitting next to my mother's drip stand as she lay dying, the silver stand that Kutu clung to, remaining there still, after she had been wheeled to the morgue.

The assistant clips headphones over my ears. The flutes and swelling Tibetan strings of Deuter's New Age music flows through them. She points out the red emergency button on my chair arm. The treatment, as she calls it, will last about an hour and a half. She dims the lights and leaves me alone. I sit watching the drug drain from the drip bag down the looping catheter into my vein, waiting for the ketamine to kick in.

• • •

It is night. I am squeezed into the cockpit of a Second World War Spitfire. The noise is overwhelming. The roar of the Merlin engine, the buzz of the rivets that fix the plexiglass canopy to the fuselage. Tracer bullets pour past. Below is a ruined city, its oxbow river on fire. Restless searchlights stab upwards through the smoke-choked sky.

I look away, upwards, and the contrast is complete. Up there, all is quiet, the peace of the slowly wheeling celestial dome. But I know that I cannot flee there, to do so is to embrace my own death. I look down again, at the destruction beneath. I know I *should* go back down there; that is my life, after all. But I'm so bloody tired—maybe the time has come for me to just let go?

No, I *must* stay focused, engaged, committed.

Then the resistance abruptly bleeds out of me. It *is* time. Fuck it. Fuck *this*. I unstrap my harness, slide open the canopy, and step out of the cockpit.

I am a deadweight, falling, falling. I can hear that sound again, the one I heard when my father told me that Jain was dead, the massive bass groan of a black hole imploding.

Then all is quiet.

———

I am a soldier, a knight in a suit of rusted armor. But my molded chest plate is too small. It constricts me. I battle to breathe. I must break out of it or my heart will burst. The chest plate is attached to me with leather straps. I stretch behind to undo them, but I can't quite reach the buckles. And with each attempt, my arms grow shorter, morphing into little T. rex arms. Finally, I manage to wrench the armor up over my head, though it cuts deep wounds across my face.

I am a bird, flying. I can see the feathered ends of my own wings, white with black tips. I adjust them minutely, effortlessly, instinctively, to keep me stable as I soar, like a swan pulling the Reverend Godwin to the moon. Now I can make out enough of myself to recognize I am not a swan, but a white stork—my totemic shuramurove. I have an arrow lodged in my neck, but it does not seem to slow me. The earth is falling away beneath, the searchlights and the ack-ack guns and the burning oxbow river grow small, insignificant. I am beyond their reach now. They cannot hurt me because I no longer belong to their world. I am in another place. A place where time is not linear.

I am flying over a thick green canopy of forest. There is a clearing ahead, and I swoop down to land in it.

My grandparents and my aunt, all the Polish side of my family, are boarding a train. They stand sepia at the windows waving, as though setting off on holiday. It is winter and they are wearing fur coats and hats and gloves and muffs and scarves. I try to shout to them, to warn that the train will take them to the Holocaust, but they cannot hear me. They just keep waving and blowing kisses. With a tremendous lurch, the train heaves forward, and they all fall down.

I am at elementary school in Chimanimani, waiting for my parents to collect me from the red cement veranda, waiting and waiting. The school falls into ruins around me, doors drop off their hinges, windows break, the swimming pool empties and fills with garbage, and still my parents do not arrive. They have left me behind. They have forgotten me.

Across the valley, on Green Mount, which is black from a veld fire, I see Jesus hanging on his cross. An iron spike is hammered through his metatarsals, pinning his overlapping feet into the rough timber vertical. Above his head, on a little wooden scroll, are burned the letters INRI. I know from the Jesuits what they stand for. "Iesus Nazarenus, Rex Iudaeorum." Jesus of Nazareth, King of the Jews—written there on the instructions of Pontius Pilate as a mocking moniker. He seems relaxed, Jesus does, considering he's being crucified. I call over to him, but he just looks up at the sky and beams beatifically.

I am flying over the forest again, and landing at the summit of Spitz Kop. Jain is there. She's a teenager. We stand together on the small concrete base of the trig point, looking down the long valley into the floodplains of Mozambique. Beyond is a low glow; it is the prospect of the Indian Ocean. My father takes photos with his complicated camera. He fiddles with the focus and the exposure dials. Jain's glee club from Marymount College is there too. The girls have freckles and long, sun-streaked hair. They strum the catgut strings of acoustic guitars and sing "The Sound of Silence."

Jain folds me in a hug, holding my head against her heart, so that I can hear it beat. And when she steps back, she suddenly ages, becoming the old woman she would be now, had she not been killed. Dad keeps asking us to move further back so that he can get a better angle for his shot, until Jain steps over the edge of the mountain. It is a long, long way down. Jain waves to me as she falls. And as she waves and smiles, she becomes young again.

I am flying, over the sea. It is the captive sea in the painting above my mother's bed, raging yet strangely still. I circle inland over the manicured vineyards of Stellenbosch and Franschhoek and Paarl, swooping up over the Hottentots Holland Mountains and down the other side, making landfall on Robben Island, the old apartheid penal colony.

Nelson Mandela stands there, leaning on a pickax at the base of the tall limestone cliffs they are forced to dig all day. In that lilting, deliberate cadence of his, he explains that the white dust blocks the prisoners' tear ducts so they cannot weep. When I get out of here, he says, then I will be able to weep again.

I am back in the military as a teenager, a boy soldier. We wear camouflage fatigues, swirling greens and browns so that we can blend in better with the Rhodesian bush. We are being ambushed, but we keep going. The only way out is through. But my leg is injured and I cannot walk, so my comrades are carrying me home, no man left behind. We are still under fire as they lug me through acacia thorns, over fallen tree trunks and across water-filled ditches.

I feel a bullet pierce my back. I look down and see that it has punched its way out through my chest, leaving a jagged red hole where my heart should be. With his extended silver antenna Colonel Jolly is pointing out my exit wound on his slide screen. He presses the remote and the carousel clatters around, and my comrades lose grip of me, and the slide falls out of Colonel Jolly's frame. I am falling, falling, down from the Chimanimani Mountains towards the Mozambican floodplain and into the Hudson River, swimming out towards the open ocean. High Holidaying Jews in black suits and wide-brimmed hats are tossing Tashlich atonement notes onto me and I can read them all—all the sins of the world—because my eyes have no lids.

Consciousness seeps back. I look at the clock. I have been out for more than two hours. I am wet through with sweat. A young man in a tan sheepskin jerkin wishes to debrief me, but I wave him away and start writing before I forget the places I have been.

The next day my scapulae and triceps are aching, and I realize that I really *was* flapping my arms like wings during my strange psychedelic safari.

I don't feel dramatically reborn afterwards; no epiphany—but quieter, perhaps, and calmer. And when I think about my trip, I don't feel the need to sift through the symbolism. Though I do feel embarrassed about the guest appearance of Nelson Mandela (who I'd interviewed, and who contributed the foreword for a book I wrote), and I wonder if it represents a white fantasy of Black forgiveness. A tabula rasa of race relations. I notice too that none of my psychedelic time was current. I saw nothing of Joanna, nothing of my children and, most remarkable, nothing of my mother. My flights were all back into my history.

Will paying homage to my past somehow subdue its strength, I wonder, tethering the wolves of memory that have consumed me? Might I be able to live in the present now—what modest portion of the present I still have in my future?

• • •

The Empress Dowager's funeral service takes place in the parish church of St. John-at-Hampstead. It is not that well attended, maybe eighty people. The last of her friends are dead, infirm, or far away.

Most of the mourners wear black. Joanna wears silver, a shimmering pantsuit of space-blanket silver. Our matchmaker, Jane, is there, and Alison, and—remarkably—my favorite elementary school teacher, Mrs. King, née Gloyne, has trekked down from Cumbria.

Nema is a no-show. We have left her text messages about the funeral date, but now her phone is "out of service." The agency says she has resigned and left no forwarding address. We suspect that, having waited for Mum to die, she has finally done her runner, fled her arranged marriage, made her bid for freedom, armed now with her shibboleth-shattering, Empress Dowager English, and her Hello Kitty notebook brimming with wine-dark metaphors and adjectival order, and Swiftian egg allegories.

A Zimbabwean choir, the Soul Singers, is in full throat, singing Shona hymns a capella—"Jerusalem Musha Wangu" (Jersualem Our Home) and "Ishe Komberera Afrika" (God Bless Africa)—astonishing the home team Hampstead parish choir with a harmonic master class.

I sit in the front pew, towered over by a son on either side. We are dry-eyed. But when the Zimbabwean choir starts to sing, I begin silently to weep. The boys both look at me in alarm, each slips an arm through one of mine, and they begin to cry themselves. Mostly, I think, because this is the first time they have seen me weep.

Xanthe reads "Remember," by Christina Rossetti. Thomas reads an extract from *When a Crocodile Eats the Sun*. A son reading from his father's book about his grandmother. Ellah reads a poem by Margaret Mead. Georgina reads "Secret Music," by Siegfried Sassoon. Fiona Watson, Mum's goddaughter, recites Psalm 121. "I will lift up mine eyes unto the hills, from whence cometh my help."

I give a tribute for which I have somehow been unable to prepare, so I must ad-lib.

I say things like, Helen Godwin didn't have a Facebook page. She didn't have an Instagram feed or a Twitter hashtag. She wasn't a Snapchatterer. She never took a selfie in her life. She wasn't about selfies. Her mental camera pointed outwards. She didn't do what she did for money—her salary was paltry. Nor for status—she was self-effacing, to a fault. Nor for praise—it made her squirm. She wasn't in the pursuit of her own happiness. Service was simply in her blood. Duty in her bones. She was a feminist without calling it that. A rebel without labeling it such. A pioneer without claiming to be one.

I say things like, her frugality was legendary. As was her conservation—though she wouldn't have used that name. She was a multiple reuser of bags, rinsing them and hanging them on the clothesline, and all containers that crossed her line of sight, a repurposer of clothing. She was a mender of shoes, a darner of dresses. The instinct to recycle runs deep in her people.

I say things like, she was the opposite of a helicopter parent. And yet she had a huge influence on us. By her example and through the people she touched. Everywhere we went we came across those who praised her treatment of them as patients and as people, with kindness and understanding. We miss her, but she lives on in the lives she saved, the lives she gave, the lives she touched with her healing hands.

I say things like that.

After the service, the congregation files up the road to the nearby cemetery, led by the Zimbabwean choir singing "Swing Low, Sweet Chariot." Their music swells into the surrounding streets and, like the Pied Piper did to Hamelin, the Soul Singers do to Hampstead, attracting a crowd to follow them. They follow all the way to the graveside, inflating the small congregation. A knot of complete strangers to see off Her Grace. She would have been amused.

I think I spot Nema mingling with the tourists, but I can't be sure because her black caul is pulled low over her face and when I move towards her, she disappears.

The granite gravestone is not here yet, it's on back order from Italy; apparently Brexit Britain has no funeral stone of its own. When it is eventually erected, letters carved in black, it has the wrong birth month for Dad—August instead of February. Georgina and I blame the stonemason, and the stonemason blames us. We had been fussing over fonts and worrying over wording and somehow none of us caught the two morphing into an eight. Either way, we can't afford to change it now. And we laugh at what our fastidious father's reaction would have been to the mistake, how we couldn't even get *this*, his earthly sign-off, right, for God's sake!

Well, he should be grateful, says Georgina. He's had six months shaved off his age; it's a kind of postmortem Botox.

The wording on the gravestone, our parents' lapidary cicatrix, is simple:

GEORGE GODWIN, Engineer
Born Warsaw 16. 8. 1924
Died Harare 8. 2. 2004
HELEN GODWIN, Doctor
Born Weymouth 25. 8. 1925
Died London 16. 3. 2018
Lived and loved in Zimbabwe
for fifty years
Stoic parents of Jain, Peter & Georgina

Almost Home

KYIV IN WINTER. BITTERLY COLD. FIVE P.M. AND IT IS ALREADY DARK. Russian missile strikes have cut electricity again and the city is mostly unlit. You can see the stars as clearly as you can from the countryside. And the moon reflects off the snow-laden roofs.

I'm here helping PEN gather evidence of Russia's efforts to destroy Ukrainian culture. It is the first time I have been back to a war zone in almost a decade. Here in Ukraine, I find both task and purpose. In the middle of war, I find a kind of peace. My brain is primed for this. This is my default. "Normal" life is what I struggle with.

The Museum of Western and Oriental Art is closed, its windows boarded up, shattered by a missile strike in the toddlers' playground opposite. Its paintings have been dispersed, hidden outside the city to protect them from war. A few statues that are too monumental to move are swaddled in sandbags. The only signs of the exhibition are the dark patches on the flock wallpaper where the art used to hang.

The curator takes us on a tour anyway. We wear our coats indoors and use our phone flashlights to see.

A museum without art is like a deconsecrated church, stripped of its essential purpose. Yet to the curator it's as if the paintings still hang. This is the consuming strength of memory. It can overpower reality.

• • •

The sleeper train out of Kyiv thunders through the night across the snow-stacked steppes, the cars darkened to offer a less enticing target. I am sharing the compartment with two sweat-sheened teen soldiers who play backgammon on a mini board.

I find myself wondering if either of them has yet to fall in love.

It takes eleven hours to reach the Polish border and another three hours' drive to Warsaw, where I want to visit the grave of my paternal grandfather. It has been found by Zosia, my second cousin, a quest made harder for her by the fact that it isn't in the large Jewish cemetery, as expected, but on Zytnia Street, in the small graveyard of the Polish Reformed Church, a tiny Calvinist sect to which he converted late in life.

Her second obstacle was the name on the headstone. By the time he died, my grandfather had changed his name from Maurycy Goldfarb to Stefan Golaszewski, to hide his Jewish origins, just as my father had changed *his* name to George Godwin and converted to the Church of England. Two name changes in successive generations—shibboleth-evading, minority-shapeshifting, the better to "fit in."

But it turns out my family is not good at fitting in, we have no talent for real assimilation. Tribe seems to elude us. We are die-hard mongrels.

The headstone is somber black marble, and the grave itself lies under a profusion of poet's ivy that shivers in the wind. I wipe the frost off the lettering. Someone—the caretaker doesn't know who—has recently placed a candle on it, in a green glass lantern with bronze yoke. There is an identical lantern on the adjoining grave of Natalia Bermanowa, my grandfather's second wife.

I pay my obsequies, and, as we leave, the caretaker intercepts us. There is money owing on the grave's upkeep, he regrets to inform me. So, I arrange to assume the annual payments, to keep the weeds cleared from the grave in the summer, and the leaves swept away in the fall, and the snow shoveled off in winter, and, most of all, to prevent my grandfather from being dug up and replaced.

Then I drive to Warsaw's Chopin Airport and fly across the world back to New York.

* * *

The yellow cab from Newark is a battered Ford Crown Victoria with a collapsed rear seat and shot suspension. It lurches down the Jersey Turnpike as the driver conducts a phone conversation at a bass bellow in West African–inflected French.

"Attends! Attends!" he shouts at his phone, and he breaks off to ask me which route I want him to take to Manhattan. We agree it's quickest to loop north over the George Washington Bridge.

"Where you from?" he asks, picking up on my accent.

"Afrique du Sud, Zimbabwe."

"Moi, je viens d'Afrique de l'Ouest, Côte d'Ivoire," he says. "We both far from home. I'm Mamadou."

"Peter," I say.

"Salut." He turns, reaches back, and we shake hands, ignoring the honking as our cab drifts out of lane.

"How long have you been here?" I ask.

"More dan twenty years."

"Me too. Will you go back?"

"No, I have my life here in New York now," he says. "And my boys, they American."

"Yeah, mine too."

His phone rings. The ringtone is from "Mariama," by Baaba Maal. I recognize the track from my tribes-without-flags playlist. Baaba Maal's Pulaar-speaking Fulani people were sundered by colonial France when it split the ancient kingdom of Futa Tooro between Senegal and Mauritania.

"It's my brother in Abidjan," Mamadou explains, and he resumes his conversation.

My own phone beeps. It's the Air Alarm Ukraine app. The icon is the standard traffic sign of a pedestrian silhouette in profile, like the one guarding the crossing to Joan of Arc outside my front window, only this one is running, trying to outpace the rocket at its back. Russian missiles are again converging on Kyiv, it warns, take shelter.

We turn east onto I-95 and the Manhattan skyline swings into sight like a towering ocean liner, a modern ship of Theseus, a vessel of reinvention, its portholes all aglitter, its prow at Battery Park slicing towards the Atlantic, its bridge on Wall Street, its funnels the 57th Street supertalls, its sleek luxury cabins the uptown co-ops, its stern ensign fluttering from the steeple of Riverside Church on West 120th Street.

After more than twenty years, the first returning glimpse of the cityscape has lost none of its luster, the sheer audacity of this nature-defying apparition, all these lives teeming together on this small granite hull, surrounded by water.

Like Mamadou, I wasn't born here, but we both have berths on the SS *New York City*, both borne along in her, on the voyage of life.

• • •

I sit in my New York study, alone now in what used to be our family home. Joanna lives downtown, in a white loft; she works in finance. And the boys have successfully lifted off into their own orbits— Thomas works in a television writers' room, Hugo is still at college and cooks three nights a week in a restaurant—their parental launching pads jettisoned, as they should be.

So, it's just Phoebe and me. She's elderly now, white around the muzzle, with poor eyesight and almost no hearing. I know she's getting ready to die, and I must steel myself for her exit. She looks up at me with her sad almond eyes, hoping for affection, for food—for any attention, really. And mostly, I comply.

The view from my desk is of a redbrick wall; torn cream cuticles of paint and crumbling mortar hang from it like lichen. In the alley below, a laundry fan exhales warm soapy fumes onto the skinny stalk of a tree that has somehow thrust its way up through the concrete. It is a tree of heaven (*Ailanthus altissima*), an invasive species from China, known for its ability to survive in poor conditions. The Chinese call it the "tree of the gods" and they see it as a symbol of spiritual resilience.

Here, in America, it is nicknamed the ghetto palm. This one has already grown sixty feet high, a bent beanstalk groping for the giant's castle, striving for the sliver of sky twelve stories above. Like the lightning-scorched, vine-sheathed oak at Indian Orchard, this tree has somehow summoned the sheer grit to survive.

A black garbage bag is snagged on one of its uppermost branches. It has been there for several years now. I like to think of the tree as a misshapen mast flying a black flag, the "no quarter flag," a signal of resolve that pirates hoist once battle begins. In ship-speak the flag says, we give no quarter; we take no prisoners. It rustles and flaps, tugged at by the breeze that blows off the Hudson and gusts through the gloomy canyons between these tower blocks. Its ugliness is evident, but it has a kind of beauty too, a brave, defiant beauty—a little victory in the quiet war against despair.

The tree of heaven's branches are still bare. But any day now, by the Ides of March—the anniversary of my mother's death—small green buds will appear, and new pinnate leaves will unfurl, against all the odds.

I think of my mother trying to describe what she saw on the cusp of death, her view from the bridge of the good ship mortality. That from up there she could no longer tell islands from clouds. One substantial, surrounded by sea. The other ephemeral, surrounded by sky.

It is time for me to leave, to brave the gale. There is a wind advisory in effect. I look through the front window to check the yellow pedestrian sign atop its metal stalk, planted in the sidewalk. It serves as my wind vane. This morning it is vibrating violently, its bolts screeching in protest. I wonder if one day it will succumb to metal fatigue and the sign will break free, flying up Riverside Drive like a lethal metal Frisbee, scattering the corded columns of Day-Glo toddlers.

I show Phoebe that I'm going out, otherwise she'll search for me the entire time I'm gone.

Then I shrug on my jacket and scoop up my MetroCard from the cracked marble of the hall table. It's a new card, and I notice it bears a single stanza from the New York subway's Poetry in Motion series: "Love in the Ruins," by Jim Moore:

> *I remember my mother towards the end,*
> *folding the tablecloth after dinner*
> *so carefully*
> *as if it were a flag*
> *of a country that no longer existed,*
> *but once had ruled the world.*

Stepping onto Riverside Drive, I hear honking above me. Through a small blue break in the clouds fly a chevron of geese, returning from their winter in Mexico.

They are flying against the wind, honking to cheer each other on, honking to boost their morale.

They have almost reached their destination.

They are almost home.

FIN

Acknowledgments

THANKS TO MY EDITORS IN NEW YORK AND LONDON, JUDY CLAIN AND Ellah Wakatama (fellow Zimbabweans both), and their respective staffs. At the newly minted Summit Books: Josie Kals, Kevwe Okumakube, Anna Skrabacz. And at Canongate: Leila Cruickshank, Rali Chorbadzhiyska, Craig Hillsley, Lucy Zhou, Alice Shortland, Natasha Gargan, Hannah Watson, and Gill Heeley. Thanks to Susan Lehman, for her critical cheerleading in the early stages. To Thomas and Hugo Godwin, Joanna Coles, and Xanthe Summerfield, for tolerating a writer in their midst. And those (listed alphabetically) who helped me, read pages, and offered advice: Prospero Bailey, Brenda Berger, Jessica Blau, Jesse Browner, Anthony Feinstein, Thomas Godwin, Christen Herbert, Marissa Kalman, Elianna Kan, Jonathan Kay, Nate Krieger, Sasha Lazard, Andy McNicol, Cambra Overend, Geoff Parcell, Steven Radowitz, Melanie Thernstrom, Uma Thurman, Rachel Ward, Graham Young, and Mike Yule. Most of all, my thanks to Georgina Godwin, who I find does not annoy me.

Notwithstanding their help, this book is entirely my own fault.

Permission Credits

About the Author

PETER GODWIN was born and raised in Zimbabwe. He is the author of six nonfiction books, including *Mukiwa*, which received the Orwell Prize and the Esquire/Apple/Waterstones Non-fiction award, and *When a Crocodile Eats the Sun*, which won the Borders Original Voices award. His book *The Fear* was selected by *The New Yorker* as a best book of the year. He has taught writing at Wesleyan and Columbia, and served as president of PEN America. He is an Orwell Fellow and a Guggenheim Fellow. He lives in New York City.